D1029719

UNDERSTANDING
ITALO CALVINO

UNDERSTANDING

ITALO
CALVINO

BY BENO WEISS

UNIVERSITY OF SOUTH CAROLINA PRESS

Published in Columbia, South Carolina, by the
University of South Carolina Press

Manufactured in the United States of America

Library of Congress Cataloging-in-Publication Data

Weiss, Beno, 1933–
    Understanding Italo Calvino / Beno Weiss.
        p.   cm. — (Understanding modern European and Latin American
    literature)
    Includes bibliographical references and index.
    ISBN 0–87249–858–1
    1. Calvino, Italo—Criticism and interpretation.   I. Title.
    II. Series.
    PQ4809.A45Z89   1993
    853'.914—dc20   92–40941

to Rachel, my beautiful and lovely mother

CONTENTS

EDITOR'S PREFACE

Understanding Modern European and Latin American Literature has been planned as a series of guides for undergraduate and graduate students and nonacademic readers. Like the volumes in its companion series, *Understanding Contemporary American Literature,* these books provide introductions to the lives and writings of prominent modern authors and explicate their most important works.

Modern literature makes special demands, and this is particularly true of foreign literature, in which the reader must contend not only with unfamiliar, often arcane artistic conventions and philosophical concepts, but also with the handicap of reading the literature in translation. It is a truism that the nuances of one language can be rendered in another only imperfectly (and this problem is especially acute in fiction), but the fact that the works of European and Latin American writers are situated in a historical and cultural setting quite different from our own can be as great a hindrance to the understanding of these works as the linguistic barrier. For this reason, the UMELL series emphasizes the sociological and historical backgrounds of the writers treated. The peculiar philosophical and cultural traditions of a given culture may be particularly important for an understanding of certain authors, and these are taken up in the introductory chapter and also in the discussion of those works to which this information is relevant. Beyond this, the books treat the specifically literary aspects of the author under discussion and attempt to explain the complexities of contemporary literature lucidly. The books are conceived as introductions to the authors covered, not as comprehensive analyses. They do not provide detailed summaries of plot because they are meant to be used in conjunction with the books they discuss, not as a substitute for study of the original works. The purpose of the books is to provide information and judicious literary assessment of the major works in the most compact, readable form. It is our hope that the UMELL series will help to increase knowledge and understanding of European and Latin American cultures and will serve to make the literature of those cultures more accessible.

J.H.

PREFACE

The reader of *Understanding Italo Calvino* should bear in mind that it was not possible to avoid altogether the highly specialized language of current literary criticism, given the fact that Calvino himself consciously made use of it in many of his writings. I have tried therefore to keep this discourse at a minimum, sufficient to facilitate the reader's understanding of Calvino's works. Finally, because Calvino has been enormously prolific as journalist, editor, and essayist, I found it necessary to include only his own fiction and his writings dealing with literature and literary theory. Publication dates for works cited in the text refer to the original Italian and other foreign language editions. The dates of English translations appear in the Bibliography. All translations are mine, unless otherwise indicated.

ACKNOWLEDGMENTS

I wish to thank the Institute for the Arts and Humanistic Studies, the Office of Research and Graduate Studies (College of the Liberal Arts, Pennsylvania State University) for grants that made possible research for this study. I also wish to express appreciation and gratitude to my department colleagues, especially Leon Lyday, for the invaluable support they have given me. I owe much to my friend Professor Louis C. Pérez for his encouragement and wise counsel in reading my manuscript, and to my colleagues and friends Alfred Triolo and Robert Lima for having patiently allowed me to use them as a sounding board for my ideas. I also wish to thank my son Alessandro for his wonderful editorial help and the University of South Carolina Press for their extraordinary patience and kindness.

Excerpts from "The Watcher" © 1963 by Giulio Einaudi editore s.p.a. and "Smog" © 1958 by Giulio Einaudi editore s.p.a. in *The Watcher and Other Stories* by Italo Calvino, copyright © 1971 by Harcourt Brace Jovanovich, Inc., reprinted by permission of Harcourt Brace Jovanovich, Inc.

Excerpts from *Invisible Cities* by Italo Calvino, copyright © 1972 by Giulio Einaudi editore s.p.a., English translation copyright © 1974 by Harcourt Brace Jovanovich, Inc., reprinted by permission of Harcourt Brace Jovanovich, Inc.

Excerpts from *The Castle of Crossed Destinies* by Italo Calvino, copyright © 1969 by Franco Maria Ricci editore, copyright © 1973 by Giulio Einaudi editore, s.p.a., English translation copyright © 1977 by Harcourt Brace Jovanovich, Inc., reprinted by permission of Harcourt Brace Jovanovich, Inc.

Excerpts from *If on a winter's night a traveler* by Italo Calvino, copyright © 1979 by Giulio Einaudi editore, s.p.a., English translation copyright © 1981 by Harcourt Brace Jovanovich, Inc., reprinted by permission of Harcourt Brace Jovanovich, Inc.

Excerpts from *Marcovaldo, the Seasons of the City* by Italo Calvino, copyright © 1963 by Giulio Einaudi editore s.p.a., English translation copyright © 1983 by Harcourt Brace Jovanovich, Inc. and Martin Secker & Warburg Limited, reprinted by permission of Harcourt Brace Jovanovich, Inc.

Excerpts from *The Uses of Literature Essays* by Italo Calvino, copyright © 1982 by Giulio Einaudi editore s.p.a., English translation copyright © 1986 by Harcourt Brace Jovanovich, Inc., reprinted by permission of Harcourt Brace Jovanovich, Inc.

Excerpts from *Under the Jaguar Sun* by Italo Calvino, copyright © 1986 by Garzanti editore, English translation copyright © 1988 by Harcourt Brace Jovanovich, Inc., reprinted by permission of Harcourt Brace Jovanovich, Inc.

CHRONOLOGY

1923   Birth of Italo Calvino in Santiago de Las Vegas, near Havana, Cuba, October 15.

1925   The Calvino family returns to San Remo, Italy.

1927   Birth of his brother Florio.

1941   Enters the University of Turin, Faculty of Agriculture.

1943   He transfers to the University of Florence. He avoids military conscription by joining a communist group in the Italian Resistance; he serves until 1945.

1945   At the conclusion of the war, Calvino resumes his education and transfers back to the University of Turin, but moves to the Faculty of Letters. He joins the Communist Party and collaborates with the journal *Il Politecnico*, the party paper *L'Unità*, and other publications of the left.

1947   Gets his degree in letters from the University of Turin with a thesis on Joseph Conrad. Publication of his first novel, *Il sentiero dei nidi di ragno* (*The Path to the Nest of Spiders*), for which he receives the Riccione Prize.

1948   Finds a job in the publicity department of the Einaudi Publishing House; eventually he joins the editorial board on which he remains until 1984.

1949   Publication of *Ultimo viene il corvo*, a collection of short stories.

1952   Publication of his second novel *Il visconte dimezzato* (*The Cloven Viscount*) and the novella *La formica argentina* ("The Argentine Ant").

1954   Publication of *L'entrata in guerra* (Entrance Into War).

1956   Publication of *Fiabe italiane* (there are two English versions: *Italian Fables* and *Italian Folktales*) and *La panchina: Opera in un atto di Italo Calvino; Musica Sergio Liberovici* (The Bench: One-Act Opera by Italo Calvino with Music by Sergio Liberovici).

1957   Publication of *Il barone rampante* (*The Baron in the Trees*) and *La speculazione edilizia* (''A Plunge into Real Estate''). From 1957–58, the serialized publication of the novel *I giovani del Po* (The Young of the Po River). As a consequence of the Soviet repression of the 1956 Hungarian uprising, Calvino resigns from the Italian Communist Party.

1958   Publication of *La nuvola di smog* (*Smog*) and *I racconti* (most of these stories are in *Adam, One Afternoon, and Other Stories;* in *The Watcher and Other Stories;* and in *Difficult Loves*).

1959   Publication of *Il cavaliere inesistente* (*The Nonexistent Knight*). During 1959–60, makes his first visit to the U.S and to the USSR. Together with Elio Vittorini Calvino founds and directs the journal *Menabò* (1959–67) in which he publishes several significant essays.

1960   Publication of *I nostri antenati* (Our Ancestors); the volume, for which he receives the Salento Prize, includes: *The Cloven Viscount, The Baron in the Trees,* and *The Nonexistent Knight.*

1963   Publication of *La giornata d'uno scrutatore* (''The Watcher'') and *Marcovaldo ovvero Le stagioni in città* (*Marcovaldo*).

1964   He marries Judith Esther Singer (affectionately called Chichita), a translator at UNESCO, and settles in Paris where he comes in close contact with leading French intellectuals; he becomes acquainted with Oulipo (Workshop of Potential Literature) and its leader Raymond Queneau. He continues his editorial work for Einaudi.

1965   Birth of their daughter Abigail. Publication of *Le cosmicomiche* (*Cosmicomics*); and *La nuvola di smog e La formica argentina* (''Smog'' and ''The Argentine Ant'').

1967   Publication of *Ti con zero* (*t zero*).

1968   Publication of *La memoria del mondo e altre storie cosmicomiche* (The Memory of the World and Other Cosmicomic Stories).

1969   Publication of Calvino's translation of *Les fleurs bleues* (*Blue Flowers*), a novel by Raymond Queneau; he publishes a deluxe Italian edition of "Il castello dei destini incrociati" in *Tarocchi: Il mazzo visconteo di Bergamo e di New York* ("The Castle of Crossed Destinies" in *Tarots: The Visconti Pack in Bergamo and New York*).

1970   Publication of *Gli amori difficili* (*Difficult Loves*) and *Orlando Furioso di Ludovico Ariosto raccontato da Italo Calvino, con una scelta del poema* (Calvino's Version of Ariosto's *Roland Mad*, and Selections from the Epic Poem).

1972   Publication of *Le città invisibili* (*Invisible Cities*), for which he receives the prestigious Feltrinelli Prize.

1973   Publication of *Il castello dei destini incrociati* (*The Castle of Crossed Destinies*) which includes also "La taverna dei destini incrociati" ("The Tavern of Crossed Destinies").

1979   Publication of *Se una notte d'inverno un viaggiatore* (*If on a winter's night a traveler*).

1980   The Calvino family leaves Paris and settles in Rome. The author intensifies his collaboration with the daily *La Repubblica;* he publishes his first collection of essays: *Una pietra sopra* (*The Uses of Literature: Essays*).

1983   Publication of *Palomar* (*Mr. Palomar*).

1984   Changes publishers; leaves Einaudi for Garzanti which publishes *Cosmicomiche vecchie e nuove* (Old and New Cosmicomics) and a new volume of essays: *Collezione di sabbia* (Sand Collection).

1985   Calvino prepares the "Charles E. Norton Lectures" to be given at Harvard University. The author dies from the effects of a stroke on September 19.

1986   Posthumous publication of *Sotto il sole giaguaro* (*Under the Jaguar Sun*).

1988   Posthumous publication of Calvino's unfinished Charles E. Norton Lectures, *Lezioni Americane: Sei proposte per il prossimo millennio* (*Six Memos for the Next Millennium*); and *Sulla fiaba* (On Fables), a collection of essays dealing with fables.

1990   Posthumous publication of *La strada di San Giovanni* (The San Giovanni Road), a collection of short stories.

1991   Posthumous publication of *I libri degli altri 1947–1981* (Other People's Books), a collection of letters to writers; and *Perché leggere i classici* (Why Read the Classics), a collection of essays.

UNDERSTANDING
ITALO CALVINO

CHAPTER ONE

Introduction: Calvino's Life and Circumstances

Italo Calvino, a master of allegory and fantasy, continues to be perhaps the most original, imaginative, and appreciated writer of post–World War II Italy. Until his untimely death in 1985 he was among a handful of major novelists of international standing. Because of his merits as an innovator on the Italian and world literary scene and because of the political and ethical dimension of his writings, his name kept cropping up as a candidate for the Nobel Prize in literature. Calvino was attracted primarily to folktales, knights, chivalry, social and political allegories, and pseudo-scientific legends of our time. Indeed, he compiled, transcribed from numerous Italian dialects, and expressed artistically the most complete collection of Italian folktales.[1] He was endowed with a lucid intellect and inspired by a fervid imagination that spanned the chivalry of the Middle Ages to the modern fantasies of space and science fiction.

During his productive literary career Calvino was loath to discuss his private life and experiences. He was a timid, solitary person who stuttered, spoke haltingly, and felt ill at ease and awkward in society, though he was open and congenial with family and intimate friends. Although he gave numerous interviews, he always refrained from revealing his intimate feelings and often spoke ambiguously about his writings. He expected his readers to know him through his works and nothing else. The French critic Paul Fournel refers to him as "a man of few words" who nonetheless explains himself through his works.[2] Ernesto Ferrero, who was associated with Calvino at the Einaudi publishing house, tells us that his friend's "reticence and unsociability" were a defense mechanism for his "actions and his nature."[3] The outcome is that Calvino, the private man, remains somewhat of an enigma, notwithstanding the fact that so much has been written about him. Often personal experiences help to understand an author. In Calvino's case the only known concrete aspects of his life that left an indelible mark on the novelist were his scientific upbringing, his experiences under the Fascist puppet regime (1943–45) during the Nazi occupation of Italy, the many years spent in the editorial offices of Einaudi, and his long residence in Paris.

Italo Calvino was born on 15 October 1923 in Santiago de Las Vegas, a suburb of Havana, Cuba, where his parents were conducting scientific experiments. His father, Mario, a tropical agronomist and botanist, had spent a number of years in Mexico and other Central American countries. His mother, Eva Mameli-Calvino, a native of the island of Sardinia, was a botanist and also a university professor. His parents chose for him the name Italo because they did not want him to forget his Italian roots. However, less than two years after their son's birth the Calvinos returned to Italy and settled permanently in San Remo, Mario's native town. Thus Italo grew up on the Italian Riviera in the midst of nature, dividing his time between his family's Villa Meridiana in San Remo, where his father directed an experimental floriculture station, and their country house in the hills, a small working farm where the elder Calvino pioneered in the growing of grapefruit and avocados. The experience of living in San Remo on the Ligurian coast among so many exotic plants and trees was to have a profound influence on the future novelist and to provide him with much inspiration for his narrative writings. Indeed, *Il barone rampante* (*The Baron in the Trees*) grew out of Italo's and his brother Florio's habit as children of climbing the numerous trees of Villa Meridiana and spending long periods of time perched among the branches. In an interview with Maria Corti, Calvino stated that "San Remo continues to pop out in my books, in the most diverse pieces of writing."[4]

San Remo, a Mediterranean seaport and popular Italian resort on the western Ligurian coast, is situated in the center of a large cove and sheltered by a natural amphitheater of green hills that slope down to the calm blue waters of the bay. East of Nice, it is located about ten miles from the French border and eighty-five miles from Genoa. The city is divided into two different parts. The old terraced town, called *la Pigna*, still characteristically medieval, developed in feudal times as a fortification when the coastal region was infested with Moorish pirates. It has steep, narrow, winding alleys called *carrugi*, often connected by arches sustaining the top of the lofty buildings, and dark vaulted arcades with flights of cobbled steps, typical of many old Italian hill towns.

The architecture of the old town contrasts sharply with the modern structures of the lower town, which is located along the sea and characterized by beautiful beaches, elegant villas and hotels, gardens, scenic promenades, and gambling casinos. For many years the annual San Remo Song Festival has taken place in the Casino Municipale. Begun in the 1700s, the modern part of the town quickly became a favorite resort for European nobility. Protected by the Ligurian Alps to the north, the region's mild winter climate and its natural beauty have made San Remo the exclusive year-round spa and tourist attraction of the Italian Riviera, vying even with Portofino and Rapallo.

Although the Calvinos were strongly anti-Fascist and freethinkers who did not give their children a religious upbringing, Italo attended nonetheless a Protestant elementary school run by the Waldensians. For his secondary schooling he attended the state-run Ginnasio-Liceo G. D. Cassini, where he followed the classical curriculum, receiving the esteemed Classical diploma. In high school, at his parents' request, he was exempted from the traditional religious training. In June 1940, after Italy's delayed entry into the Second World War, when the Nazis were approaching Paris and Mussolini wanted to take part in the spoils of victory, Calvino participated in the Italian occupation of the French Riviera as a compulsory member of the Young Fascists. In 1941 he enrolled at the University of Turin, where his father was teaching. Although he already had some inclination toward becoming a writer—his first passion was to write for the theater—he chose to study agriculture to please his parents, but quickly lost interest after the first examinations, turning his back on the scientific world of his family. Nevertheless, he always retained the benefits of having been nurtured in a liberal and enlightened scientific atmosphere.[5]

When the Germans occupied Liguria and the rest of northern Italy in 1943 (under the guise of protecting Mussolini, who after his downfall had established there a puppet Fascist Social republic), Italo Calvino first evaded the Fascist draft and then joined the Italian Resistance together with his younger brother Florio. He was a partisan for twenty months and fought in the Ligurian mountains with the "Garibaldi Brigades" until 1945, when the Germans and the Fascists surrendered. During the last part of the liberation struggle his parents were held hostage for some months by the Germans. The war experience with all its horror left an indelible mark on Calvino's social consciousness and provided him with the raw material for his first successful literary attempts. In fact, his first novel, *Il sentiero dei nidi di ragno* (*The Path to the Nest of Spiders*), is set among the partisans in the Ligurian mountains and depicts their activities as observed by a small boy named Pin.

At the end of the war he joined the Italian Communist Party and began contributing to *Il Politecnico,* whose mission was to fill the cultural void created by the extended Fascist rule and to bring Italy back into the European cultural mainstream; he also collaborated with other leftist journals, especially *l'Unità,* the official party newspaper. He joined the Party not merely for ideological reasons, but because he felt that the Communist Party seemed to have the most realistic program for remaking Italy and for opposing a resurgence of fascism. At the same time he resumed his university studies, changing from agriculture to English literature; he wrote a thesis on Joseph Conrad and graduated in 1947. That year he found a job in the publicity department of the Turin publishing house Giulio Einaudi, where he eventually became an editor and where virtually all his works were published. He remained with Einaudi until 1984.

During the late forties and early fifties, Calvino began writing and publishing stories dealing with his wartime experiences as a partisan and as an anti-Fascist. When he finished *The Path to the Nest of Spiders* at the end of 1946, he showed it to his friend Cesare Pavese, who was by then already well known as a writer, and who together with the novelist Natalia Ginsburg was trying to bring the Einaudi publishing house back to life. Pavese, though not too enthusiastic, recommended its publication. The book achieved a respectable success (6,000 volumes sold—quite a feat in postwar Italy) when it was published in 1947, and launched Calvino on his career as a writer. For his first novel he won the prestigious Premio Riccione.

Calvino's experiences in Turin, a vital industrial city and center of proletarian struggle, as well as in the offices of Einaudi Editore, were fundamental to the intellectual and artistic formation of the young writer. He was put in touch with the controversial ideological, political, and literary ideas that were being discussed in the recovering nation, and he became personally familiar with their leading exponents. But above all, the nature of his work as a consulting editor—reading manuscripts—not only gave him the opportunity of promoting the writings of the most significant authors of modern Italy,[6] but also conditioned him to become a reader of texts.[7] This experience would allow him to create great works of fiction as well as of metafiction, most notably *Se una notte d'inverno un viaggiatore* (*If on a winter's night a traveler*), his most extensive analysis of the relationship between author, reader, and text. His first collection of short stories, *Ultimo viene il corvo* (The Crow Comes Last), published in 1949, deals with the Resistance and life in postwar Italy.

On the basis of his first publications, Calvino was associated with Pavese and with the novelist Elio Vittorini as a member of the Italian neorealist movement. Although the movement was not organized and did not have a specific artistic program, most writers of the period came under the influence of Herman Melville, Ernest Hemingway, Sinclair Lewis, Sherwood Anderson, Edgar Lee Masters, John Dos Passos, Theodore Dreiser, William Faulkner, and other American writers. Pavese and Vittorini were ardent promoters of these realistic writers, having translated into Italian many of their works; for the two anti-Fascist novelists America represented cultural and political freedom.

During the 1950s Calvino's narrative veered away from neorealism with his trilogy of novels: *Il visconte dimezzato*, 1952 (*The Cloven Viscount*), *Il barone rampante*, 1957 (*The Baron in the Trees*), and *Il cavaliere inesistente*, 1959 (*The Nonexistent Knight*). Although these highly fantastic novels, for which he received the Salento Prize in 1960, are not set in current society, they nevertheless offer allegorically a deep concern for contemporary social and political issues. In 1957 Calvino left the Communist Party, as did many Italians, as a result of the Russian intervention in the 1956 Hungarian revolution, his personal disillusionment with the socialist reforms in Italy, and his conviction that an artist should remain detached from politics. This political disinclination is best expressed in his satirical and allegorical novellas *La formica argentina*, 1952 (*The Argentine Ant*), *La speculazione edilizia*, 1957 (*A Plunge into Real Estate*), *La nuvola di smog*, 1958 (*Smog*), and many other stories, but most notably in the extremely realistic *La giornata d'uno scrutatore*, 1963 (*The Watcher*) where Amerigo Ormea, the disheartened "poll-watcher" of the story, muses: "Morality impels one to act; but what if the action is futile?"[8]

In 1959, together with Elio Vittorini, the leading left-wing intellectual of postwar Italy, Calvino founded *Il Menabò*, which published interesting and timely debates on the role of the intellectual vis-à-vis the ideological crises of the leftist political parties, bent on solving social, historical, and literary problems. The journal's most compelling program was to point out that the ever-increasing role of science in modern society is not necessarily in conflict with our humanistic values.

Under the influence of the Argentine author of exotic prose fiction Jorge Luis Borges, the Swiss founder of modern linguistics Ferdinand de Saussure, the modern critics Roland Barthes and Vladimir Propp, semiotics, structuralism—the entire spectrum of recent theories of narrative and even comic strips—Calvino once again changed course when he wrote *Le Cosmicomiche*, 1965 (*Cosmicomics*) and *Ti con zero*, 1967 (*t zero*). He abruptly pulled away from his familiar themes, making use of modern science as a means of creating illusory circumstances in order to communicate a new vision of reality.

In essence, so to speak, his new stories are cosmogonic fairy tales constructed around scientific propositions that permit him to narrate tales of science fiction reaching all the way back to our primordial universe.

In 1964 Calvino moved to Paris, without giving up his work at Einaudi, and married the Argentine-born Esther Singer—nicknamed Chichita—who worked as a translator at UNESCO headquarters. One year later their daughter, Abigail, was born. Calvino liked living away from Italy: "The ideal place for me," he wrote, "is the one in which it is most natural to live as a foreigner."[9] In Paris he became acquainted with the activities of Oulipo (*Ouvroir de littérature potentielle:* Workshop of Potential Literature) led by Raymond Queneau, poet, novelist, mathematician, and by the mathematical historian François LeLionnais. The group's intentions were to explore all the potentialities of writing and to apply mathematical structures to writing. As a result of this, in 1969 Calvino published *Il castello dei destini incrociati* (*The Castle of Crossed Destinies*), in which he focused on narrative language and interpretation. In this work, stories are created via the magical reading of tarot cards, used not to predict the future, but to re-create the past. In 1969 he also translated into Italian Queneau's novel *Les fleurs bleues* (*Blue Flowers*). A subsequent significant work published in 1972, *Le città invisibili* (*Invisible Cities*), presents a mythical Marco Polo who entertains an aged Kublai Khan by describing to him various imaginary cities of his decaying empire.

In 1979 Calvino once again broke stride with the publication of *If on a winter's night a traveler*, a narrative tour de force, a self-referential literary game as in Borges's recursive labyrinths. A male and a female reader set out to read a new novel by Calvino; their task is constantly interrupted to the extent that they are maneuvered, almost perversely, to read ten unfinished novels written by different authors.

In 1980 the Calvino family moved back to Italy and settled in Rome, where the author intensified his collaboration with the daily *La Repubblica*. Also his first major collection of essays, *Una pietra sopra: Discorsi di letteratura e società* (*The Uses of Literature*) was published in 1980.[10] In *Palomar*, his last significant book, published in 1983, the protagonist observes and describes various aspects of nature, questioning via an inner dialogue the arcane similarities between man and the cosmos, nature and human communication.

On 19 September 1985 Calvino died in a hospital in Siena from the effects of a stroke suffered twelve days earlier. At the time of his death he was almost sixty-two years old and on the point of departing for Harvard University, where he was supposed to deliver the Charles Eliot Norton Lectures for 1985. Although the last of the projected six lectures was never completed, five were published posthumously in 1988 under the title *Six Memos for the Next Millennium*. The loss of Calvino's creativity and talent was not Italy's alone, but also the world's.[11]

Throughout his career Calvino, like Mr. Palomar, the protagonist of his last novel, tried to defy with his technical virtuosity and fantastic characters the malaise of daily life in a dehumanizing, modern world controlled by science. He was a seeker of knowledge, and like Ariosto a visionary in a sublime and absurd world. His quest was to grasp the entire universe, to gain a cosmic sense of harmony and inner tranquility for himself and for his readers—all this through a continuous interplay between fantasy and reality and in a language that never changed.[12] In the final chapter of *Mr. Palomar*, properly called "Learning to be Dead," the protagonist, wondering what it means to be dead, realizes that it "is less easy than it might seem," and that it constitutes "himself plus the world minus him."[13]

NOTES

1. *Fiabe Italiane* (Turin: Einaudi, 1956). There are two English versions: *Italian Fables* (1961) and *Italian Folktales* (1980).

2. Paul Fournel, "Italo Calvino: cahiers d'exercice," *Magazine Littéraire* (June 1985): 84.

3. Ernesto Ferrero, "Edizioni Calvino," *L'Espresso* (19 May 1991): 109.

4. Maria Corti, "Intervista: Italo Calvino," *Autografo* 2 (Oct. 1985): 51.

5. In a 1960 interview Calvino stated that he hid his literary aspirations "from his intimate friends . . . and almost even from himself" (Contardo Calligaris, *Italo Calvino* [Milan: Mursia, 1985] 171). In a more recent interview (1985) with his English translator William Weaver, Calvino added: "I began writing fairly early. When I was around sixteen I tried to write pieces for the theater; the theater was my first passion, perhaps because at that time one of the links with the outside world was radio. And so I started writing—by trying to write—plays. When I was eighteen, something I wrote won a mention in a student competition" (William Weaver, "Calvino: An Interview and its Story," *Calvino Revisited*, ed. Franco Ricci [Toronto: Dovehouse, 1989], 25).

6. Among others, Calvino signed up for the Einaudi publishing house Bernard Malamud, Saul Bellow, and Julio Cortázar.

7. In his "By Way of an Autobiography," Calvino states: "Working in a publishing house, I spent more time with the books of others than with my own" (*The Uses of Literature* [New York: Harcourt Brace, 1986] 341).

8. *The Watcher and Other Stories* (New York: Harcourt Brace, 1971) 37.

9. "By Way of an Autobiography" 341.

10. His other collection of essays, *Collezione di sabbia* (Collection of Sand; Milan: Garzanti, 1984), was written mostly in the 1980s and published in *La Repubblica*.

11. Two collections of Calvino's narrative works were also published posthumously: *Sotto il sole giaguaro* (*Under the Jaguar Sun*, 1988); and *La strada di San Giovanni* (*The San Giovanni Road*, 1990). *I libri degli altri: Lettere 1947–1981* (a collection of letters written by Calvino to various authors while working for Einaudi) and *Perché leggere i classici* (Why Read the Classics) were published in 1991.

12. In "By Way of an Autobiography" Calvino writes: "Everything can change, but not the language that we carry inside us, like a world more exclusive and final than one's mother's womb" (341).

13. *Mr. Palomar* (New York: Harcourt Brace, 1985) 121, 122.

CHAPTER TWO

A Neorealistic Path to Literary Exordium:
The Path to the Nest of Spiders

Even though my natural tendency would be toward fantasy and invention, the first things I wrote were realistic.[1]

Calvino wrote his first novel during the postwar period marked by not only a remarkable resurgence in Italian fiction, but also by turmoil, unrest, desperation, hunger, revenge, and profound economic, social, and political instability. The Second World War changed the moral life of the nation; as Salvatore Quasimodo, the 1959 Nobel Prize winner for literature, said in 1953, the "individual, upon his return, no longer found any measure of conviction within his inner self because it had been diminished and ironically undermined during his confrontations with death."[2] Although American audiences are not well versed in Italian literature, they nevertheless know, on the whole, that postwar Italy was extraordinarily rich in imaginative and courageous realistic films that brought about a much-needed and better understanding of the country and its problems. When we consider that period we inevitably think of film directors such as Roberto Rossellini, Vittorio De Sica, and Luchino Visconti, among others, whose great films were categorized as neorealistic because their principal characteristic was a representation of life in its immediate reality. The films, imbued with a clear social and political commitment, not only represented realistic situations in contemporary Italy but also were filmed on location, in popular settings, with nonprofessional actors who, more often than not, spoke their local dialect instead of standard Italian. These films had a documentary quality which, according to Peter Bondanella, "contained a message of fundamental human solidarity fostered by the anti-Fascist Resistance within which most of the greatest Italian directors came of age."[3]

Similarly, in literature the compelling motives that urged Italian neorealist authors to write were a deep-felt need and obligation to present in a realistic mode their narrative testimonies of the recent war, as well as its calamitous consequences to the nation. Neorealism, however, was not really a well-defined movement, but rather a meeting of different artistic personalities who had various aspirations in common. It was an attempt to replace old literary narrative materials with others containing democratic, social, and historical values, and whose subject matter would be the people and the events of recent and current history: workers, farmers, partisans, and city dwellers presented in their struggle for survival. This was to be done in a new and practical language, untouched by traditional aesthetic considerations, almost akin to the spoken language of the country, and in some cases in sheer dialect. In a very significant and enlightening essay written by Calvino as a preface to the 1964 edition of *The Path to the Nest of Spiders,* we see his own hesitancy regarding the definition of neorealism:

> Having emerged from an experience, a war and a civil war that had spared no one, made communication between the writer and his audience immediate. . . . With our renewed freedom of speech, all at first felt a rage to narrate . . . [the] stories we had personally enacted or had witnessed mingled with those we had already heard as tales, with a voice, an accent, a mimed expression. . . . But the secret of how one wrote then did not lie only in this elementary universality of content . . . [but primarily] in a desire to *express.* . . . We knew all too well that what counted was the music and not the libretto. . . . "Neorealism" was not a school. . . . It was a collection of voices, largely marginal, a multiple discovery of the various Italys, even—or particularly—the Italys previously unknown to literature.[4]

In short, neorealism had no formal, structural, or thematic limitations for the authors whose main concern was above all to be witnesses to the ills of fascism and to the recent conflagration that had virtually destroyed their country.[5] What all neorealist Italian writers *did* have in common was not only a disgust for the moral emptiness prevalent in fascist culture and its bombastic rhetoric, but above all a compelling desire to relate their experiences under the tyranny of fascism and to promote objectively the idea of a reformed and better society in a clear, simple language, unconcerned with aesthetic literary standards.

The Path to the Nest of Spiders clearly reflects Calvino's experiences as a young partisan fighting in a communist brigade against the Fascist and German occupation of Italy. It narrates the war adventures of a young street urchin, a boy of about twelve or thirteen, mischievously wicked and at the same time naïve. He lives in the slums of a war-torn Ligurian town with his sister Rina, a young prostitute. Their mother is dead and their father has long abandoned them. Pin, who has no friends of his own age, fends for himself, working as a cobbler's apprentice, stealing and getting free drinks from the men at the local tavern whom he entertains with bawdy songs and, at the same time, mocks with his biting tongue. When he is enticed by one of the men to steal a pistol from a German sailor, one of Rina's customers, he is questioned, beaten, and put in jail by the Germans. In prison Pin meets an older boy, a communist member of the underground by the name of Lupo Rosso (Red Wolf). They both escape, and Pin joins a group of Resistance fighters in the Ligurian mountains. His detachment, however, instead of being typically composed of valiant, patriotic fighters, is made up of a sorrowful pack of misfits, including their leader Dritto (Straight or Righteous), who do not fully understand why they are fighting the enemy. Although the boy continues to face the same loneliness as before, he is nevertheless fascinated by the colorful existence of the group and, for the first time in his life, enjoys a sense of belonging. When Pin's unit is ordered into combat, Dritto, claiming to be ill, refuses to join his men, preferring instead to remain at the encampment where he goes to bed with the wife of one of the fighters. This takes place virtually in the presence of Pin who, because of his age, has also remained behind. When the partisans have to clear out of the area, Pin is once again on his own. He returns to the spider's nest where he had hidden the sailor's pistol for safekeeping, but it is no longer there. He surmises that it was stolen by Pelle, a former partisan who has joined the Fascists, and to whom Pin had revealed his secret. Eventually Pin recovers the weapon from his sister, who had gotten it from Pelle during a sexual encounter. Alone again, the distraught Pin runs into Cousin, the partisan who had first introduced him to the Resistance movement. As the novel comes to an end, the protective man and the boy walk hand in hand toward an unknown destiny, looking forward to a time when nature will heal all the horrors of war.

While postwar Italian art and letters typically dwelled on positive heroes,[6] dedicated to fighting social and political evils, Calvino, in his first short stories and in *The Path to the Nest of Spiders*, partially broke away from this stance. Instead, he presented his protagonists in a negative light, degraded and living on the margins of society—thieves, swindlers, unsavory characters—rebellious not only against the Fascists but also against the economic and social ills resulting from capitalistic bourgeois society. Artistically he presented his protagonists in an expressionistically distorted manner, making them negative because he "found a poetic meaning only in 'negativity' " (xi). Unlike his more engagé writer friends, who believed that their work had to contribute primarily to the betterment of society, Calvino was unwilling to overlook in his art the factionalism and the ill-feelings that were gripping the nation, not even for the sake of the country's need for brotherhood, redemption,and reconstruction. His aim was to challenge "the Resistance's detractors and, at the same time, those high priests of a hagiographic and edulcorated Resistance" (xiii), as he himself was to state years later.

In selecting Pin as his hero Calvino purposely eschewed the traditional pattern of contemporary Italian writers, who invariably selected heroic characters as representative of their political, social, and literary ideas. Pin possesses none of these admirable qualities and is too young to fully comprehend the reality of the situation during the 1943–45 oppression; he does not even "know the difference between when there's war and when there isn't" (87). For Pin, a truly pathetic reject from society, all adults are the same whether they are the Germans who go to bed with his sister or the local people whom he despises and yet defiantly entertains with bawdy songs. Pin joins the Ligurian partisans in order to escape from jail, and not because of conviction. In fact, several other partisans as well are totally devoid of any ideology or understanding and do not seem to know why they are participating in the struggle against tyranny. Pelle offers a good example of this opportunism when he leaves the partisans, joins the Blackshirts, and then betrays his former companions. "Calvino does not idealize his partisans," writes Frank Rosengarten; "they are not stalwart Sir Galahads, but ordinary flesh-and-blood people who are quite prone to vulgarity, lust, and cowardice."[7] However, unlike the men of the tavern, the partisans despite their failings treat Pin kindly, with genuine affection and generosity—sentiments he has never known before.

The title of the novel is intriguing and magically mysterious. The path symbolizes movement, transition, expression of an urgent desire or need for discovery and change that underlies the adolescent's life. It also presages Pin's escape from his dreadful life and entry into a different one where he will live new experiences intensively. The spiders, on the other hand, with their ceaseless weaving and killing, building and destroying, symbolize the continual alternation of forces on which the stability of Pin's universe depends. The idea of spinning a web implies fostering life. The Parcae in classical mythology were spinners who spun the thread of life and cut it short as they presided over the destiny of human beings. Pin's destiny revolves around this mysterious and magical place where he hides the pistol stolen from the German sailor. For him it symbolizes power, authority: "A real pistol. A real pistol. Pin tries to excite himself with the thought. Someone who has a real pistol can do anything, he's like a grownup. He can threaten to kill men and women and do whatever he likes with them" (14–15). Indeed, the weapon and its hiding place have all the qualities of a rite of passage practiced in primitive societies. The evocation of the secret event (stealing the pistol) and of the sacred place (spiders' nest) allow Calvino to dissolve the realistic elements of the novel—the Nazis, the Fascists, the war and all its consequences—into fabulous tones, and enchantment. Like the Latin American practitioners of magic realism, Calvino converts reality into fantasy without distorting the former. The magical effect is realized by juxtaposing scenes and details of great realism with fantastic and magical situations. This he does very artfully through the dislocation of time, place, and identity, and by zooming in on and fading out from reality.

The first critic to have captured the essence of Calvino's narrative was the novelist Cesare Pavese, who, in his review of *The Path to the Nest of Spiders*, underscored the fairy-tale quality of his writing and praised him as a *scoiattolo della penna* (squirrel of the pen) because, unlike other writers of the Resistance, he astutely "climbed into the trees, more for fun than fear, to observe partisan life as a fable of the forest, clamorous, multicolored, different."[8] Pavese also singled out the author's *sapore ariostesco* (Ariostoesque flavor) inasmuch as Calvino, too, used in his novel a kaleidoscope of episodes based on fact, magic, and fantasy. Ludovico Ariosto (1474–1533) had done so in his great epic, *Orlando Furioso*, as a means of escaping from the turbulent times in which he was living into a world of fantasy and freedom. However, adds Pavese, the "counterparts of our modern-day Ariosto are Stevenson, Kipling, Dickens and Nievo, successfully disguised as a young boy."

In fact, from the very beginning of the novel we are introduced into a romantic world of fantasy replete with echoes of Stevenson's *Treasure Island*, where Pin, like Jim Hawkins, experiences his adventure into the adult world in which he finally is accepted because of his displayed competence; Calvino's choice of the name Kim reminds us of Kipling's novel in which the protagonist, an orphan fending for himself in the slums of Lahore, swirls through the exotic beauty and squalor of India and its people, and the principal theme focuses on the chasm between the world of action and the world of spirit.[9] Likewise, Dickens's Pip of *Great Expectations* and his adventures in overcoming obstacles in life, as well as Ippolito Nievo's patriotic and romantic fervor, dramatized in his famous novel *Confessions of an Italian*, set in the period of Italian unification, resonate in Calvino's novel.[10] Moreover, the selection of monosyllabic names in *The Path to the Nest of Spiders*, like Kim and Pin, clearly is determined by other well-known literary names, such as Pip, Kim, Jim, Tom, Tim, Huck, Joe, Nick, found in English and American fiction.[11]

Calvino modulates the novel on two distinct tones: on the one hand we have Pin's wretched life inserted into the Nazi–Fascist oppression and the civil war; on the other hand we have a lyrical evocative tone that emerges from the Ligurian landscape and mountains where the boy's spiders operate in their secret hiding places. From the very beginning the Ligurian background—Calvino says "My landscape was something jealously mine" (viii)—sets the tone of the novel, and it becomes an essential part of the story, providing a sense of focus and continuity. Whenever described, it is always in luminous terms and presented as a bucolic sylvan garden profaned only by the ugliness of war. It is in the second tone that Calvino's poetic qualities are used in showing off the knowledge of the Ligurian flora and fauna acquired from his scientist parents. In modulating the two tones Calvino mingles realism, poetic feeling, social conviction, and sympathy in a dialogue between Pin's symbolic and evasive world and the war's actuality.

Like his literary archetypes Pin, too, is a picaresque character—though lacking compared to the shrewd talents of the classical picaro, Lazarillo de Tormes. Just as the Spanish picaro uses his wits and native intelligence as a defense against society as a whole, Pin—who has good qualities yet often is wicked, deceitful, crafty, sly, mischievous, though always winning in his innocence—uses his sarcasm and acerbic wit whenever he strikes back at those who have mistreated him, first against the taunting habitués of the local tavern and then against his comrades in the mountains. Everybody is afraid of him because he can be ruthless and "hurt them without any pity" (131). Only Cousin, who first introduced him to the partisans and then at the end becomes his guide and mentor, escapes somewhat unscathed from Pin's sadistic ill-will.

Pin, through whose innocent eyes we see the unfolding of the narrative events, has been shaped by the environment he has been condemned to live in. More than all the other characters in the novel he truly is an outcast and suffers from a sense of abandonment and isolation; his greatest urgency is for human fellowship and understanding, which he will partly find among the partisans and more fully with Cousin. He desperately longs to be with children of his own age with whom he could play and even show where spiders make their nests. "But Pin is not liked by boys of his own age; he is the friend of grown-ups, [and] he can say things to grown-ups that make them laugh or get angry, while other boys can't even understand what grown-ups say to each other." And so, "in order to disperse the cloud of loneliness which settles around his heart" (6–7), Pin is forced to be with adults who are friends and enemies at the same time, "turn their backs on him and are as incomprehensible and far-removed from him'' (7) as they are from the other rascals of the neighborhood. No matter how hard he tries, he does not know how to take part in games either of children or grown-ups. The only game he *does* play is with the stolen pistol and with the spiders.

Most intriguing is Cousin, a loner and Pin's affectionate mentor, who is always ready to undertake all by himself the dangerous task of killing collaborators, traitors, and spies. Because of his wife's infidelity, which he blames on the war, he now hates all women to the extent of blaming them for having started the war: ''Women, women I tell you, they're behind everything. Mussolini got the idea of the war from the Petacci sisters'' (93).[12] Cousin is the only one who shows affection to the boy. As his ''Great Friend'' he represents the boy's salvation, and ''is the last person Pin has left in all the world'' (144). At the end of the novel, amidst the flickering fireflies around the nest of spiders, ''they walk off into the country, with Pin holding Cousin's big soft calming hand'' (145). Cousin and the spiders' nest represent hope and redemption both for Pin and for Italy, which will be rebuilt into a progressive nation based on humanitarian ideals, just as the spiders have always rebuilt when their nest is destroyed.

Calvino originally began to write the novel without a precise plot in mind, save for the character of Pin. In order to give it a fictional base he added the sister, the pistol, and the partisans. Eventually from a projected picaresque tale he found himself compelled to turn it into a ''collective epic'' (xv). Calvino wanted to show that even the most fierce and primitive people, such as the misfits of Pin's group, who fought without any political conviction and were driven by ''an elementary impulse of human rescue'' (xiii), could be indoctrinated into becoming class-conscious. The Resistance movement provided the people of Italy a reason for being that went beyond their struggle in the civil war; and ultimately, because of the conflict, goodwill and trust could overcome hatred and deceit. As Rosengarten puts it, ''A messianic fervor permeates this novel: great hope for redemption animates its humble characters.''[13] In fact, Commissar Kim, Calvino's eloquent spokesman to whom the novel is dedicated[14] and the only intellectual in the novel, is portrayed as a medical student who yearns for logic and has a great interest in humanity. He is not well liked by the men because with his logic he forces them to come to terms with their own beliefs. He sees behind all human beings a ''great machine of class movement.'' Unlike the other commander of the partisans, Kim defends his idea of having put together a detachment of misfits who cannot be trusted, because they present him with a laboratory for political work where he can turn them into proletarians with a new class consciousness; for in spite of their shortcomings, they all fight against the enemy "with the same sort of urge in them. . . . Each has a an urge of his own . . . but they're all fighting in unison now, each as much as the other. . . . That's what political work is . . . to give them a sense" (100). Above all, they fight because of a deep-seated "resentment" that comes from

> the squalor of their lives, the filth of their homes, the obscenities they've known ever since babyhood, the strain of having to be bad. . . . An elementary, anonymous urge to vindicate all our humiliations; the worker from his exploitation, the peasant from his ignorance, the petty bourgeois from his inhibitions, the outcast from his corruption. This is what I believe our political work is, to use human misery against itself, for our own redemption, as the Fascists use misery to perpetuate misery and man fighting man. (102, 104)

In spite of his own reservations about the novel being too political, as well as severe criticism from some of his literary friends, Calvino nonetheless felt compelled to "satisfy the necessity of the ideological insertion," arbitrarily placing it in chapter 9, which, by his own admission, is the least felicitous of the novel.[15]

The novel is constructed as a series of episodes consisting of restrained events that never lead up to a powerful climax. There are no big scenes except for the uplifting account of the final episode that takes place in Pin's magical and emblematic path and which leads to a sort of resurrection. Calvino's language is colloquial and dialectal inasmuch as it is "clotted into patches of color" and includes a "documentary-like repertory (sayings, songs) which almost arrives at folklore" (x). The entire narrative, written in the present tense and told with "extraordinary lightness,"[16] is replete with repetitions and, except for the political parts, reflects the mentality of a child through whose innocent eyes everything is perceived. According to John Gatt-Rutter, "The boy protagonist, Pin, knows everything—that men fornicate and kill— but understands nothing."[17] The omniscient point of view allows the author to shift freely from the external to the internal worlds of Pin; the only time the point shifts from that of the omniscient narrator is in the case of Kim.

It is difficult to classify *The Path to the Nest of Spiders*. The author, who wrote it at the young age of twenty-three, did not yet have a precise idea of what he was doing and consequently did not follow rigorously any literary trend. He seems to have been intuitively led toward certain themes and forms that already foreshadowed his subsequent works: a certain inventiveness and mystification, a fablelike fantasy, a keen interest in nature, in the cosmos and mankind's place in it, as well as a propensity to be free from traditional literary schemes and structures. Calvino himself recognized the importance of his first novel, stating in the preface that his story as a writer was already contained in that beginning: "Your first book already defines you, while you are really far from being defined. And this definition is something you may then carry with you for the rest of your life, trying to confirm it or extend or correct or deny it; but you can never eliminate it" (xxiii). Calvino's originality is to be found in his inspired manner of presenting his vision of life, in the force of the expression and perspicacity of his observations on human nature and suffering, and in an almost absolute control of language.

NOTES

1. Alexander Stille, "An Interview with Italo Calvino," *Saturday Review* Mar.-Apr. 1985: 39.

2. Salvatore Quasimodo, *Poesie e discorsi sulla poesia,* ed. G. Finzi (Milan: Mondadori, 1971) 281.

3. Peter Bondanella, *Italian Cinema: From Neorealism to the Present* (New York: Continuum, 1983) 66.

4. *The Path to the Nest of Spiders* (New York: Ecco Press, 1987) v-vii. All quotations from the novel come from this edition. Page numbers referring to this edition are shown in the text in parentheses.

5. Rosengarten uses the term "The Italian Resistance Novel" in grouping the authors who dealt with the theme of resistance against Fascism and Nazism from different points of view and styles of method, and worked independently of each other. See Frank Rosengarten, "The Italian Resistance Novel (1945-1962)" in *From Verismo to Experimentalism,* ed. Sergio Pacifici (Bloomington: Indiana University Press, 1969) 212-16.

6. In the preface, Calvino writes: "You want 'revolutionary Romanticism,' do you? Well, I'll write a partisan story in which nobody is a hero, nobody has any class consciousness" (xiv).

7. Rosengarten 225.

8. Cesare Pavese, review of *Il sentiero dei nidi di ragno, L'Unità* 26 Sept. 1947.

9. "Our heads are still full of magic and miracles, thinks Kim. Sometimes he feels he is walking amid a world of symbols, like his namesake, little Kim in the middle of India, in that book of Kipling's which he had so often re-read as a boy" (105). At the end of the chapter we find out that Kim "feels like the hero of that novel read in his childhood; the half-English half-Indian boy who travels across India looking for the river of purification" (108).

10. In the preface, Calvino points out the similarity of the encounter between Pin and Cousin with that of Carlino and Spaccafumo in Nievo's novel. *Il sentiero dei nidi di ragno* (Milan: Garzanti, 1987) 18. Weaver's English translation of the preface fails to include this reference.

11. As far as Pelle is concerned, I would suggest that Calvino must have been familiar with Martin Andersen Nexos's novel *Pelle the Conqueror,* where a picaresque peasant boy becomes a trade unionist and strike leader. Like Pin, he starts out as an apprentice to a shoemaker and is made the butt of all sorts of heartless practical jokes by his elders. I should also point out the significance of Red Wolf, whose name not only stands in contrast to the Fascist Black Wolf, but contains allusions to the wolf in the story of Little Red Ridinghood.

12. Claretta Petacci was Mussolini's mistress. The two were captured by the partisans and shot on 28 April 1945.

13. Rosengarten 224-25.

17

14. It is somewhat puzzling that Calvino's dedication "A Kim, e a tutti gli altri" [to Kim, and to all the others] should have been left out of the English translation.

15. Calvino's writer friends advised him to eliminate the entire chapter. But, as he wrote in the preface, "I held out: the book had been born like this, with this composite, illegitimate element" (x).

16. Sergio Pacifici, "Italian Novels of the Fifties," *On Contemporary Literature*, ed. Richard Kostelanetz (New York: Avon, 1964) 171.

17. John Gatt-Rutter, *Writers and Politics in Modern Italy* (New York: Holmes & Meier, 1978) 47.

CHAPTER THREE

Fantastic and Realistic Webs of Prose

The art of writing tales consists in an ability to draw the rest of life from the nothing one has understood of it, but life begins again at the end of the page when one realizes that one knew nothing whatsoever.[1]

Between the summer of 1945, only a few months after the end of the war, and the spring of 1949, the period encompassing the writing and publication of *The Path to the Nest of Spiders,* Calvino wrote many short stories dealing with the war and its aftermath. Some appeared in the Turin and Genoa editions of *l'Unità,* the official newspaper of the Italian Communist Party. In 1949 thirty of these stories were published by Einaudi in a volume bearing the title *Ultimo viene il corvo* (The Crow Comes Last; most of the content appears in *Adam, One Afternoon, and Other Stories*).[2] Written "with a deep distrust and a deeper faith,"[3] as were the works of his contemporary Beppe Fenoglio, the narratives reflect on the whole Calvino's anguish and hope for a better society. As a result of the war, most of Italy lay in ruins; the economy was destroyed, and the nation suffered the loss of 440,000 people, among them soldiers, partisans, and civilians.[4] Consequently, during the postwar period Calvino was concerned with the lack of progress toward a truly democratic system, and was somewhat taken aback by the Italian Communist Party's dogmatic insistence that writers should toe the party line, represent positive heroes, and proclaim the intellectual and moral superiority of socialism.[5] In an article "Ingegneri e demolitori" (Engineers and Destroyers), he categorically made it known to his comrades that he was unwilling to become an "engineer of souls" as required by socialist realism: "We love more the ruins than the trusses and the bridges, the awareness of our society's ills has affected us down to the bone but has remained stagnant, the zealous study of these ills has bound us to them with either a secret or open attachment."[6]

In addition to his concern with the relations between writers and politics, he was disheartened by the lack of a viable political program he could believe in. He was weary—as becomes clear in the stories "Chi ha messo la mina nel mare?" ("Who Put the Mine in the Sea?") and "Impiccagione di un giudice" ("A Judgment")—that in spite of the collapse of fascism, its ideology continued to deeply influence Italian consciousness. He feared also that Italy's problems would continue to be more or less the same as they were before. In fact, due to national dissension and the unfulfilled promises of the political parties, the country was suffering from rampant unemployment, an economy in shambles, a high number of homeless and displaced people, political corruption, illiteracy, severe poverty, unequal distribution of wealth, labor unrest, self-destructive tendencies of rival parties, and finally the incipient Cold War.

Ultimo viene il corvo

The thirty stories brought together in *Ultimo viene il corvo* once again reflect the author's own experiences during the last phases of the war as well as describing the panorama of postwar Italy. Although they do not appear in chronological order, they seem to provide an overview of Calvino's political and artistic progress during a crucial period. In them we hear echoes of shouting Germans banging their fists against doors; we see the Blackshirts committing cruel deeds with no shame or remorse; we experience life in the mountains among the persecuted peasants and the disorganized partisans; we witness revenge and retaliation, hunger, survival, and acts of heroism. Indeed, although the collection contains diverse stories, unity is provided by shared temporality. The backdrop is still San Remo and Liguria, as was the case with *The Path to the Nest of Spiders,* and the protagonists, other than the ubiquitous proletarian partisans, are mainly the homeless, the unemployed, the peasants, laborers, children, and smugglers. Occasionally, as in "I fratelli Bagnasco (Dopo un po' si riparte)" ("Leaving Again Shortly") and "Pranzo con un pastore" ("A Goatherd at Luncheon"), we find bourgeois types with their typical class foibles. The characters weave out of one story and into another in a satisfying way, reminiscent of children's fables in which the protagonists reappear but in different situations. Of course, as has already been shown in the analysis of his first novel, Calvino's great appeal is inextricably bound to the fablelike quality of his works, in which he offers vivid and realistic portraits of life that operate, at the same time, on the very edge of fantasy. He does this in the manner of a fugue, arranging contrapuntally within each story the realistic/fabulous elements of his vision; also, the sequence of the stories forms a texture which consists of different individual voices that ultimately blend into a polyphonic sound.

"Un pomeriggio, Adamo" ("Adam, One Afternoon") and "Il giardino incantato" ("The Enchanted Garden") present an idyllic world of fantasy and adventure, but it is always underscored by a realistic awareness. In the first story, set in an Edenlike garden, we find an anarchist lad by the name of Libereso (which in Esperanto means "liberty") who works as a gardener and introduces a young servant girl to the fantastic world of nature; he showers her with gifts ranging from a pair of mating frogs to a hedgehog. On Sunday, instead of going to church, he tells Maria-nunziata,

> my father reads out loud from Kropotkin.[7] My father has hair down to his shoulders and a beard right down to his chest. And he wears shorts in summer and winter. And I do drawings for the Anarchist Federation windows. The figures in top hats are businessmen, those in caps are generals, and those in round hats are priests; then I paint them in water colors. (15)

In "The Enchanted Garden" two young children, Giovannino and Senerella, accidentally enter the garden of what they think is an abandoned villa where they frolic amidst the opulent surroundings. They do so with the apprehension of one who enters an unknown and enchanted forbidden world. As they play Ping-Pong, the ball hits a gong. At once two servants appear carrying trays filled with delicacies. The children uneasily partake of the food but cannot enjoy it because nothing seems to have any taste. "Everything in the garden was like that: lovely but impossible to enjoy properly" (22). When they peer through a window of the villa, they see a pale little boy who is looking into a book, "sitting there and turning the pages and glancing around with more anxiety and worry than their own" (22). They realize that all this wealth cannot be enjoyed by the sick boy, and so they flee because the realistic scene has disturbed their carefree life, and they fear that a spell, "the residue of some injustice committed long ago" (23), is hanging over the mysterious villa and its garden. The beauty of the story is that even when evil seems to be lurking in the background—i.e., the war and the foreboding garden—the fablelike quality of the narrative continues to work its magic, as nature with its regenerative capacity represents the positive in life. As Calvino himself has pointed out, the fantastic shows that the world is complicated beyond our comprehension.[8]

In "La stessa cosa del sangue" (The Identity of Blood Ties), "Attesa della morte in un albergo" (Awaiting Death in a Hotel Room), and "Angoscia in caserma" (Anguish in the Barracks), written immediately after the war's end, Calvino dwells on reprisals, deportations, hostages, betrayals,[9] and escape from forced military service. In the first story we recognize autobiographical elements when the mother of two teenagers is taken hostage by the German SS, as had actually happened to Calvino's own parents.[10] Although the story is powerful in depicting the dilemma of the Resistance in trying to prevent the taking of hostages, Calvino borders on propaganda as he extols the virtues of communism. The same is true in the second story when he hails the partisans as "Titans who are generating new laws," and men "who walk, go hungry, shoot, not for pay or because they are forced to do so, or because it amuses them, for they are men who have become evil by dint of being good."[11]

From a structural point of view, "Uno dei tre è ancora vivo" (One of the Three Is Still Alive) is a good example of Calvino's approach to narrative point of view. James Gardner comments that in these stories Calvino indulges "in those tricks that would later make him famous. One of these is the inverted perspective, whereby he, the author, adopts the point of view of the character who is narrating the tale, even when that viewpoint is diametrically opposed to his own."[12] In this narrative three naked soldiers are about to be executed by several peasants whose relatives have been brutally killed by the enemy and whose village has been destroyed. Their plan is to lead the prisoners up to a high ledge and shoot them. As the first two are shot and fall down the precipice, the third one leaps into the abyss before being shot. He survives, because his fall is cushioned by the bodies of his companions. Before the execution the narrative point of view is that of the Italian peasants as they debate the correctness of their actions, but then we suddenly are compelled to look through the eyes of the condemned men as they confront death. We know that the narrator and the reader agree with the action of the avengers, but we eagerly take the side of the surviving naked man when he refuses to believe the peasants' promise not to harm him if he climbs up the rope they have thrown him. He rightly refuses, knowing that "they wanted to save him at all costs so as to be able to shoot him all over again; but at that moment they just wanted to save him, and their voices had a tone of affection, of human brotherhood" (79). In the end he escapes through an underground passage, and we find ourselves rooting for him as he emerges from the darkness and beholds a valley of woods and shrub-covered slopes. In the distance he sees white smoke coming from a house: "Life, thought the naked man, was a hell, with rare moments recalling some ancient paradise" (82). Calvino waves a wand, and dares the reader to follow his magical sleight of hand as he finds refuge, once more, in the regenerative powers of nature.

The title story, "Ultimo viene il corvo" ("The Crow Comes Last"), could easily have become a chapter of *The Path to the Nest of Spiders* in view of similarities in character and circumstance. A band of hungry partisans, stopped at a trout stream, debate whether to use hand grenades as a way of killing the fish so they can have a good meal. A young boy, who has been watching, approaches the men, borrows a rifle, carefully takes aim, and in rapid succession kills several trout without missing a shot. The partisans praise his marksmanship and ask him to join their unit. He accepts, provided he is allowed to keep the rifle. On their way to camp he is told not to shoot unless it is absolutely necessary, in order to conserve ammunition and hide their position from the enemy. However, the boy starts shooting at different animals that come into his sight, and the men take back the gun. At daybreak he steals away from camp, taking their best rifle and filling his haversack with cartridges. Then, we see him shooting birds, squirrels, snails, lizards, frogs, and even mushrooms, never missing his mark. As he wanders among "unknown fields," he sees German soldiers coming toward him with arms at the ready; but upon seeing the smiling boy, they shout at him as if they want to greet him. He shoots at one of them aiming at one of his uniform buttons. Eventually the partisans hear the guns and come to the boy's rescue. In the skirmish one German soldier manages to reach a position above the boy, who with the first shot puts the soldier's rifle out of order, and with another tears off a shoulder strap from his uniform. The boy plays with his prey, pursuing it with accurate and deadly aim, until he corners him behind a big rock in the glade. At this point we have another inversion of perspective when the narrative point of view becomes that of the German soldier as he confronts the situation he is in. In spite of several failed escape attempts, he still feels safe hidden behind the rock because he has several grenades left. Suddenly as birds appear in the sky, the boy brings them all down with his rifle. Thinking that he is now distracted by the birds, the German throws a hand grenade, but quickly a shot explodes it in midair. As the German dives for cover, he notices a crow wheeling in the sky above him. The boy starts to shoot at pine cones, and the soldier thinks that he may not have noticed the bird. As the crow is circling with impunity lower and lower, he wonders if it is not a hallucination, and that perhaps the crow's appearance portends that one's time has come. The man feels that he must warn the boy, who keeps firing at the pine cones. He jumps up and points to the bird, shouting in his language. He is immediately struck "in the middle of an eagle with spread wings embroidered on his tunic," while "slowly the crow came circling down" (73).

Although the protagonist of this story is a young "Apple Face" boy, the point of view is no longer that of the picaresque but innocent Pin, because, as Contardo Calligaris points out, in all the stories of *Ultimo viene il corvo* we no longer find "the essential formal quality of fables: the infantile perspective."[13] The boy is intriguing because of his riflery, but remains a mystery to the reader. We know only that he is glad to leave his home, "a blotch of slate, straw, and cow dung at the bottom of the valley," and venture into the world "because there were new things to be seen at every turn, . . . false distances . . . that could be filled by a shot swallowing the air in between" (69). The weapon and the boy's deadly accuracy are paradigmatic of how in wartime soldiers become callous to killing, while at the same time they are fascinated by the deadly instruments of war, losing all touch with human qualities. The machines of destruction become toys to be played with, the way "Apple Face" plays with his gun and targets. Like Pin's stolen pistol, the rifle allows the boy to enter the world of adults, where he surpasses them in courage and marksmanship; above all, it allows him to escape from his hovel, as the poor have historically done by joining the military, because by going "from one target to another, perhaps he could go around the world doing it" (70). Since he seems to be totally taken with his superhuman marksmanship, and so are we as readers, the war is almost forgotten in this game for targets—animal, vegetable, and human. Ironically and tragically, at the end of the drama, the German asks the boy to kill the circling crow, thus providing with his body a final target for the deadly aim of the shooter. As Giorgio Baroni points out, "The entire scene seems to be really more a shooting party than a war action."[14] Nevertheless, one should note that until this moment the boy has killed only animals, and that the soldier in uniform becomes the first human casualty of his marksmanship when he stops being a mere target and, as Giovanna Cerina observes, the killing "sanctions" the hero's ultimate recognition "of the soldier as the enemy."[15]

In his close psychological reading of "The Crow Comes Last," A. H. Carter finds that "the realistic and fantastic elements interrelate, mutually supporting each other in the development of the narrative." Calvino takes us from "a realistic texture to a mixture of realism and fantasy," and he extends the boy's skill as a rifleman to "superhuman proportions."[16] Indeed, there is something cold and logical in this Kafkaesque story and in the boy's superhuman abilities which put him on a parallel with the encircling and approaching bird. The crow unquestionably senses and announces death with its flight pattern,[17] undisturbed by the loud sound of the rifle. Death is the last thing that happens to us. We are all born into a pattern where life itself is a game, which is how the boy sees life when he shoots at targets. His function, however, is to interfere with the pattern of life by eliminating all existing things that come into view. The only thing he cannot interfere with is the black crow, which symbolically represents death, and therefore cannot be eliminated. This explains, perhaps, why he does not shoot the crow. But why does the German soldier make himself a target by indicating to the boy the bird's presence above him? Is it to distract him, so that he can kill him with one of the remaining hand grenades? Or is it to warn him about death's presence? Furthermore, whose death does the bird foreshadow? The text is ambiguous in this regard, since it tells us that the crow was circling "over him" without specifying over whom—the boy, the soldier, or possibly both.

Ironically, by killing the soldier, the boy unwittingly becomes next in line for the crow's ritualistic prophecy. It is even possible that the soldier may be sacrificing his own life for that of the boy when he thinks, moments before being shot: "Perhaps when one is about to die one sees every kind of bird pass; when one sees the crow it means one's time has come. He must warn the boy" (73). But then, we don't really know if the German is actually having these thoughts or if they are part of his imagined hallucination. Even the open-ended finale of the story—"Slowly the crow came circling down"—is full of ambiguity. Is the bird going to feed on the soldier's body, or is it choosing its next victim? The crow could be hovering over the boy because they both strike indiscriminately. Perhaps the boy does not see the German as the enemy but as a target, much like the crow. Is life senseless? Are the enemies on our side as well as the other? Are there sides? Or only circumstances?

And finally, not only do we have once more in "The Crow Comes Last" the paradox of violence set against a backdrop of an almost idyllic nature— "The current was a network of light ripples with the water flowing in the middle"—but in this instance nature seems to be a willing accomplice in the art of destruction and death. According to Carter, the thematic power of the story is the presentation of death as the ultimate force: "Nature appears to cooperate with the force, sending over birds, providing unknown meadows and valleys, and sending the scavenger crow as a messenger of death. The boy may be the agent of the shooting, but his skill seems mysteriously a part of some larger order."[18]

"The Crow Comes Last," only five pages long, is more complex and ambiguous than the other stories of the collection; it is densely packed with metaphors and allusions that clearly suggest something straight out of Kafka. Calvino approaches everything in the spirit of play, but his phrasing of the story is in a language that brings us extremely close to reality.[19]

I giovani del Po

In the last phase of his so-called social neorealistic period. Calvino wrote a novelette, *I giovani del Po* (The Young of the Po River), which appeared serially during 1957–58 in the periodical *Officina.*[20] The first draft dated back to 1947 and the actual writing was done in 1950 and 1951. Dissatisfied with the work, Calvino refused to let it come out in book form. In his introduction to the first installment, Calvino points out that in writing it, "I was aiming to provide an image of human disintegration; but it resulted in an unusually grey book, in which the fullness of life, even though much is said about it, is barely felt: therefore I have never wanted to publish it as a volume."

Clearly a bildungsroman, it is also an epistolary novel set in the neorealistic period. The predominant first-person narrative voice alternates with the third. The plot unravels from a correspondence between the protagonist, Nino, and his friend Nanin, who has remained home in his village. Nino has left his native Ligurian town for Turin, in search of work in an industrial factory, which he regards as the matrix for social change. He finds a job as a machinist and eventually participates in the class struggle of the labor movement, hoping to help fulfill the ideals and dreams of postwar Italy. Nino meets Giovanna, a student, and her parasitic bourgeois friends, and falls in love. Because of their class differences—her jealous Fascist friends resent her involvement with a proletarian—Nino must reconcile his love for the girl, whose family is strongly anticommunist, and his obligations as a militant worker. Concurrently he is also torn between his need to be in touch with nature and the dreary life in the industrial city. Confused about his own political ideas, he wishes to clarify them, and the act of writing the letters permits him to do so. In the factory he attains a certain notoriety with his fellow workers, though he is admired more for his character than for his sociopolitical ideas. Eventually his commitment to the struggle helps him overcome his sentiments for the girl, and the relationship ends in failure. During a labor dispute led by Nino, Giovanna is accidentally killed, and her death brings about the successful resolution of the strike. In spite of this, and unlike Calvino's position in *The Path to the Nest of Spiders,* Nino remains a positive hero as required, at that time, by the Italian Communist Party.

I giovani del Po is patently autobiographical; it parallels Calvino's own experiences when he left San Remo and went to work for the Einaudi publishing house in Turin. It also describes his longings for his idyllic San Remo, the political involvement in the city, his doubts and search for identity, as well as his existentialistic wistfulness for the unfulfilled promises of the Resistance movement. This is best described by Nino, when he writes to his friend:[21]

> I don't seem to be able to have a life without it being in pieces: in my hometown I felt the absence of the working class, here I miss the sea and the woods; with my

girl I don't have the kind of intellectual exchange I have with my companions; with them I don't have that sense of amazement I experience with my girl.[22]

Because the major part of the novel is in the first person, the language is close to colloquial Italian and often shows little regard for proper grammatical structure. Prior to the writing of this novel, Calvino had often expressed in newspaper articles and essays his concerns and experiences regarding "the city, industrial civilization, the workers" and above all "an arduous search for natural happiness." Yet when he tried to express in narrative form the same concerns, he was totally dissatisfied with *I giovani del Po* because he felt that it had turned out to be "a rather muddled neorealist grotesque" novel.[23] Alas, Calvino was quite right. However, as has been pointed out, the usefulness of this narrative is "as a document to Calvino's attempts, between 1950 and 1951, to find a follow-up" to his first novel.[24] The artificiality and failure of the novel is best summed up by Cristina Benussi when she points out that Calvino lacked a true understanding of the worker's plight; that his disguise as the proletarian Nino is immediately undone, "because working at Einaudi or at Fiat, was not, is not, the same thing."[25] Be that as it may, after Nino has become a minor shop union leader, he speculates on the role of the worker in the larger scheme of world problems. He writes to his friend: "I feel that the story of the world depends also on what I do. Only remotely, you understand. Nonetheless, it does depend on me somewhat."[26] Ernesto Ferrero, who also worked for many years at Einaudi and was closely associated with the author, notes that Nino's concerns and ideas express the core of Calvino's ethical and methodological principle, both as man and writer. These are

> his total concentration in the apparent insignificance of a small industrial crafts-man, with the full awareness that the world can change only through the concomitance of so many loving and precise small gestures; and at the same time knowing that it takes only a bit of wind to upset any project, that the inevitable setbacks, and any attempt to overcome them, are the only stoic, desperate, proud and subdued privilege that twentieth-century man can afford to do.[27]

I racconti

In 1958 Calvino published his second collection of stories, *I racconti* (The Stories). The anthology, consisting of forty-nine short stories and three novelettes, is divided into four parts: "Gli idilli difficili" (Difficult Idylls), "Le memorie difficili" (Difficult Memories), "Gli amori difficili" (Difficult Loves), and "La vita difficile" (Difficult Life). There are nineteen stories previously included in the 1949 edition of *Ultimo viene il corvo*, and many of the other narratives had appeared earlier in various Italian newspapers and periodicals. Calvino knew very well the art of recycling his material and getting as much advantage as possible out of it. The following may shed some light on Calvino's recycling of previously published material and shifting styles. Asked by Maria Corti if he followed a process of coherent development in his narrative activity, Calvino replied:

> I change track in order to say something I would not have been able to express with a previous conceptualization. That does not mean that I have exhausted a previous line of approach: it can happen that I may go on for years in planning other texts to add to the ones I have already written, even though I might already be interested in something quite different; in fact, I do not consider an undertaking completed until I have given it a meaning and a structure that I deem definitive.[28]

Indeed, the three novelettes constituting Part 4 had already been published in two separate volumes (*La speculazione edilizia*, and *La formica argentina* which includes *La nuvola di smog*), as well as in prominent journals. The short stories "L'entrata in guerra" (Entrance into War), "Gli avanguardisti a Mentone" (The *Avanguardisti* in Menton), and "Le notti dell'UNPA" (The Nights at UNPA),[29] were previously published in 1954 in a separate volume, *L'entrata in guerra*.

In the three war stories, written in a still pronounced neorealistic manner, Calvino goes back to 10 June 1940, when Italy finally decided to join Nazi Germany and enter World War II, in order to explore the recent past and "trace the itineraries of the individual and collective conscience" of the people during the Fascist regime.[30] The teenage protagonist is patently Calvino himself who, as a member of a Fascist militia composed of high school students, underwent similar war experiences on the French–Italian border. At first the young man of the title story sees only the ceremonial and exhilarating aspects of war—adventure, the excitement of danger, parades, shining uniforms, a visit by Mussolini—as he moves through various vicissitudes, totally detached from the events and the consequences of war. However, when he finally takes off his uniform, he becomes again aware of his bourgeois nature and loses the apathy with which he had been viewing the horrors of war. In "Le notti dell'UNPA," the protagonist has a far more dramatic and emotional change of heart as he struggles with a guilty conscience brought about by his carefree attitude toward the cruelties of war:

> The city with its uncertain lights lay before me. I was sleepy and unhappy. The night was rejecting me. And I expected nothing from the day. What was I to do?

I wanted to lose myself into the night, empty my body and soul into its darkness, to rebel, but I understood that what drew me to it was only the deaf, desperate negation of the day.[31]

In "Gli avanguardisti a Mentone," Calvino not only shows the protagonist's disgust in seeing the Fascists pillage the French town, but above all he parodies Mussolini's dream of enlarging continental Italy at the expense of the French. Ironically, unlike the rapidly sweeping German military forces, Italy was too late and managed to gain only a tiny, insignificant strip of land near the French border. In these remembrances of the momentous war events during the summer of 1940, Calvino presents himself as an anti-heroic character opposed to the regime but incapable of taking any decisive action—Franco Ricci characterizes him well as "an immature spectator gnawed by anxiety."[32]

Marcovaldo

Ten narratives from *I racconti* dealing with the protagonist Marcovaldo were eventually augmented with a number of similar stories and published in 1963 in a separate volume intended for Italian secondary school children: *Marcovaldo ovvero Le stagioni in città* (*Marcovaldo or the Seasons in the City*).[33] In a note accompanying the English version of the collection, Calvino writes that the first ten stories were written in the early 1950s and "thus are set in a very poor Italy, the Italy of neorealistic movies," and the additional ten "date from the mid-60s, when the illusions of an economic boom flourished" (v). In addition to the chronological, social, and economic differences, Maria Corti finds that the earlier tales are ideologically simple, Cinderella-like fables—*racconti-favole*—where Marcovaldo struggles for the most basic needs for survival, and where the city with all its negative aspects is pitted against the idyllic countryside. The second series of stories, those written in the 60s, grow in sophistication, are more surreal, and present more conflicting values where "the antithesis city–countryside has become archaic," yielding to "technological reality vs power of invention." This is so because Calvino's ideological motivation has become "less contingent, more universal, subtle and complex."[34]

The stories take place in an unnamed northern Italian industrial city—very likely Turin; each is dedicated to a season, and all follow five cycles of the four yearly seasons. Marcovaldo, who apparently has become a stock character in Italian letters in the manner of Sancho Panza, Don Abbondio, Don Camillo, or Charlie Chaplin's little tramp, is a manual laborer who works in a warehouse, lives with a nagging wife and six children in crowded quarters, barely earns their keep, and always longs for life in the country, which he abandoned by coming to the inhospitable city. He bears a high-sounding medieval chivalric name (Marcovaldo was the giant slain by Orlando in Luigi Pulci's *Morgante*) just like all the other adult characters appearing in the stories—Domitilla, Amadigi, Tornaquinci, Guendolina, Sigismondo, Astolfo, Fiordaligi,—whereas the children have simple, normal names. He is best described in the first story:

> This Marcovaldo possessed an eye ill-suited to city life: billboards, traffic-lights, shop-windows, neon signs, posters, no matter how carefully devised to catch the attention, never arrested his gaze, which might have been running over the desert sands. Instead, he would never miss a leaf yellowing on a branch, a feather trapped by a roof-tile; there was no horsefly on a horse's back, no worm-hole in a plank, or fig-peel squashed on the sidewalk that Marcovaldo didn't remark and ponder over, discovering the changes of season, the yearnings of his heart, and the woes of his existence. (1)

Marcovaldo expresses our uneasiness in a constantly and rapidly changing society that makes us outcasts by marring our existence. He stands for the plight of the individual who, paradoxically, though repelled by this way of life, at the same time knows that he is an integral part of the very system he so abhors. In his preface to the 1963 school edition of Marcovaldo, Calvino states that the protagonist is a "Man of Nature," exiled to an industrial city where he is an "immigrant" in an "estranged world from which there is no escape."

Typically, the *Marcovaldo* stories adhere to the following structure: (1) Marcovaldo notices the coming and going of the seasons by observing both the animal and the vegetal kingdoms; (2) he dreams of return to a natural state; (3) he faces inevitable disappointment because it is impossible to turn back to an idyllic condition which exists only as an illusion, as Calvino explains:

> The book certainly does not invite us to lull ourselves into an attitude of superficial optimism: contemporary man has lost the harmony between himself and the environment in which he lives, and the overcoming of this disharmony is an arduous task, because expectations that are too easy and too idyllic always turn out to be illusory.[35]

Despite "the woes of existence," Marcovaldo succeeds in preserving the pristine qualities of his nature: innocence, modesty, frankness, goodness, resignation to his fate, vivid fantasy, and hope that springs eternal. As an immigrant to a both technological and more culturally sophisticated society, he hasn't fully grown up and therefore, just like our contemporary consumer-oriented society so ready to abuse the environment and deplete our scarce natural resources, Marcovaldo too is incapable of measuring his actions or foreseeing their often dangerous consequences.

In "The Poisonous Rabbit," while being discharged from a hospital, Marcovaldo steals a rabbit from a laboratory not knowing that it has been injected with a dreaded illness. He brings it home and thinks it will make a good meal. But first the animal must be fattened up. Unbeknownst to him, his wife, Domitilla, decides to have it killed the same day because all their money has been spent on medicines and there is no food left in the house. The children take the rabbit to Signora Diomira to have it killed and skinned, but instead they let it go free. For the poor animal this is an entirely new experience: "It was an animal born prisoner: its yearning for liberty did not have broad horizons. The greatest gift it had known in life was the ability to have a few moments free of fear. Now, now it could move, with nothing around to frighten it, perhaps for the first time in its life" (57).[36] At work Marcovaldo is suddenly surrounded by a multitude of orderlies, doctors, and policemen anxious to reclaim the stolen rabbit. Eventually, the animal is rushed back to the hospital in an ambulance, together with Marcovaldo and his family who are going "to be interned for observation and for a series of vaccine tests" (59). The fact is, the rabbit would certainly be better off dying a quick death rather than having to suffer the agonies resulting from further painful scientific experiments. But it is not the only creature to exist in a system aptly characterized by John Updike as "a world of deferred disaster."[37] Both man and animal are victims, yet the victimizer is always man.

Although the narratives are set in the 50s and early 60s, they have a characteristic fablelike quality that manifests itself in the simplicity of language and structure, in the poetic and fantastic aura of the situations, and primarily in the stories' indeterminate localities and situations. The city is not identified, Marcovaldo's job is not well defined, and his place of work is not determined. Calvino explains that the city is nameless because it represents *all* industrial cities, and Sbav & Co., the establishment where his character is employed—we never find out what it produces—is "*the* company, the firm, the symbol of all the firms, the enterprises, and the corporations that today control people and events."[38] In short, the calculated abstractions convey the feeling that modern life has become too abstract, and that we have lost the precious human contact with things and nature that is crucial for even a relatively minimal but satisfying existence.

This is why Marcovaldo always seeks the presence of nature even in the difficult and disfigured world of an industrialized metropolis. Just like children, who because of their innocence and fantastic abilities are capable of seeing and believing certain realities that adults no longer perceive, so only Marcovaldo notices even the slightest traces of nature in the asphalt and concrete jungles of the city. In the first tale, "Mushrooms in the City," the wind blows spores in from the countryside. Marcovaldo spots sprouting mushrooms near his trolley stop, and to him "the gray wretched world surrounding him seemed suddenly generous with hidden riches; something could still be expected of life, beyond the hourly wage of his stipulated salary, with inflation index, family grant, and cost-of-living allowance" (2). He bides his time, waiting for the mushrooms to mature, and refuses to divulge the location of the patch even to his family, fearing that they might tell others. After a downpour, together with his children he runs to the patch and they begin to gather the full-grown mushrooms. When he notices the local street cleaner with a basket full of mushrooms, momentarily he gets angry; but then he quickly succumbs to "a generous impulse" and tells the passersby to partake in the harvest. That evening all the mushroom gatherers meet again in the same hospital ward where they are being treated for food poisoning. Fortunately, "it was not serious, because the number of mushrooms eaten by each person was quite small" (4). Clearly, Calvino is trying to tell us that nature is still powerful enough to break through the barriers created by man and penetrate into the heart of the city. At the same time, he is warning us that nature too has its dangerous side, and that we face today the potential of both natural and man-made disasters.

In "A Journey with the Cows," one hot summer night, while the whole family is asleep, Marcovaldo hears a distant clank of bells and the sound "of hundreds and hundreds of steps, slow, scattered, hollow" (46). He instinctively knows that a herd of cattle is passing through the city on its way to pasture in the mountains. The herd evokes for him "the odor of dung, wild flowers, and milk," and the animals do not seem to be touched by the city because they are "already absorbed into their world of damp meadows, mountain mists and the fords of streams" (46–47). Marcovaldo's children, born and raised in the city and totally unfamiliar with their father's rustic beginnings, ask him: "Are cows like trams? Do they have stops? Where's the beginning of the cow's line?" When he tells them that the cows are going to the mountains, to eat grass, they inquire: "Can they wear skis?" and "Don't they get fined if they trample the lawns?" (47). This idyllic scene, however, backfires on Marcovaldo because his eldest son, Michelino, follows the herd to the mountains without telling his parents. Weeks later, when the boy returns home, he complains that he worked like a mule and that he never had a chance to do what he had wanted more than anything else: to enjoy the green meadows. And so we learn that like the city, even the irresistible country has its drawbacks.

Marcovaldo has the vital language and inventiveness of plot that characterize Calvino's other fiction, but it also has a sharper focus of intention and a deeper level of understanding and compassion. Marcovaldo, the Italian little tramp, is clearly a favorite of Calvino, who always presents him wittily, with great affection, commiseration, and admiration. The author always inserts a note of pathos that makes the hero not only amusing but endearing to younger and older readers alike: "A book for children? A book for teenagers? A book for grownups?" asks Calvino in his preface, and then rhetorically replies by wondering, "Is it rather a book in which the Author through the screen of simple narrative structures expresses his perplexed and questioning relationship with the world? Perhaps even this."[39] Indeed, the stories of his Marcovaldo cycle can be viewed as parables about both the vulnerability and the resiliency of human dignity. That we find ourselves laughing at Marcovaldo's miseries and mishaps does not in any way diminish their impact, for ours is the laughter of recognition and empathy, melancholy yet cathartic.

In Calvino's view, "A background of melancholy colors the book from beginning to end."[40] In "The City Lost in the Snow," Marcovaldo is awakened one morning by silence. He finds the city gone and replaced "by a white sheet of paper." Walking to work in the fresh snow, he feels "free as he had never felt before. In the city all differences between sidewalk and street had vanished; vehicles could not pass" (16). He feels unshackled because he can freely walk in the middle of the street, trample on flower beds, and cross wherever it pleases him. At work he is told to clear the snow from the sidewalk. He shovels with gusto because he "felt the snow was a friend, an element that erased the cage of walls which imprisoned his life" (17). As he contemplates a snowman, he suddenly finds himself buried by a mass of snow that has fallen off the roof. The children, who had made the snowman, marvel at the presence of a second snowman. When they stick a carrot into its head, Marcovaldo, who has not eaten all day, chews on it and makes it disappear. And when they try to give him a nose made out of coal, he spits it out, causing them to run away thinking the snowman is alive. Because of the frigid temperature Marcovaldo sneezes so powerfully that he causes "a genuine tornado" that completely clears the courtyard, and "the things of every day" reappear to him "sharp and hostile" (20).

Despite the comical and hard-to-swallow plot situations of these stories, Calvino is always striving for a meaningful realism: "But in presenting this book to the schools, we wish to offer to the young a writing in which the themes of contemporary life are treated with a pungent spirit, without rhetorical indulgences, and with a constant invitation for reflection."[41] In "Santa's Children," the concluding story of the collection, the author presents a bitter and sarcastic indictment of the commercial exploitation of Christmas and a parody of our consumer-oriented capitalistic society that will stop at nothing in order to make a profit. One winter the Public Relations Office at Sbav & Co. decides that the Christmas presents for the most important persons associated with the firm should be home-delivered by someone dressed as Santa Claus. Marcovaldo is chosen and promised a bonus if he makes fifty deliveries per day. His first trip is to his home, wanting to surprise his children. But they easily recognize him and barely look up because they have become accustomed to seeing Santa Clauses: it seems that many other firms have also recruited a large number of jobless people to dress as Santa Claus, and these have been roaming the city streets delivering packages. When they tell their father that they are preparing presents for poor children, he remarks that "poor children don't exist any more!" But Michelino inquires: "Is that why you don't bring us presents, Papà?" (115). Feeling guilty, Marcovaldo takes Michelino along on his round of deliveries. Although he is getting nice tips, Marcovaldo regrets that the recipients of the gifts show no excitement, curiosity, or gratitude. At a luxurious house they meet a nine-year-old boy who is totally bored and unconcerned about getting a present from Santa. The governess explains that he has already received three hundred and twelve presents. Outside, Michelino asks, "Papà is that little boy a poor child?" (117), and Marcovaldo tells him that he is the son of the president of the Society for the Implementation of Christmas Consumption. Hearing this, Michelino runs away. That evening Michelino explains to his father that he had run away in order to go home and fetch presents for the poor boy, "the one that was so sad . . . the one in the villa, with the Christmas tree" (118). He gave the boy three presents that made him very happy: a hammer with which he broke all the toys and the glassware; a slingshot with which he broke the balls on the Christmas tree; and a box of kitchen matches that "made him the happiest of all," with which he destroyed everything by burning down the house (119).

The next day, returning to work, Marcovaldo thinks that he is going to be fired. But instead he is told to change all the packages because the Society for the Implementation of Christmas Consumption has launched a new campaign to push the "Destructive Gift." He learns that the president's son had received some "ultramodern gift-articles, Japanese, and for the first time the child was obviously enjoying himself" (119). This reversal in company policy, however, is not determined by the child's happiness, but by a more practical business consideration: "the Destructive Gift serves to destroy articles of every sort: just what's needed to speed up the pace of consumption and give the market a boost" (119–20). With this story Calvino dramatizes the ills of our society where all our values can be bought and sold and everything is valued in terms of production and consumption. The aim of the powers that control the economic system is not to provide the consumer with useful and necessary goods, but rather to manufacture only what will result in greater profits. Calvino seems to be saying also that if the system continues in this manner, it will eventually self-destruct, the way the villa was demolished by the boy's Destructive Gift. In fact, "Santa's Children" reminds us of the goose that laid the golden egg, another fable where greed resulted in a needless loss.

Laden with a bag of Destructive Gifts, Marcovaldo returns to the streets filled with shoppers, bright lights, Christmas trees, Santa Clauses; but then, abruptly, both he and the city disappear from the text. The narrative transports us to a snow-covered field near a black forest, where a white hare is made invisible by the snow and a wolf by the dark forest. The victim's presence is seen only by his footprints, while that of the victimizer can be seen from his white teeth when he opens his mouth. The wolf chases the hare, who seems to escape; but we are not sure: " 'Is he here? There? Is he a bit farther on?' Only the expanse of snow could be seen, white as this page" (121).

"Santa's Children," like many of the other Marcovaldo stories, starts with reality and then shifts to fantasy once the meaning emerges. The Author typically pulls back with his characteristic elusiveness, confident that the important meaning of a story is the one the reader gets on his own; at this juncture, adds Calvino, the Author "hastens to remember that it has all been a game." This clarification allows us to understand why this story more than the others—with the exception of "The Wrong Stop," where Marcovaldo thinks he is getting on a bus but then finds himself on a plane headed for India—ends with a surrealistic scene and why the concrete images of the city and Marcovaldo dissolve; and like Russian dolls or Chinese boxes "the detailed grotesque sketch turns out to be inserted in another design, a drawing of snow and animals that we find in children's books, which then transforms itself into an abstract design, then into a white page."[42] The conscious display of coloristic effects, the fact that the narrative richness is visual, and the repeated use of *disegno* (a drawing, design, sketch), are clear references to

Calvino's strong interest in cartoons and comic books that dates back to his youth. Indeed, he informs us that his Marcovaldo stories follow the classical narrative structure of children's comic books.

In *Marcovaldo,* Calvino has artfully created a preposterous but endearing antihero who struggles farcically against the caprices of fate and the irrational abuses of capitalistic and technological society where the normal relationships between cause and effect disintegrate. Marcovaldo, the lost soul often shown in the context of the wealthy—especially in "Marcovaldo at the Supermarket"—is not a rebel or a dissident but only a misfit, a nonconformist, who shows only natural human responses to the situations he is in. He is an urban pícaro who meets and pits his wits against a variety of people—bosses, his wife, children, policemen, doctors, maids—and his naïve approach to life entangles him in risky situations from which he removes himself effortlessly, ingeniously, and by goodwill and good luck. He never gets a real chance in life, and like Chaplin's wistful little tramp he too is perpetually and mercilessly knocked about by modern times. But Marcovaldo does not despair or look for an easy way out, because he represents the mass of poor immigrants who leave the impoverished South and come to the industrialized North in search of a better life. He tries very hard to "adapt and conform," writes Ilene T. Olken, "but will never succeed, as his children may do; he is too divided between the two worlds, ill-prepared and therefore victimized."[43] And yet, though Marcovaldo is always confused and clobbered in the collection's twenty amusing satires, he is never totally beaten, and the reader is always rooting for him.

NOTES

1. *The Nonexistent Knight and The Cloven Viscount* (New York: Random House, 1962) 61.

2. *Adam, One Afternoon, and Other Stories* (London: Secker & Warburg, 1983). The English edition, first published by Collins in 1957, contains only twenty of the thirty stories found in the Italian edition, plus "The Argentine Ant." Page numbers referring to the 1983 edition are given in the text in parentheses.

Of the thirty original stories, only nineteen were included by the author in his collection *I racconti,* published in 1958. In 1969, Calvino published a new edition of *Ultimo viene il corvo,* in which twenty-five stories from the original printing were included, plus five other ones written after 1949. *Difficult Loves,* the English translation of *I racconti* published in 1984, presents a total of twenty-eight stories, but only fourteen come from *Adam, One Afternoon, and Other Stories.*

3. Quoted from Walter Mauro, *Realtà mito e favola nella narrativa italiana del Novecento* (Milan: Sugar Co Edizioni, 1974) 152.

4. For a detailed account of the war's devastation, see Alberto Traldi, *Fascism and Fiction* (Metuchen, NJ: Scarecrow Press, 1987).

5. In his story "Isabella e Fioravanti," Calvino satirizes the Party's sense of superiority. The narrative appeared in *L'Unità*, 31 Oct. 1948: 3.

6. Italo Calvino, "Ingegneri e demolitori. Il compito di 'ingegnere delle anime' che la società socialista dà allo scrittore," *Rinascita* 11 Nov. 1948: 400.

7. Prince Peter Alekseevich Kropotkin (1842–1921), Russian anarchist, who after 1917 rejected bolshevism. He is best known for *Memoirs of a Revolutionist* and *The Anarchists in the Russian Revolution*.

8. Introduzione, *Racconti fantastici dell'Ottocento* [Nineteenth-Century Fantastic Short Stories] (Milan: Mondadori, 1983).

9. In "Attesa della morte in un albergo" the traitor is once again Pelle. However, unlike in *Il sentiero*, here he is called Pelle-di-biscia, Snake-Skin. To the best of my knowledge, the three stories have not been translated into English.

10. Calvino has stated that when he deserted the Fascist army and joined the partisans, his "father and mother were arrested by the Fascists and for several months were the hostages of the SS." Alexander Stille, "An Interview with Italo Calvino," *Saturday Review* Mar.-Apr. 1985: 37.

11. *Ultimo viene il corvo* (Turin: Einaudi, 1949) 106, 104.

12. James Gardner, "Italo Calvino 1923–1985," *The New Criterion* 4 (Dec. 1985): 7–8.

13. Contardo Calligaris, *Italo Calvino* (Milan: Mursia, 1985) 20.

14. Giorgio Baroni, *Italo Calvino: Introduzione e guida allo studio dell'opera calviniana* (Florence: Le Monnier, 1988) 31.

15. Giovanna Cerina, "L'eroe, lo spazio narrativo e la costruzione del significato. Lettura di 'Ultimo viene il corvo,' " in *Dalla novella rusticale al racconto neorealista*, ed. Sandro Maxia and Giovanni Pirodda (Rome: Bulzoni Editore, 1979) 138.

16. Albert Howard Carter III, *Italo Calvino: Metamorphoses of Fantasy* (Ann Arbor: UMI Research Press, 1987) 16.

17. According to Cirlot, the crow has "certain mystic powers and in particular the ability to foresee the future" (J. E. Cirlot, *A Dictionary of Symbols* [New York, Philosophical Library, 1962] 68–69).

18. Carter 23.

19. In his interview with Maria Corti, Calvino informs us that "Ultimo viene il corvo" was inspired by one of Gustave Flaubert's stories: "Recently, re-reading the scene of the hunt in the 'Légende de saint Julien l'Hôpitalier' I relived profoundly the moment in which I became aware of my fondness for the gothic and animalistic, which surfaces in a story such as 'Ultimo viene il corvo' as well as in other stories written at that time and after" (Corti, "Intervista: Italo Calvino," *Autografo*, 2 [Oct. 1985]: 48). For a detailed comparison of Calvino's and Flaubert's stories, see Lucia Re, *Calvino and the Age of Neorealism: Fables of Estrangement* (Stanford: Stanford University Press, 1990) 164–69, 378. According to Re, "Calvino's 'deconstruction' of Flaubert's story implies in turn a deconstruction of the Resistance mystique" (166).

20. *I giovani del Po* appeared in *Officina* 8 (Feb. 1957), 9–10 (June 1957), 11 (Nov. 1957), and 12 (Apr. 1958). It has not been translated into English.

21. Typically, Calvino and his narrator are the same. See Giovanni Falaschi, "Ritratti critici di contemporanei: Italo Calvino," *Belfagor* 27 (1972): 547, and Calligaris 84.

22. *Officina* 12 (Apr. 1958): 547.

23. *Officina* 8 (Feb. 1957): 331.

24. J. R. Woodhouse, *Italo Calvino: A Reappraisal and an Appreciation of the Trilogy* (Hull: University of Hull, 1968) 91.

25. Cristina Benussi, *Introduzione a Calvino* (Rome-Bari: Laterza, 1989) 24.

26. *Officina*, 9–10 (June 1957): 407.

27. Ernesto Ferrero, "Edizioni Calvino," *L'Espresso* (19 May 1991): 108–09.

28. Corti, 48.

29. The *Avanguardisti* was a Fascist paramilitary youth organization for males 14–18 years old. UNPA was a Fascist civil defense group charged with the protection of civil installations during the war.

30. *L'entrata in guerra* (Turin: Einaudi, 1986) back cover.

31. "Le notti dell'UNPA," *L'entrata in guerra* 84.

32. Franco Ricci, *Difficult Games: A Reading of "I racconti" by Italo Calvino* (Waterloo, Ont.: Wilfrid Laurier University Press, 1990) 49.

33. The English edition, which I have followed, is *Marcovaldo or the Seasons in the City* (New York: Harcourt Brace, 1983). Page numbers referring to this edition are shown in parentheses.

34. Maria Corti, "Testi o macrotesto? I racconti di Marcovaldo," *Il viaggio testuale* (Turin: Einaudi, 1978) 196. Actually there are two different types of antithesis. As has been pointed out by Ossola, Marcovaldo cannot escape from the stereotype "nature vs culture, country vs city" (Carlo Ossola, "L'invisibile e il suo 'dove,' " *Lettere italiane* 39 [April-June 1987]: 225).

35. "Presentazione e note a cura dell'autore," *Marcovaldo ovvero Le stagioni in città* (Turin: Einaudi, 1966) 8.

36. In 1984 Calvino will return to the theme of freedom in his short story "Un re in ascolto" ("A King Listens").

37. John Updike, "Modernist, Postmodernist, What Will They Think of Next?" *The New Yorker* (10 Sept. 1984): 141.

38. "Presentazione e note a cura dell'autore" 7. One should keep in mind that "società anonima" is the Italian term for a legal business corporation (Inc.).

39. "Presentazione" 11.

40. "Presentazione" 8.

41. "Presentazione" 11.

42. "Presentazione" 11.

43. Ilene T. Olken, *With Pleated Eye and Garnet Wing: Symmetries of Italo Calvino* (Ann Arbor: University of Michigan Press, 1984) 122.

CHAPTER FOUR

Our Ancestors: A Viscount, a Baron, and a Knight

My intent was to fight all the possible sunderings of humanity, and to champion the total individual, this much is certain.[1]

The philosopher and critic Adriano Tilgher was instrumental in identifying the antithesis of *life* and *form* as a constant in Pirandello's works. Although Pirandello had expressed this contrast in his early writings, apparently he had done so unconsciously. Thus, it could be argued that the playwright profited from this awareness as he further developed his art and thought, best expressed today by the term "Pirandellian ideas." A similar scenario occurred in the case of Calvino, who was unquestionably influenced by Cesare Pavese's and Elio Vittorini's early assessments of his first writings: that his originality and artistic nucleus were to be found in the adventurous and fabulous elements of his fiction. Pavese had called the author a "squirrel of the pen" who "climbed into the trees," while Vittorini characterized his work as "realism with a fairy-tale timbre" and "fairy tale with a realistic timbre."[2] Consequently, having failed in his attempt to realize with *I giovani del Po* a truly neorealist novel, with the creation of the trilogy *Il visconte dimezzato*, 1952 (*The Cloven Viscount*), *Il barone rampante*, 1957 (*The Baron in the Trees*), and *Il cavaliere inesistente*, 1959 (*The Nonexistent Knight*)— published collectively as *I nostri antenati*, 1960 (Our Ancestors)—Calvino veered away from realism in favor of a more fabulous realm—very much in the vein of Ariosto's fanciful, extravagant, and implausible adventures. Among all the poets Ariosto was Calvino's favorite. He never tired of reading him because, as he stated in 1959,

Is my love for Ariosto an evasion? He teaches us how intelligence lives above all of fantasy, irony, and accuracy of form; and how none of these attributes is an end to itself but how they can all become part of a conception of the world, and serve to better value virtue and human vices. These are all contemporary lessons, necessary today, in an age of electronic brains and flights into space. The energy that propels Orlando, Angelica, Ruggiero, Bradamante, Astolfo . . . faces the future, I am certain of it, and not the past.[3]

In the first novel Calvino presents a grotesque Viscount who has been split into halves; in the second, the hero, very much like a squirrel, lives out his life in the trees; and in the third, the protagonist Agilulfo is actually a suit of white armor with nothing inside it. All three novels are viewed by Milanini as consequences of common metaphors—"to behave like half a man," "to remain suspended," and "to be empty on the inside."[4] All three take place in distant bygone times—the ninth, seventeenth, and eighteenth centuries—as if Calvino were stepping back to "grasp from a privileged position (that of the observer who looks down), the whole complexity of social, political, and even moral relationships of circumambient reality, which virtually bore down on him in the act of writing."[5]

The Cloven Viscount

In *The Cloven Viscount*, Viscount Medardo of Terralba joins the Christian forces to fight against infidels in Bohemia during the late-seventeenth-century war between Austria and Turkey. Approaching the royal encampment, the still innocent and inexperienced warrior encounters the horrors of war and its accompanying pestilence. When he finally joins in the battle, he is quickly halved by a cannonball. The mutilated body not only lacks one arm and one leg, "but the whole thorax and abdomen between the arm and leg had been swept away. . . . All that remained of the head was one eye, one ear, one cheek, half a nose, half a mouth, half a chin and half a forehead; the other half of the head was just not there" (156).[6]

Unaware of each other, the two parts of the Viscount live on autonomously. The right half of Medardo, after being sealed with pitch, returns to his Ligurian estate in Terralba and establishes a reign of terror among the local populace by cutting in half plants and animals, setting fires, and condemning several of his subjects to death for minor infractions. He leans on a crutch and is covered by a black cloak and hood, while on the left everything seems "hidden and wrapped in edges and folds" of black drapery (159). Near Terralba is the village of Pratofungo, where lepers live. In spite of their disease they live happily, playing strange instruments invented by them and indulging in carnal pleasures which make them forget their forced isolation from society. Not far away, and in contrast to the carefree lepers, there is a colony of Huguenots. They have fled from France, where they were persecuted by the king. They are suspicious, hardworking, and extremely puritanical in their ways. The elder Ezekiel, forever reproaching and urging his followers to work harder, continuously shouts at them with his fists raised to the sky: "Famine and plague! Famine and plague!" (183). Eventually the other half of the Viscount, endowed with exemplary qualities, arrives at Terralba and protects the populace from the evil segment. At first, however, the people fail to recognize that it is the left side of Medardo that has returned. When the two sides fight a duel for the love of a young shepherdess, Pamela, both are badly wounded. But Doctor Trelawney sews the cloven parts together, thus making the Viscount whole again, "neither good nor bad, but a mixture of goodness and badness, apparently not dissimilar to what it had been before the halving" (245).

The story is told by the Viscount's bastard nephew, who at the beginning of the narrative is a seven- or eight-year-old child but at its conclusion has become an adolescent. Thus the events span several years. The boy loves to roam the fields and the woods in the company of Doctor Trelawney, a bizarre shipwrecked Englishman and formerly ship's doctor to the legendary Captain Cook.[7] Rather than being concerned with healing the sick, the doctor is more interested in drink and in a rare "crickets' disease caught by one cricket in a thousand and doing no particular harm" (168). His great passion, however, is catching will-o'-the wisps.

In the preface to *The Cloven Viscount,* Calvino informs the reader that when he began writing the novel in 1951, it was as a pastime, and he intended it to be merely a fantastic tale. Yet he found himself unable to escape the impact of the turbulent times in which he was living:

> We were in the heat of the cold war, in the air there was a tension, a deaf sundering, which was not manifest in visible images, but nonetheless bore down on our hearts. . . . Much to my surprise I found myself expressing not only the suffering of that particular moment, but also the urgency of escaping it.[8]

This was certainly a very trying moment for Europe and the world. In 1946 Winston Churchill declared that an Iron Curtain had fallen across Europe, and in 1948 the Soviets seized Czechoslovakia and blockaded the Allied sector of Berlin; in 1949 the Chinese Communists defeated Chiang Kai-shek and gained control of mainland China, while on the European continent the Western allies formed NATO; in 1950 North Korea with China's support invaded South Korea, bringing the world powers to the brink of a nuclear conflagration; finally, in 1952 the United States, after many atomic tests, exploded its first hydrogen bomb. In his 1955 essay "Il midollo del leone" (The Lion's Marrow), discussing his own existentialistic anguish as well as the "literature of negation," Calvino wrote: "This awareness of living at the most tragic and lowest point of a human parabola, to live between Buchenwald and the H-bomb, is the point of departure of all our fantasies, all our thoughts."[9] In spite of these traumatic events that would lead us to believe that Medardo's two parts are in effect representative of this struggle, Calvino insisted that he was not interested merely in the problem of good and evil, but in *dimidiamento* (sundering, rift, splitting, halving, estrangement); that he used the two traits solely to create a contrast, just as a painter employs colors to accentuate a particular form. The two opposite sides of Medardo served to accentuate the pervasive *dimidiamento* of the individual and of society: "Sundered, mutilated, and enemy to himself is contemporary man; Marx called him 'alienated,' and Freud 'repressed.' "[10] Man's old harmony has vanished, Calvino concluded in this essay, and we must strive for a new wholeness. Certainly Medardo's disharmony and division are meant to underscore the inability of contemporary man to see clearly what is happening to the world and to himself. Although the author readily offers helpful ideas about interpreting the novel, he admits that his characters may be interpreted differently from his own suggestions.

As an organic and whole individual, the Viscount is unable to see reality as it truly exists. He must therefore be severed, dissected, and subjected to rigorous analysis in order to be able to see his own merits and faults, and humanistically perceive life with all its contradictions. Indeed, both of Medardo's parts recognize the utility of being halved; and the evil side of Medardo would like to split everything, as he tells the young narrator, in order

> that everyone could escape from his obtuse and ignorant wholeness. I was whole and all things were natural and confused to me, stupid as the air; I thought I was seeing all and it was only the outside rind. If you ever become a half of yourself . . . you'll understand things beyond the common intelligence of brains that are whole. You'll have lost half of yourself and of the world, but the remaining half will be a thousand times deeper and more precious. And you too would find yourself wanting everything to be halved like yourself, because beauty and knowledge and justice only exists [sic] in what has been cut to shreds. (191–92)

Ironically and paradoxically, Medardo's good side agrees with this outlook, although he sees everything in terms of suffering and its elimination:

> One understands the sorrow of every person and thing in the world at its own incompleteness. I was whole and did not understand, and moved about deaf and unfeeling amid the pain and sorrow all around us, in places where as a whole person one would least think to find it. It's not only me, Pamela, who am a spoilt being, but you and everyone else too. Now I have a fellowship which I did not understand, did not know before, when whole, a fellowship with all mutilated and incomplete things in the world. If you come with me, Pamela, you'll learn to suffer with everyone's ills, and tend your own by tending theirs. (216–17)

One is reminded of the novelist Italo Svevo's *Confessions of Zeno,* where Zeno, the neurotic and hypochondriac protagonist, is convinced that healthy people have no conception of what health really is. His contention is that health, wholeness, cannot analyze itself, and that it "is only we invalids who can know anything about ourselves."[11] Svevo uses the symptomatic characteristics of Graves' disease—hyperactivity and hypoactivity—to formulate a vision of life and man's place in it. It is the balance between the active and inactive, the healthy and the ill, the hero and antihero, that makes society survive and move forward. The same could be said about the two contrasting sides of Medardo. Both are imperfect and equally resented by the people: the bad for his obvious cruelty and the good for his blindness in believing that the only way of reforming society, including his evil counterpart, is by good example and by "showing ourselves kind and virtuous" (231). The result of his naïveté—some would call him today a classic bleeding-heart liberal—is that many Terralbians engaged in fighting evil are killed needlessly. Above all he is despised for his moralizing dogmatic fervor, and for interfering in other people's affairs to such an extent that they have ended up being "lost between an evil and a virtue equally inhuman" (235). And yet, both sides have positive qualities, best summarized by Calvino himself in "Il midollo del leone." With obvious reference to Medardo's disfigured face, he states that as a writer he is not interested in an affective rapport with reality, but rather prefers "the bitter and somewhat crooked face of someone determined not to disguise from himself anything at all concerning the world's negative qualities."[12] Additionally, on the basis of his readings of Antonio Gramsci, one of the founders of the Italian Communist Party in 1921, Calvino further clarifies for us the formal duality of Medardo: one side represents "pessimism of the intelligence," and the other "optimism of the will."[13] Similarly, another analogy can be made with what Sartre called the man of good faith vis-à-vis the man of bad faith. In the first instance, the individual is honest with himself, understands the human condition, and fully accepts responsibility for his actions. In the other instance, the man of bad faith is a hypocrite who uses the pretext of good intentions as an excuse to escape responsibility for his conduct, which always involves the suffering of others.

The *dimidiamento* is not limited to the protagonist of the novel, but is reflected in the other characters as well. Mastro Pietrochiodo, the carpenter who zealously constructs the gallows and other instruments of torture for Medardo's victims, plies his trade with hardly any concern for the evil to which he is contributing. He is typical of the modern scientists who undertake sophisticated experimentation without regard for its potentially evil results.

Ironically, Pietrochiodo is quite industrious when it comes to creating machines of evil purpose, but reluctant and doubtful "whether building good machines was not beyond human possibility" (229). Modern scientists—Calvino undoubtedly has in mind the builders of nuclear weapons—although essentially well-meaning, are likewise tempted by their desire for knowledge to experiment selfishly with life and to end up in a hell of their own making.

Doctor Trelawney, the eccentric English physician who has totally forgotten his Hippocratic oath, presents yet another form of *dimidiamento*. In addition to his drink, he prefers to pursue "pure science"—the useless search for will-o'-the-wisps[14] and the study of an almost nonexistent disease affecting crickets—instead of practicing "meaningful" medicine. In other words, the doctor is very attentive to animals, yet disgusted by "human beings and their infirmities" (177). One is reminded of *The Tin Drum*, Günter Grass's satire of Nazi violence, in which a storm trooper who has participated in the Reich's atrocities is nevertheless drummed out from the military because of his "inhuman cruelty to animals." Even at the end of *The Cloven Viscount*, after Dr. Trelawney has reconnected Medardo's two halves and finally does take some interest in the sick, he still refuses to go near the lepers. And as soon as the opportunity arises, he abandons Terralba, where he knows very well that he is desperately needed as a doctor. He rejoins his old crony, Captain Cook, "whose gunwales and rigging were full of sailors carrying pineapples and tortoises and waving scrolls with maxims on them in Latin and English." And to what purpose? To respond to the Captain's summon: "Come on board at once, Doctor, as we want to get on with that game of cards," a game interrupted years before by the shipwreck (246). For Calvino, Trelawney clearly represents the "scientist devoid of any integration with living humanity."[15] J. R. Woodhouse properly observes that in the political and social essays Calvino was writing during the composition of *The Cloven Viscount*, "machines very often assume human proportions while human beings become cogs in their wheels," and society with its increasing reliance upon specialists ends up "isolating that specialist from his fellow man, and hence helping to destroy the structure of society itself, certainly causing a rift between the individual and his environment."[16]

Unlike the unfulfilled men of Terralba, the two principal female protagonists are presented as complete and wholesome characters, totally lacking in *dimidiamento*. Sebastiana, the Viscount's old nurse, is the only one who fails to see him as having two separate natures. As an integrating force representing human nature, she sees him only in his totality, and accepts him the way he is, despite the hardships he imposes on her. The same can be said of Pamela, the young shepherdess for whose affection the two parts of Medardo carry on the bloody duel. She too represents, in Calvino's words, the notion "of feminine concreteness," for it is because of her that the two male counterparts coalesce.[17]

Dimidiamento is not limited to the individual, but is also inherently present in society. This is best expressed by the lepers and the Huguenots, two isolated groups living apart on the fringes of Terralba who are "isolated physically by a hillside and a hedge respectively, as well as by their unapproachable natures."[18] In Calvino's view the lepers represent man's hedonistic qualities: "irresponsibility, happy decadence, the nexus aesthetism–disease, and in a certain way contemporary artistic and literary decadentism, as well as that of all times (Arcadia)."[19] They too, like the cloven parts of the Viscount, are split not only in their progressively decaying bodies, reflective of Medardo's frenzy for halving everything; above all, they are severed from society, which regards them as outcasts and to which they can never return. But unlike Medardo, they can't be put together again. This is why they have forgotten "the human community from which their disease had cut them off" (176), and find solace in their licentious and decadent way of life, never complaining about their punishing affliction.

The Huguenots, who stand in direct contrast to the lepers, are meant to represent austere moralism: "They exemplify (both in a satiric and admiring way) the Protestant origins of Capitalism according to Max Weber, and, by analogy, any other society based on an active moralism." Calvino, who often cites the likely possibility that his family name had its origin in Calvinism, adds that they also represent "a religious ethic without religion."[20] In fact, after their expulsion from France, they came to the area of Terralba without their sacred books and objects, "and now had neither Bibles to read from nor Mass to say or hymns to sing nor prayers to recite" (181).[21] They are no longer familiar with their original religious practices, and have even stopped proselytizing. When they want to sing a psalm, they do not remember the words, only the melody. Since they do not know what constitutes sin, they have imposed upon themselves many prohibitions lest they make mistakes. "But with time the rules of their agricultural labors had acquired a value equal to those of the Commandments, as had the habits of thrift and diligent housekeeping to which they were forced" (182). The puritanical work ethic and the profit motive are paramount in their way of life. When Ezekiel is asked to lower the price of rye so that the hungry can be fed, and to consider the good he can do, he replies impassively: "To do good, brother, does not mean lowering prices" (226).

The power of *The Cloven Viscount* lies in its simple style and subtle humor; in its fantastic Ariosto-like vision; in the unmasking of contemporary man's false identities, and the fragmentation and mutilation of his world, as well as in the realistic exposure of his follies and fears; and finally, in the author's courage in recognizing absurdity and confronting it with a sophistication that seems naïve and childlike, but remains ever rooted in reality. In addition to the novel's political and moral implications, Calvino, like all good storytellers, wants to entertain his readers and at the same time stimulate them to probe deeper into the text.[22]

Finally, it should be noted that the novel brings to mind Rudolph Eric Raspe's *Adventures of Baron Munchausen,* the celebrated collection of popular, humorous, and highly colored German tales with which Calvino was familiar.[23] Very much like Medardo, Baron Munchausen, when his horse is split in two by a suddenly dropped portcullis, has his farrier bring "both parts together while hot," and sew them up "with sprigs and young shoots of laurel that were just at hand."[24] Not only do we have here the presence of *dimidiamento*—albeit that of an animal—and the rejoining of two split parts, but also a scene very much reminiscent of Medardo's description of the "cavalry stables where the veterinarians were at work patching up hides with stitches, belts and plasters of boiling tar, while horses and doctors neighed and stamped" (149). Indeed, in the macabre scene of the littered battlefield, when Medardo is on his way to join his comrades, he quickly learns that horses are first to die in combat at the hand of low-statured Turks, who wield scimitars made "to cleave their bellies at a stroke" (147). Later on, the Viscount's horse is disemboweled even before he is struck and split by the fateful cannon ball: "All its guts were hanging to the ground. The poor beast looked up at its master, then lowered its head as if to browse on its intestines, but that was only a last show of heroism; it fainted, then died" (154). Baron Munchausen's horse, however, is luckier for it is not aware of its own sustained loss: "They had dropped the port-cullis," narrates the Baron, "and unperceived by me, and the spirited animal, it had totally cut off his hind part, which lay still quivering on the outside of the gate."[25] What captures the reader of both *The Cloven Viscount* and the *Adventures of Baron Munchausen* is that the unimaginable events—rather than the events themselves—come in a rush, are received with a willingness to suspend judgment despite disbelief, and become pure and innocent fantasy. These palpable absurdities represent, perhaps, a satiric revenge of Calvino's and Raspe's prodigal fantasy against the hard, overbearing, pessimistic reality of their respective worlds.

The Baron in the Trees

It has been said that honesty with oneself is paramount as a common value in all existentialist thinking, and that all existentialist writings describe the emotional travail of trying to attain it. Unquestionably Calvino wishes to convey this notion when he clarifies to the reader the real essence of his narrative theme: "A person willfully imposes on himself a difficult rule and he follows it no matter where the consequences lead him, because without this rule he would be untrue to himself and to others."[26] This is precisely what happens in *The Baron in the Trees,* when a young boy, after a minor disagreement with his father, climbs up a tree and lives an arboreal existence for the rest of his life. *The Baron in the Trees,* Calvino's longest novel, was written between 10 December 1956 and 26 February 1957, when the author, still trying to define for himself the role of the intellectual in contemporary society as well as his own moral commitment to the Italian Communist Party, was contemplating breaking with it after the Soviets' brutal 1956 intervention in the Hungarian revolution and its repression. Regarding this period, Calvino writes in 1960 that it had been one of "reevaluating the role we can have in the historical movement, when new hopes and new afflictions succeed one another. In spite of this, the times are showing improvement; it's a matter of finding the right accord between the conscience of the individual and the course of history."[27]

The Baron in the Trees is a most unusual story. On 15 June 1767 Cosimo Piovasco di Rondò, twelve-year-old son of a noble family, having been scolded by his father the Baron for refusing to eat a dinner consisting entirely of snails prepared by his sadistic sister Battista, climbs up a tree in an apparent fit of rebellion. At first, the family thinks that he is just having a tantrum and will come down by nightfall, given that with his "powdered hair, three-cornered hat, lace stock and ruffles, green tunic with pointed tails, purple breeches, rapier, and long white leather gaiters halfway up his legs," the young Baron is certainly not properly dressed for this occasion.[28] But soon it turns out that the boy has decided never to come down again. In fact, from this moment on, Cosimo will spend the rest of his days living in the trees on his father's large wooded estate, traveling with Tarzan-like speed and sureness along the branches of the immense Ligurian sylvan landscape of Ombrosa. Of course, the action takes place when the Riviera and the San Remo region had not yet been cleared of their forests.[29] Like Daniel Defoe's Robinson Crusoe, he too meets the challenging difficulties of a primitive existence with wonderful ingenuity and fortitude.[30] With innate intelligence and inventiveness, he succeeds in creating for himself a life not too dissimilar from the one he would have led had he remained on the ground. Thus, he leads a creative, adventurous, and rewarding life: he goes hunting and fishing, has a pet dog, turns into an avid reader and becomes a scholar and author, falls in love and has sexual encounters with women, goes mad and then regains his sanity, fights against pirates, becomes a Freemason and duels with Spanish Jesuits, participates in the Revolution and the Napoleonic wars (he even meets the emperor), corresponds with the leading thinkers of the Enlightenment (Voltaire is one of his many admirers), prints newspapers, fights forest fires, is elected to public office, and helps the poor and the downtrodden. The "lightness" and rapidity with which these events are presented by Calvino exhilarate the reader, precluding boredom and skepticism.

Among his many adventures the Baron meets a group of Spanish noblemen and their families who have been exiled by the king of Spain. They live in the trees in the nearby town of Olivabassa, because the Republic of Genoa, which is offering them asylum, does not want to violate its treaty with the king, which states that no exiles are "to touch the soil" of Genoese territory (127). In this beautiful satire of the art of diplomacy and of the privileged classes— "they never moved a finger the whole day long" (127)—when Cosimo first introduces himself to his fellow tree-dwellers, they ask him in Spanish, *"desterrado también?"* He replies, "No, sir. Or, at least, not exile by anyone else's decree." And when they ask if he travels in the trees for fun, he explains: "I do it because I think it suits me, not because I'm forced to" (126). Instead of using the word *exiliado*, Calvino, tongue in cheek, prefers *desterrado* because in Spanish it literally means to be away from the ground or one's land. Woodhouse regards both Cosimo's and the Spaniards' tree existence as being indicative of freedom because their normal code of behavior is "relaxed by the irresponsible life of exile they lead,"[31] so that Cosimo can court one of the Spanish women with no intention of marrying her.

Throughout his life Cosimo unfailingly remains true to his ideals, never questioning his original resolve to remain in the trees and showing noble qualities of character: kindness, courage, patience, ingenuity, industry, and a profound sense of justice. When he reaches old age, the Baron remarks: "I too have lived many years for ideals which I would never be able to explain to myself; but I do something entirely good. I live on trees" (213). The narrator muses about Cosimo's old age: "Youth soon passes on earth, so imagine it on the trees, where it is the fate of everything to fall: leaves, fruit" (208).

At the age of sixty-five, when he is dying, some Englishmen who happen to be flying in a balloon over the trees of Ombrosa drop an anchor in order to control their flight. The moment it passes near Cosimo, he grips the rope, and with his feet on the anchor he flies away and vanishes out to sea. When the balloon finally lands, there is no trace of the Baron. His family tomb bears the inscription: "Cosimo Piovasco di Rondò—Lived in trees—Always loved earth—Went into sky" (216).[32]

What are we to make of the Baron's resolve to live in the trees? Unlike his prototype, Robinson Crusoe, Cosimo is not shipwrecked and compelled to lead such an extraordinary existence. He does so of his own volition and conviction. The boy first leaves his parents' residence because the home environment is too strict, bizarre, unwholesome, and devoid of meaning. Cosimo's unfashionable father, Baron Arminio Piovasco di Rondò, clad in a long wig that falls over his eyes in the style of Louis XIV, is a bore. His entire life is dominated by a desire to regain the lost title of Duke of Ombrosa. He constantly thinks of "nothing but genealogies and successions and family rivalries and alliances with grandees near and far" (5). At dinner he watches his children like a hawk, making sure their demeanor follows royal rules. Not only is he frustrated by not being able to obtain the desired title, but he is convinced that the Jesuits are always plotting against him. The mother, Baronessa Corradina di Rondò, daughter of General Konrad von Kurtewitz formerly in the service of Empress Maria Theresa, is referred to by all as the "Generalessa" on account of her brusque military manners. She dreams of a military career for her two sons and is far more interested in discipline than etiquette.

Living with them is Cavalier Avvocato Enea Silvio Carrega, the illegitimate brother of the father, who dresses in Turkish robes, supervises the waterworks, and administers the estate even though he "scarcely ever exchanged a word with bailiffs or tenants or peasants, due to his timidity and inarticulateness" (57). Once a lawyer, he had lived for many years in Turkey, where he learned hydraulics, the only task he now actually performs at Ombrosa. Ostensibly a Moslem, he was found in chains, rowing in an Ottoman galley captured by a Venetian ship. Set free, he lived for some time in Venice, where he got into trouble and ended up in prison. Eventually he was ransomed by his brother Arminio, who was very fond of him and who brought him back to Ombrosa.

Then there is Cosimo's sister Battista, "a kind of stay-at-home-nun" (4), now confined to the house for having once tried to rape one of her suitors. She dresses like a nun and expresses her evil schemes and "macabre fantasy" (10) by preparing exotic meals for her unsuspecting family, such as paté toast of rats' liver, grasshoppers' claws, pigs' tails, and porcupines. It is her "snail soup and snails as a main course" (11) that trigger Cosimo's rebellion. And finally there is Biagio, the protagonist's younger brother and confidant,—he is eight years old at the beginning of the novel—who narrates the baron's arboreal adventures, at times even taking part in the action of the novel.

Eventually, as Cosimo's anger at his family begins to fade, his flight into the trees evolves into a protest against society, becoming moreover a means of affirming his moral, social, and philosophical commitment to the betterment of society. At first glance the reader of *The Baron in the Trees* may consider it to be a novel of evasion, of flight from reality and society. Yet it quickly becomes clear that Cosimo's "rampant"[33] existence in the trees is only a strategic retreat with multiple implications. For one, his life-style represents a constant search for a higher order which increases in intensity the more the world below and around him seems uncertain and in turmoil. When Voltaire, who has heard of Cosimo's achievements, asks Biagio whether his brother lives in the trees in order to be nearer to the sky, he replies: "My brother considers that anyone who wants to see the earth properly must keep himself at a necessary distance from it." Pleased with this response, the philosopher remarks: "Once it was only Nature which produced living phenomena. Now 'tis Reason" (144).[34]

Although he now lives on a higher plane—albeit in physical isolation and spiritual loneliness—Cosimo never leaves society, and, indeed, even more than before, he fully takes an active part in it by assisting the people of Ombrosa. "Despite that escape of his," comments Biagio, "he lived almost as closely with us as he had before. He was a solitary who did not avoid people. In a way, indeed, he seemed to like them more than anything else" (64). The brother adds later on that by using his arboreal talents Cosimo became "at the same time a friend to his neighbor, to nature and to himself" (103). This altruistic commitment is best expressed in his association with the bandit Gian dei Brughi, whom he reforms by imparting to him a "passion for reading and for all human knowledge" (92).

One cannot help but argue that there is a clear similarity between the young Baron's flight into the trees and Calvino's own break with the Italian Communist Party as well as that of many other intellectuals.[35] In his own instance the determined act of separation—*dimidiamento*—from its hegemony over Italian intellectual life was not necessarily one of evasion or outright rejection. Granted, Calvino felt alienated from his surroundings, a sense of being artistically strangled (like Cosimo refusing to eat the snails), and a constant need to explain himself and defend his act of repudiation. Nonetheless, by leaving the "official" party, Calvino did not necessarily abandon the principles that originally had brought him into its fold and had guided him as a young member of the Resistance movement. "One should remember," Biagio tells us, that his brother "was just as contrary to every kind of human organization flourishing at the time, and so he fled from them all and tried experiments with new ones" (190–91).

Indeed, very much like Cosimo in the trees, Calvino too continued to take an active part and play a vital role in the intellectual, political, and social life of his country despite his sense of alienation. Similarly, the Baron's feeling of alienation is the hidden motive of all his efforts, and the search for a higher law is what draws him to his amazing but sensible adventures. Whereas in the novel Cosimo finds his own voice in the trees, Calvino accomplished the same by moving away from the rigid precepts of the party or any orthodoxy, lest they compromise his intellectual and artistic independence. Cosimo's determined act is very much like that of Henry Thoreau, the essayist and nature writer who was convinced that by living alone in a cabin at Walden Pond his life could be simplified so that its meaning would become clearer; he also maintained that above all, government is best when it governs the least, and a person's first loyalty is to his own nature. The noncomformist Thoreau, however, refused to be cut off from society, and in fact, like Cosimo, entertained friends, worked his land, recorded observations of natural phenomena, and became an acute observer of social behavior. In this highly inventive narrative of Cosimo's inexhaustible feats, as he lives in unconstrained and cordial familiarity with nature and its surrounding people, the fantastic element, though at times bizarre, is not based on magic; nor does it ever turn absurd or ludicrous, because practically all the events are rooted in the history of the eighteenth century, the era of the Enlightenment. There is always a balance between fable and reality, as we have already observed in *The Path to the Nest of Spiders*. Enrico Ghidetti hits the mark when he categorizes the fantastic in Calvino's art as always being "well-temperate," because his attitude toward it is balanced by an innate rationalistic sense, bound by an illuministic approach.[36] We have already seen how Cosimo's elevated angle allows him to enjoy a different and assymetrical viewpoint from which to scrutinize nature and human society; analogously, the use of the fantastic permits Calvino the author to achieve similar optical advantages.

A familiar tautology states that "one observes a lot by watching." Perched in his trees, Cosimo observes, interprets, and takes an active part in the age of Voltaire, first as it unfolds, then as it goes by, and finally as it is replaced by a new era. His act of defiance undoubtedly reflects the century's revolt against every constraint—the church and state, intolerance, superstition, poverty, ignorance—whereas his technical innovations above ground correspond to the remarkable scientific progress made during that same period. Furthermore, Cosimo's keen interest in *all* matters results in the unfinished treatise *Project for the Constitution of an Ideal State in the Trees* (142), as well as in the publication of *Constitutional Project for a Republican City with a Declaration of the Rights of Men, Women, Children, Domestic and Wild Animals, Including Birds, Fishes and Insects, and all Vegetation, whether Trees, Vegetable, or Grass* (205). This is typical not only of the Encyclopedists such as Diderot, but of all the adherents to the Enlightenment movement, especially Condorcet's ideas on the perfectibility of mankind and his optimistic view of the destiny of human society.[37]

Among the many exploits of the ingenious Baron, that of his love relationship with Viola is both amusing and revealing. He first meets the capricious, aristocratic girl—she lives on a neighboring estate—shortly after his ascension into the trees. They become friends, but soon she moves away. Many years later she returns to her estate, having just lost her husband, a much older man whom she had married for money and not love. Cosimo and the restless and coquettish Viola fall in love and for months carry on a passionate affair in the trees. They make love "suspended in the void, propping themselves or holding onto branches, she throwing herself upon him, almost flying" (161). However, their clashing personalities provoke frequent quarrels and separations, because Cosimo is a rationalist and a true product of illuministic readings. A puritan when it comes to making love, he is repelled by Viola's exuberant passion and by "everything that clouded or replaced the wholesomeness of nature." Although his love fulfills Viola sensually, it leaves "her imagination unsatisfied" (161) and eventually she leaves for France, never to be seen again. Alas, when it is too late, he realizes that "all her whims and dissatisfactions were but an unsatiable urge for the increase of their love and the refusal to admit it could reach a limit, and it was he, he, he, who had understood nothing of this and had goaded her till he lost her" (179). And when, like Ariosto's Orlando who loses his sanity over a woman, Cosimo goes mad with despair over the loss of Viola, the puzzled Ombrosians wonder: "How can someone go mad who's always been mad?" (180).

The Baron's amorous puritanism is best explained by Calvino in his introduction to the 1965 school edition of the novel: "The first lesson we can draw from the book is that disobedience acquires meaning only when it becomes a moral discipline more rigorous and arduous than the one one is rebelling against."[38] Although Cosimo has rebelled against traditional values and certainly, to say the least, leads a very nontraditional life, when it comes to his sense of propriety he feels compelled by his position as philosopher and committed intellectual to champion wholesomeness, integrity, self-discipline, and independent thought.[39] Although it is never made clear in the novel, what Cosimo fears the most is that his love and passion for Viola will eventually cause him to renounce the arboreal life which is fundamental for him. He is reminded of Viola's own admonition when they both were children: "You have the lordship of the trees, all right? But if you touch the earth just once . . . you lose your whole kingdom [and] it's the end of you!" (21). Indeed, Cosimo seems to be mighty as long as he stays in the trees from which he gets his compelling strength, power, and determination. He is like the mythological giant Antaeus: each time Hercules threw him, he gained fresh strength from touching the earth; and as long as he could touch the earth he was invincible.

Caught in a conflict between his own passions and his civic responsibility, Cosimo is faced by what Constance Markey calls "the existential dilemma: the paradox of choice."[40] Eventually what he learns from this experience is not only "to love without inhibition," but also "to master himself and attain self-sufficiency when she has gone."[41] He is forced to confront the equation of freedom and solitude, that one can be free only if one is alone. Calvino solves Cosimo's dilemma by causing him to go mad and become like a bird living in the trees, adorning himself with bright-colored feathers and making speeches in defense of birds. It is during his madness that he writes about birds in *The Song of the Blackbird, The Knock of the Woodpecker, The Dialogue of the Owls,* and learns how to print books and newspapers in the trees. Eventually the quixotic Baron regains his sanity by fighting off an invasion of wolves that threaten Ombrosa. The question of Cosimo's madness is clearly reminiscent of Caballero del Verde Gabán's opinion concerning Don Quixote, whom he perceives to be sane and very well versed in all issues save for the mania he has for chivalric matters.[42]

In *The Cloven Viscount* and in *The Baron in the Trees* the eyewitness raconteurs are semi-reliable not only because they are just eight years old at the onset of the novels and narrate with open-eyed innocence events whose implications are both tragic and humorous, but also because they do not share the protagonists' perspectives. Furthermore, since they participate in some of the narrated events, they become involved in their consequences. This creates a disparity in their narrative points of view, though far less in the case of the Viscount's nephew than in that of the Baron's brother, who at times becomes unreliable as narrator—after all, his spectrum is terrestrial and not arboreal.

For example, when their uncle is killed by the pirates, Biagio blames his brother for the different versions of the event. According to Jill Margo Carlton, "Cosimo observes some of the events leading to the beheading, but he doesn't hear what the participants say. He must, therefore, deduce meaning from what he sees." Similarly, Biagio is "several times removed from the source when he tells the Spanish exiles' story, which is based on Cosimo's reconstruction of two original versions: 'una laconica esclamazione' and 'una circostanziata versione' '' (a laconic exclamation and a detailed account).[43]

As in most of his writings, Calvino plays with the notion of point of view, modulates and alters the mode of the narrative, and gracefully creates ironical contrasts which are essential for satire. But his authorial deceptions leave the reader with insufficient guides for making judgments about the characters and the actions. Indeed, we never find out the full story of the Cavaliere: is he a traitor? Is Zaira truly his beloved for whose ransom he is forced to spy for the pirates? What causes the behavior of the self-possessed and eccentric Viola? Eventually, even Biagio becomes skeptical of his brother's fabulous achievements: "So many and so incredible were the tales told about his activities in the woods during the war that I cannot really accept outright any one version. So I leave the word to him, and just faithfully report some of his stories" (198).

For Constance Markey, Calvino plays "mischievous games" which make us forget, for example, that "it is Biagio who is the typical eighteenth-century man with the mind and perspective of the Enlightenment," and not the Baron or the author.[44] In fact, in his concluding musings at the end of the novel, Biagio not only indicates Cosimo's achievements, but also offers his commentary concerning the past and present centuries: "The hopes of our eighteenth century—all are dust" and "I have no idea what this nineteenth century of ours will bring, starting so badly and getting so much worse" (213). In essence, the message is that even the utopian illuministic harmony between man, nature, and history already contained the seeds of contemporary society's problems. Moreover, for the first time we glimpse Biagio's own character, rather different from that of his brother: "I have always been a balanced man, without great impetus or yearnings, a father, a noble by birth, enlightened in ideas, observant of the laws. The excesses of politics have never shocked me much, and I hope never will. And yet within, how sad I feel!" (213). At the end we surmise further that Biagio is not merely the narrator of Cosimo's life, but that he is the intellectual alter ego who understands and identifies with his brother's life-style but nonetheless remains somewhat detached from active involvement. Thus Biagio concludes that Cosimo understood "something that was all-embracing, and he could not say it in words but only in living as he did. Only by being so frankly himself as he was till his death could he give something to all men" (214). It would appear, then, that Biagio's task is to say in words what Cosimo expresses only in living. Clearly, there are parallels between *The Baron in the Trees* and Voltaire's *Candide*—even though Calvino's intent was not to parody any philosophical tenets. Cosimo's life in the trees could be seen as a response to Voltaire's positive advice contained in the famous dictum: "But we must cultivate our garden." Indeed, Cosimo shows that experience, energetic action, and hard work are necessary in order to remedy the ills of society, as well as to build and sow for a better future.[45]

Mystifyingly, Calvino the fable maker does not want his story to have the obligatory happy ending. In fact, Cosimo's disappearance corresponds to that of an idyllic sylvan Ombrosa, with forests that now are no more, because "trees seem almost to have no right here. . . . Since men have been swept by this frenzy for the ax . . . Ombrosa no longer exists" (217). Regretfully the author underscores the devastation of nature in the Ligurian region during Biagio's old age, and by extension the urbanization and exploitation of his own San Remo, so well dramatized in the story "La speculazione edilizia." Furthermore, Calvino grieves that we have become dehumanized and live today in a world without eccentrics. Unlike Cosimo's era, "the great century of eccentrics . . . our individuality has been denied to us," he continues, and the "problem is no longer a question of having lost part of ourselves, but rather of our absolute loss, our total alienation."[46] Calvino concludes his novel by making an analogy between Cosimo's existence in nature, which perhaps was only there so that he "could pass through it" (217), and the physical act of writing,

> embroidered on nothing, like this thread of ink which I have let run on for page after page, swarming with cancellations, corrections, doodles, blots and gaps, bursting at time into clear big berries, coagulating at others into piles of tiny starry seeds, then twisting away, forking off, surrounding buds of phrases with frameworks of leaves and clouds, then interweaving again, and so running on and on and on until it splutters and bursts into a last senseless cluster of words, ideas, dreams, and so ends. (217)

As the rampant Baron gives shape and form to mythical Ombrosa, so does pen and ink create a corresponding paper reality with life. In Benussi's view, "The nothingness that is hidden by life corresponds to the nothingness that is hidden by *écriture*, which, nevertheless, is the only reality that can be forged by someone who ascends nimbly" above the ground.[47] In essence, what Calvino wants is that the reader become cognizant of the fact that both writing and reading are complicated processes; and, at the same time, he anticipates and toys with the metaliterary interest that he will eventually develop further in *The Nonexistent Knight*, the last novel of the trilogy, as well as in *If on a winter's night a traveler* and *The Castle of Crossed Destinies*.

The Nonexistent Knight

Readers of the *Odyssey* will remember the amusing scene in Book 9, when Odysseus, who, together with his companions, is kept prisoner by Polyphemus, speaks with the giant: " 'My name is Nobody [Odysseus]. That is what I am called by my mother and father and by all my friends.' The Cyclops answered me with a cruel jest. 'Of all his company I will eat Nobody last, and the rest before him.' "[48] Obviously, Homer's Odysseus *does* exist in spite of the nonexistence proclaimed by his name. However, Calvino's hero in *The Nonexistent Knight*, in spite of his playful and lengthy name—Agilulfo[49] Bertrandin of the Guildivern and of the Others of Corbertranz and Sura, armed Knight of Selimpia Citeriore and Fez—does *not* exist. He is just a suit of white shining armor with nothing inside. He exists only because of what the author calls "nonexistence endowed with self-awareness and will power."[50]

Written and published in 1959, the novel concludes Calvino's chivalric cycle. The knight symbolizes for the author

> artificial man who, being equivalent to consumer goods and situations, is nonexistent because he no longer creates friction [*attrito*] with anything, he no longer has a connection (struggle and through struggle harmony) with that which (nature or history) surrounds him; he 'functions' only abstractly.[51]

The knight, representing contemporary "robotized man,"[52] does not exist because he lacks what Kierkegaard considers essential: "The existent individual is first of all he who is in an infinite relationship with himself and has an infinite interest in himself and his destiny."[53]

The action of *The Nonexistent Knight* begins under the walls of Paris with a description of Charlemagne's army as he inspects his Christian paladins, all bearing familiar legendary names found in chivalric epic poetry, including Ariosto's immortalized Orlando and Bradamante. At the end of the reviewing line, when the emperor asks Agilulfo, dressed "entirely in white armor," why he doesn't raise his visor and show his face, he is told: "Sire, because I do not exist!"[54] Later, looking inside the knight's helmet and seeing that indeed it is empty, the emperor inquires: "And how do you do your job, then, if you don't exist?" Agilulfo replies: "By will power . . . and faith in our holy cause!" (6-7). Although the valiant knight cannot eat, drink, sleep, or scratch because "he hasn't got a place to itch," he nonetheless becomes the most valorous and zealous warrior in the Christians' conflict against the Saracens, and all "without needing to exist" (17). According to A. H. Carter, his "mentality is a precise codification of the chivalric and military values around him."[55] In fact, his dedication to knighthood and all the relevant codes of behavior turn him into an uncompromising doctrinaire whose perfection causes him to be disliked by his companions, even though he longs for human contact.

Juxtaposed to Agilulfo there is his squire, who also has many names that change, this time according to season and place: Gurdulù, Gudi-Ussuf, Ben-Va-Ussuf, Ben Stanbùl, Pestanzùl, Bertinzùl, Martinbon, Martinzùl, Omobon, Omobestia, il Brutto del Vallone, Gian Paciasso, Pier Paciugo, Boamoluz, Carotun, Balingaccio, and Bertella.[56] In short, "he's a man without a name and with every possible name" (53). He perceives everything backward[57] and "whatever he is called it's the same to him. Call him and he thinks you're calling a goat. Say 'cheese' or 'torrent' and he answers 'Here I am' " (28). In fact, when he is given a tin of soup, he puts his head into it unaware that he must eat the soup and not be eaten by the soup (30). The same happens when he is given the task of burying a fallen soldier and instead buries himself. And yet, despite these aberrations, mad is "not quite the right word for him. He's just a person who exists and doesn't realize he exists" (28). The squire, very much like the contemporary individual, signifies "complete identification with the objective world";[58] he has lost his uniqueness, is unable to discriminate, and has become a pawn to be played with by the system: "It was not rare then to find names and thoughts and forms and institutions that correspond to nothing in existence" (33). Ironically, we have on the one hand Agilulfo, the *nonexistent* but *conscious* individual, and on the other hand the *existent* but *unconscious* Gurdulù. The knight represents modern man whose depersonalized existence and propensity for stolidly rationalizing everything has turned him into a mechanical robot. The squire in his almost beastly primitiveness lacks any sense of proportion or propriety. He expresses, according to Giorgio Pullini, uncivilized and animal instinct and lacks "self-awareness to the extent of confusing himself with external reality."[59] And yet, however antithetical the two might be, they are complementary to each other, the way Don Quixote and Sancho Panza are for Miguel de Cervantes; the combination of the squire's realism and the knight's idealism represents the complete man and undoubtedly helps to give his great novel almost uncanny universality.[60]

Among the many paladins, there is Rambaldo di Rossiglione, one of Agilulfo's few admirers, who has joined the Frankish army in order to avenge his father, killed in Seville by the Argalif Isohar. Rambaldo represents the untiring man of action who "acts upon history through his own practical and empirical vocation."[61] Before he can kill the enemy leader, he is told that he must first get permission from the "Superintendency of Duels, Feuds and Besmirched Honor" (14), lest the emperor be engaged in negotiations with Isohar. In spite of this bureaucratic and diplomatic snag, during a fierce battle Rambaldo shatters the Argalif's "war spectacles," thus rendering him defenseless and causing him to be killed. When Rambaldo is ambushed by two Moors, he is saved by a mysterious knight who immediately gallops off without identifying himself. Thereafter at a river bank, upon seeing the knight "naked from the waist downward" and in the process of beginning "quietly and proudly to pee" (46), Rambaldo learns that it is a woman. Without ever having seen her face, which is still covered by the helmet, he falls head over heels in love with the warrior, who turns out to be the beautiful and legendary Bradamante, who loves Agilulfo without knowing that he loves her too. When the Amazon knight, who for Calvino stands for "love as struggle or war,"[62] notices Rambaldo, she rejects his love, calls him foul names, and barely misses him with her dagger.

At a paladins' banquet, with Charlemagne presiding, Torrismund of Cornwall contests the legitimacy of Agilulfo's knighthood, obtained fifteen years earlier for having saved from rape the King of Scotland's virgin daughter Sophronia. He announces that she could not have been a virgin because she is his mother, who bore him twenty years before, when she was thirteen. The consequences are that all of Agilulfo's names and titles are annulled and each of his "attributions" becomes "as nonexistent as his person" (80). In order to redeem himself, he sets out for England and then for Morocco in search of proof of Sophronia's virginity. After various adventures, suggestive of those of Odysseus and Aeneas, he saves Sophronia from the clutches of the sultan, takes her back to Breton, and shelters her in a cave; he leaves her there while he plans to go to Charlemagne, announce her virginity, and reclaim all his names and titles.

Charlemagne is portrayed as an incompetent ruler, a shallow figure too old and weary to fully understand the exigencies and consequences of warfare. The real Charlemagne, who had been crowned emperor in 800 by Pope Leo III, had expected to reconstitute the fallen Holy Roman Empire. But when he put his ideas to the test, they turned out to be unworkable, an unattainable goal, an artificial creation—just as hollow as the armor of Agilulfo—kept together merely by self-awareness and will power, and only abstractly achievable. The only talents of Calvino's Charlemagne, characterized by Cristina Benussi as King Muddle-head,[63] are presiding over inane ceremonies and the ability to remember titles and offices.

Concurrent with Agilulfo's adventures, Torrismund's vicissitudes unfold. For Calvino he illustrates "absolute morality that comes true by means of something outside of the individual, from what has existed before him, from the whole from which he stems."[64] Having announced himself to be a bastard in contesting Agilulfo's knighthood, Torrismund faces dismissal from the Frankish army. Therefore, he sets out for Scotland in search of his paternity, ostensibly "the Sacred Order of the Knights of the Holy Grail." There he joins the Order, though they refuse to acknowledge their paternity. Torrismund quickly tires of their hypocritical and mystical life and joins the oppressed local populace in rebelling against the Order. The Knights of the Holy Grail exemplify "existence as mystical experience, as the annulment in everything, Wagner, the Buddhism of the samurai."[65] In opposition to the Knights, Calvino creates the historical experience of the Curvaldi, who, having been oppressed and left out of history for so long, are no longer cognizant of their human rights; only through struggle will they acquire this awareness. These people, Calvino tells us, are like the poor peasants in Carlo Levi's sad but realistic novel *Christ Stopped at Eboli;* they are so neglected, that even Christ never reached their small village in the mountains.[66]

Upon his return to Breton, Torrismund finds shelter in a cave and, lo and behold, falls in love with the woman left there by Agilulfo. When the latter and Charlemagne come to the cave—accompanied by an old midwife expert in matters of virginity—they find the two lovers in *flagrante delicto.* When Torrismund learns that the woman is Sophronia, he is at first horrified by the thought of having had "foul incest" with his own mother. At the same time Agilulfo is also distraught by this revelation, and rides off believing he has lost forever his name and honor. But then Torrismund remembers that the woman he has just seduced was indeed a virgin. Sophronia, who stands for "love akin to quietude and nostalgia for prenatal slumber,"[67] reveals that no incest has occurred because there are no blood ties between them. It turns out that Torrismund is her step-brother, the son of the Queen of Scotland and the Knights of the Holy Grail, adopted by the king; she is not the daughter of the queen, but rather the illegitimate issue of the king and a peasant woman. Torrismund is made a count and marries Sophronia, whereas Agilulfo is given back all his names and titles. "All seems to be working out for the best" (131),[68] but when Rambaldo is ordered to find the distraught Agilulfo and inform him that he has been fully redeemed, he finds only his armor, in pieces—the knight has killed himself. Rambaldo puts the pieces together, dons the suit, and uses Agilulfo's sword in a fierce battle against the Saracens. When Bradamante sees Rambaldo, she makes love to him thinking that he is Agilulfo. When she finally recognizes Rambaldo, she stuns him by striking him on the head with her sword—"but with the flat" part (135)—and, as always, disappears.

Surprisingly, the novel ends with the revelation by the narrator, Sister Theodora, that she is none other than the Amazon Bradamante who has taken refuge in a convent in order to forget her love for Agilulfo. There, for penance, she had decided to narrate the adventures of the Christian knights and paladins. Now, however, she yearns for the young and amorous Rambaldo. Eventually he finds her and helps her flee from the convent. Hence, the culmination of their turbulent love story coincides with that of all the other events and characters.

In *The Nonexistent Knight* Calvino retains the storyteller's concern for a well-balanced, orderly recitation of a chivalric tale, in a logically arranged narrative structure. However, he is not merely interested in relating a parody of medieval knights, battles, and courtly love, and, by extension, a parody of his own society. Moreover, he wants to examine the process of writing and the subversion that grows out of a close reading of implications and contradictions within a text itself. Consequently, Calvino presents a text which the reader can pry open and discover there various "codes" of reading or interpretation. Also in *The Nonexistent Knight,* which has a far looser structure than his earlier novels, the simple linear plot is supplanted by a chronological sequence of events which are recorded retrospectively by Sister Theodora. In the novel there is a temporal coexistence of both diachrony and synchrony, since it presents a succession of events in the past and in the ongoing present. Time works as a continuous flow in which past and present are combined into a continuous becoming. In other words, there are two distinct temporal planes at work: one of actuality, of the present (the nun's "now as I write . . ."), in which the actual writing of the recollections, personal experiences, and the penance imposed by the convent occur contemporaneously; and the other level, which concerns the recollected events that go back to the beginning of the novel, with the first appearance of the nonexistent knight. Sister Theodora's own tale and personal experiences, her comments on the nature of narrative writing, and the medieval era as platform and background all become a frame that "motivates the relation of and lends structural unity to a series of otherwise diverse and unrelated stories."[69]

Throughout *The Nonexistent Knight* the narrator constantly warns the reader that she is unreliable, that her knowledge of the events is limited to her own personal observations, that she has to rely on other unreliable sources, or that what she records is sheer invention, albeit logical invention:

> I who recount this tale am Sister Theodora, nun of the order of Saint Columbia. I am writing in a convent, from old unearthed papers or talk heard in our parlor, or a few rare accounts by people who were actually present. We nuns have few occasions to speak with soldiers, so what I don't know I try to imagine. How else could I do it? Not all of the story is clear yet to me. I must crave indulgence. We country girls, however noble, have always led retired lives in remote castles and convents. Apart from religious ceremonies, triduums, novenas, gardening, harvesting, vintaging, whippings, slavery, incest, fires, hangings, invasion, sacking, rape and pestilence, we have no experience. What can a poor nun know of the world? So I proceed laboriously with this tale whose narration I have undertaken as a penance. (34)

In essence, Calvino seems to be anticipating Roland Barthes's theory that literature should be seen as an open text, an "infinite process that is both meaning-generating and meaning-subverting."[70] The nun's long apologia ends with an admonition that she won't be able to represent accurately the battle scenes of the story because "of battles, as I say, I know nothing" (34). This and many other pronouncements of hers are sheer lies, as the reader eventually finds out in chapter 12.

> Yes, my book. Sister Theodora who tells this tale and the Amazon Bradamante are one and the same. Sometimes I gallop over battlefields after adventures of duels and loves, sometimes I shut myself in convents, meditating and jotting down the adventures that have happened to me, so as to try to understand them. (140)

And yet she continues to spin her tale, "inventing the unknown," according to Salman Rushdie, "and making it seem truer than the truth, and providing Calvino with a marvellous metaphor for himself."[71] From the combination of self-revelation and self-justification, as well as from her repeated caveats that in many instances the narrative is suspect, the cloistered storyteller actually "valorizes and disqualifies writing at the same time."[72] Finally, the problem of credibility intensifies when the narrative stops being retrospective and suddenly turns ongoing, notably when the narrator's own action parallels the text:

> When I came to shut myself in here I was desperate with love for Agilulfo, now I burn for the young and passionate Rambaldo. That is why my pen at a certain point

began running on so. I rush to meet him. I knew he would not be long in coming. A page is good only when we turn it and find life urging along, confusing every page in the book. The pen rushes on, urged by the same joy that makes me course the open road. A chapter started when one doesn't know which tale to tell is like a corner turned on leaving a convent, when one might come face to face with a dragon, a Saracen gang, an enchanted isle or a new love. (140)

What happened to the claim that she knew nothing about warfare? And why did she have to make use of "old unearthed papers" when the events she is narrating are relatively recent? Is Calvino implying here the intertextual nature of his narrative—that he has made use of both text and characters culled from ancient sources such as Ariosto, Cervantes, and Arthurian and Carolingian narrative cycles?

Calvino recognizes the artifice of all writing and plays with it. He also debunks the theory that language is a "transparent medium through which the reader grasps a solid and unified 'truth' or 'reality.' "[73] First, he skillfully convinces the reader to accept the reality, the existence of the nonexistent knight; and then by cunningly subverting other parts of the tale, he causes the reader to believe the big fabrication but to doubt the small ones—especially those pertaining to the Amazon/nun/narrator. This occurs because in the former instance we accept on faith the presence of the knight, the way we accept the presence of Pirandello's *Six Characters in Search of an Author.* However, in the latter instance, the narrative becomes suspect, especially because there are facts against which to check. Thus Calvino causes his text to undo itself, to comment on itself, and eventually to become its own subject.

At the beginning of chapter 6, Calvino notes that the art of writing "tales consists in an ability to draw the rest of life from the nothing one has understood of it, but life begins again at the end of the page when one realizes that one knew nothing whatsoever" (61). But why does he feel compelled to write tales? Is it because, as we are told repeatedly by Theodora, that it is good for the soul, that it is salvation and penance, and a way of arriving at the truth? It would appear that, for Calvino, writing is a *pharmakon* which, when used wisely, has curative qualities, and when used unwisely functions as a poison. It is, perhaps, in his 1959 essay, "Il mare dell'oggettività" (The Sea of Objectivity), that one can find another key for a better understanding of *The Nonexistent Knight.* Let us remember that when Calvino was writing this novel, he was still traumatized by his separation from the Italian Communist Party. He was also still trying to find an answer to the dilemma of being both an artist and, at the same time, a committed and concerned individual. In 1959 he writes:

> From a culture based on the relationship and contrast between two limits, on the
> one hand the individual's conscience, will, and judgment, and on the other hand,
> the objective world, we are now passing into a culture in which the first limit is
> submerged by the sea of objectivity, by the uninterrupted flux of what exists.[74]

He is referring to the irreversible changes occurring in the arts, where objectivity drowns the individual; "the volcano from which the lava flows is no longer the soul of the poet, but rather it is the boiling crater of otherness into which the poet plunges."[75] For Calvino the writer's plight is very similar to that of Agilulfo, although, unlike the contradictory knight, he does not intend to give up and destroy himself. Even when confronted by a complex world and a sea of objectivity, of which he has become an integral part (when Torrismund dons Agilulfo's armor, their two natures become one), Calvino still suggests that the writer has become "necessarily complementary to the vision of the world that avails itself of a simplifying and schematizing splitting open what is real."[76] Sister Theodora, like Calvino, learns that writing is not the expected salvation for her. "Indeed she is lost to it. Ultimately, though, it *is* her salvation, in a different way. By remembering, reconsidering, and recounting her past, she reaffirms who she is much in the manner Eliade shows that myths of origins give knowledge and control. To the end her writing creates this control."[77] The underlying premise of the novel is that although Calvino, representative of the modern and concerned Italian intellectual, shows a definite diffidence vis-à-vis any radicalism or fanaticism, he nonetheless feels the same way toward those who acquiesce and renounce their obligations toward a more just society. When Torrismund tries to rule as Count of Koowalden, the people do not accept him as such, preferring instead to live as equals. When he asks them if he should consider himself an equal to Gurdulù, who is unaware of his own existence, the citizens reply: "He will learn too. . . . We ourselves did not know we existed. . . . *One can also learn to be*" (138, my italics).[78] It is this positive outlook for a better future that brings an end to Calvino's trilogy, as Sister Theodora, now once again Amazon Bradamante, informs the reader that

> from describing the past, from the present which seized my hand in its excited
> grasp, here I am, O future. . . . What new pennants wilt thou unfurl before me
> from towers of cities not yet founded? . . . What unforeseeable golden ages art
> thou preparing—ill-mastered, indomitable harbinger of treasures dearly paid for,
> my kingdom to be conquered, the future. (141)

In his introduction to *I nostri antenati,* Calvino writes that what the novels of his trilogy have in common is that the stories lack verisimilitude; they take place in the distant past and in imaginary lands. He also states that he felt the need for a first-person narrator in order to "counter the objective coldness, typical of fabulous narrative, with an element capable of inducing rapport and lyricism, something that modern narrative cannot do without."[79] One can add to this, that the trilogy also contains elements of the Hegelian principle of *negativity* inasmuch as Calvino constantly finds his truth via a series of triads: thesis, antithesis, and synthesis. Every thesis or fact can be understood only when related to its opposites, to those elements which the thesis is not. If we assume that an idea is true—for example, that Medardo and Agilulfo exist—then we encounter the opposite, its contradiction. Indeed, it is precisely from this contradiction, from this negative relation which defines Calvino's *antenati,* that the novels impart meaning.

NOTES

1. Prefazione, *I nostri antenati* (Turin: Einaudi, 1962) xiii.

2. For Pavese, see Chapter Two, footnote 10 of present study. For Elio Vittorini, see cover jacket of Italo Calvino, *Il visconte dimezzato* (Turin: Einaudi, 1952).

3. "Tre correnti del romanzo italiano," *Una pietra sopra: discorsi di letteratura e società* (Turin: Einaudi, 1980) 57. Originally in English, it was first read as a paper at Columbia University 16 Dec. 1959 and at several other American universities in 1960.

4. Claudio Milanini, *L'utopia discontinua: Saggio su Italo Calvino* (Milan: Garzanti, 1990) 38. The Spanish poet and satirist Francisco Quevedo (1580–1645), in his *Los sueños (Dreams),* takes well-known sayings and proverbs concerning fictitious characters and then animates them and deals with them as if they were real people: Pero Grullo, Chisgaravís, Calaínos, Cantimpalos, Dueña Quintañona, etc.

5. Giuseppe Bonura, *Invito alla lettura di Italo Calvino* (Milan: Mursia, 1987) 71.

6. *The Nonexistent Knight and The Cloven Viscount* (New York: Harcourt Brace, 1977). Page numbers referring to this edition are shown in parentheses.

7. In R. L. Stevenson's *Treasure Island* the principal protagonists are Jim Hawkins, Dr. Livesey, and a squire named Trelawney.

8. Prefazione x–xi.

9. "Il midollo del leone," *Una pietra sopra* 14. Originally the essay appeared in *Il Paragone* 66 (1955).

10. Prefazione xii.

11. Italo Svevo, *Confessions of Zeno,* trans. Beryl De Zoete (New York: Vintage, 1958) 146.

12. "Il midollo del leone" 14.

13. "Il midollo del leone" 15.

14. Ironically, the doctor's laboratory is near the cemetery: it was believed that the will-o'-the-wisp phenomenon resulted from the ignition of gases emanating from decomposing bodies.

15. Prefazione xii.

16. J. R. Woodhouse, *Italo Calvino: A Reappraisal and an Appreciation of the Trilogy* (Hull: University of Hull Publications, 1968) 8.

17. Prefazione xiii.

18. Woodhouse 34.

19. Prefazione xiii.

20. Prefazione xiii.

21. It is unclear why, being Protestant, the Huguenots would "say Mass"—or perhaps they hadn't fully broken away from that practice.

22. For Calvino, "the formula *divertimento* has always meant that the reader is the one who must be entertained" (Prefazione xviii).

23. *Singular Travels, Campaigns and Adventures of Baron Munchausen.* Although Raspe (1737–94) is regarded as the author, there remain some doubts of authorship. The collection, originally published in England in 1785, was elaborated and translated into German by Gottfried Bürger in 1786. In his essay "Lightness," Calvino remarks that the eighteenth-century imagination was "full of figures suspended in air." Likewise, this drive toward unbridled imagination is found in Baron von Munchhausen's adventures: he flies on a cannon ball, he is carried aloft by ducks, he comes down from the moon on a rope, etc. ("Lightness," *Six Memos for the Next Millennium* [Cambridge: Harvard University Press, 1988] 23).

24. *Adventures of Baron Munchausen* (New York: Dover, 1960) 22. In Calvino's novel the two parts of the Viscount are "tightly bound together" and the doctor takes "great care that all guts and arteries of both parts correspond" (244). Both the Viscount's and the Baron's healing are reminiscent of a similar episode in Cervantes's *Don Quixote.* In the novel, Sancho is told that in the event Don Quixote should be halved in battle, the squire should make use of Fierabrás's balm to make him whole again.

25. *Adventures of Baron Munchausen* 22.

26. Prefazione xiv. Jean-Paul Sartre, in his *Being and Nothingness,* discusses the notion that life has no meaning or purpose beyond the goals that each man sets for himself.

27. Prefazione xiv. Nikita Khruschev's denunciations of Stalinism at the 20th Congress of the Soviet Communist Party in 1956 contributed to Calvino's disenchantment with the party.

28. *The Baron in the Trees* (New York: Random House, 1959) 12. Page numbers referring to this edition are shown in parentheses.

29. In the 1965 introduction to the school edition, writing about the beautiful natural surroundings of the region, Calvino states that the landscape "is both a detailed and transfigured remembering of something which the Author does not invent because it belongs to his real experience, to his youthful memories" (*Il barone rampante* [Turin: Einaudi, 1965] 47). The preface and the notes are by Tonio Cavilla, an obvious anagram of Italo Calvino.

30. No doubt Calvino was inspired by Defoe's novel. In fact, when Viola returns to Ombrosa a mature woman and finds Cosimo still living in the trees, the following exchange takes place: " 'You look like Crusoe!' 'Have your read it?' he said at once, to show he was up to date" (155).

31. Woodhouse 50.

32. It should be noted that in 1784-85 Europe experienced a short-lived craze for ballooning. In a sequel to the *Adventures of Baron Munchausen,* published under the title *Gulliver Revived* (1786), there are several episodes that ridicule the French balloonist Jean-Pierre-François Blanchard, the first to cross the channel in a hot-air balloon in 1784, and Vincenzo Lunardi, the Italian aeronautical pioneer, who the same year made the first aerial ascent from English soil in a hydrogen-filled balloon. In 1808, on a flight over The Hague, Blanchard suffered a stroke and fell more than fifty feet, never to recover again. Several years later his widow died when her balloon fell to the ground. Certainly Cosimo's aerial ending echoes the manner in which both Blanchards came to an end.

33. It is interesting to note the use of the adjective *rampante,* the meaning of which is the same in English: growing luxuriantly, flourishing, creeping, as in rampant plants or climbing plants. In heraldry it denotes an animal rearing up on the hind legs with forelegs extended.

34. Once again we see echoes of *Don Quixote,* especially of Sancho Panza's humorous claim to have seen the whole earth from on high; that he "had a peep at it from one angle and saw it all."

35. In an article published in *la Repubblica* (16-17 Dec. 1979), Calvino writes: "I am one of those who left the Communist Party in 1956–57 because it failed to de-Stalinize itself fast

enough" (quoted Milanini 64). Actually, Calvino left the party on 1 August 1957. His letter of resignation appeared in *l'Unità* 7 Aug. 1957. In another letter, written to his friend Paolo Spriano on the day of his resignation, he states: "I am neither a social democrat nor an *olivettiano*, [liberal socialist], you very well know that. It is difficult being a communist by oneself. But I am and I will remain a communist. If I can prove this to you, then I shall also have proven to you that *Il Barone rampante* is a book not too far removed from things that matter to me" (Spriano, *Le passioni di un decennio (1946–1956)* [Milan: Garzanti, 1986] 25). Spriano states that Calvino continued to vote for the Communist Party for more than twenty years.

36. Enrico Ghidetti, "Il fantastico ben temperato di Italo Calvino," *Il ponte* 43 (1987): 109–23.

37. Marie Jean Antoine Nicolas Caritat, Marquis of Condorcet (1743–94), author of *Sketch for a Historical Picture of the Progress of the Human Mind* (1794).

38. *Il barone rampante* 10.

39. See J. R. Woodhouse's "Introduction" to Italo Calvino, *Il barone rampante* (Manchester: Manchester University Press, 1970) xxvii.

40. Constance Markey, "Calvino and the Existential Dilemma: The Paradox of Choice," *Italica* 60 (1983): 55.

41. Woodhouse 51.

42. Discussing his interest in the Enlightenment, which he found "increasingly rich and many-faceted and full of contradictory ferments that are still going on today," Calvino adds that for him *Il barone rampante* is "a kind of Don Quixote of the 'Philosophy of the Enlightenment' " ("Two Interviews on Science and Literature," *The Uses of Literature*, [New York: Harcourt, Brace, 1986] 35).

43. Jill Margo Carlton, "The Genesis of *Il barone rampante*," *Italica* 61 (1984): 198, 199.

44. Markey 56–57.

45. *"Candide*: An Essay on Velocity," *Uses of Literature* 175–81; originally a preface to the Italian edition of *Candide* (Milan: Rizzoli, 1974). Regarding Voltaire's exhortation Calvino writes: "From this stem both an ethic of strictly 'productive' work, in the capitalistic sense of the word, and an ethic of practical, responsible, and concrete commitment without which no common problems can be solved. The real choices of man today, in a word, start from this point" (181).

46. Prefazione xvi.

47. Cristina Benussi, *Introduzione a Calvino* (Rome-Bari: Laterza, 1989) 49. The term *écriture*, used in deconstructionist criticism, here refers to the narrative stratum through which the Baron's adventures are told.

48. Homer, *The Odyssey*, trans. E. V. Rieu (Baltimore: Penguin, 1960) 149.

49. In Boccaccio's *Decameron* III.2, king Agilulf is unable to discover in his own household the man who is having an affair with his wife.

50. Prefazione xvii.

51. Prefazione xvi.

52. Bonura 74.

53. See Jean Wahl, *A Short History of Existentialism* (New York: Philosophical Library, 1949) 4.

54. *The Nonexistent Knight and The Cloven Viscount* 5.

55. A. H. Carter III, *Italo Calvino: Metamorphoses of Fantasy* (Ann Arbor: UMI Research Press, 1987) 45.

56. Rather than using Archibald Colquhoun's English rendition, I prefer the squire's names in Italian because they are far more dramatic and amusingly revealing in the original. In fact, not only do the names have Ligurian, Piedmontese, Tuscan, and Near Eastern echoes, but Calvino's onomastic imagination also suggests various possible meanings to them: Gurdulù= *guardalo* (just look at him); Gudi-Ussuf= *godi o soffri* (enjoy or suffer) and *godi Ussuf* (enjoy yourself Ussuf); Ben-Va-Ussuf (Ussuf is doing all right); Ben Stanbùl= *ben stai a Istanbul* (Istanbul is

nice for you); Pestanzùl= *pesta in giù* (beat him [or it] further down); Bertinzùl= *verti in giù* (turn downward), Martinbon= *Martino buono* (good Martin); Omobon= *uomo buono* (good man), Omobestia (animal man), il Brutto del Vallone, (the bad or wild man of the valley); Gian Paciasso = *Gianni il pascià* (Gianni who lives extravagantly like a lord or Pasha); Pier Paciugo = *Piero pasciuto* (well-fed Piero) or from the Mexican *pachuco* (flashy, coarse, common); Carotun= *carotone* (big carrot or someone with red hair and freckles); Balingaccio = *berlingaccio* (carnival day); Bertella= *bertuccia* (Barbary ape) or *bertoldo* (simpleton). Berta, sung in Carolingian poems as Bertrada or *Berta au grands piés* (Big-footed Bertha), was the mother of Charlemagne.

57. This condition brings to mind "Tante domande" (So Many Questions), Rodari's charming story concerning a child who asks logically inverted questions: Why do drawers have tables? Why do whiskers have a cat? Why does a beard have a face? (Gino Rodari, *Favole al telefono* [Turin: Einaudi, 1961]). Calvino was very familiar with Rodari's writings (also published by Einaudi) and, indeed, wrote: "Rodari e la sua bacchetta magica," *La Repubblica* 6 Nov. 1982.

58. Prefazione xvii.

59. Giorgio Pullini, *Il romanzo italiano del dopoguerra: 1940–1960* (Padua. Marsilio Editori, 1965) 357.

60. The relationship between the "vacant" knight and "pure being" squire, according to Almansi, "gives Calvino wide opportunity for binary combinations. . . . Like Don Quixote and Sancho Panza, they represent extreme cases of spirituality (thinned down to non-existence and carnality (puffed-up to non-consciousness)." Guido Almansi, "The Gnac Factor," *London Magazine* 20 (Oct. 1980): 61-62.

61. Franco Di Carlo, *Come leggere "I nostri antenati' di Italo Calvino* (Milan: Mursia, 1978) 63.

62. Prefazione xvii.

63. Benussi 69.

64. Prefazione xvii.

65. Prefazione xvii. It is interesting to note that in *Perceval, ou le conte du Graal* by Chrétien de Troyes, the Grail is a hollow dish, accompanied by a bleeding lance.

66. Prefazione xvii–xviii.

67. Prefazione xvii.

68. Clearly an allusion to Candide and Cunégonde in *Candide,* Voltaire's satire of Leibniz's philosophical belief that all is for the best in the best of all possible worlds. The entire episode dealing with Sophronia and her virginity alludes to Voltaire's parody of romances of adventure.

69. Robert J. Clements and Joseph Gibaldi, *Anatomy of the Novella: The European Tale Collection from Boccaccio and Chaucer to Cervantes* (New York: Gotham Library, 1977) 45.

70. Barbara Johnson, "Writing," in *Critical Terms for Literary Study,* ed. F. Lentricchia and T. McLaughlin (Chicago: University of Chicago Press, 1990) 40.

71. Salman Rushdie, "Calvino," *London Review of Books* 17-30 Sept. 1981: 16–17.

72. Derrida uses these terms in his reading of Rousseau's *Confessions.* (Jacques Derrida, *Of Grammatology* [Baltimore: Johns Hopkins University Press, 1974] 141).

73. Raman Selden, *A Reader's Guide to Contemporary Literary Theory,* 2nd ed. (Lexington: University Press of Kentucky, 1989) 78.

74. The essay, written in 1959, first appeared in *Il Menabò* 2 (1960). Rpt. *Una pietra sopra.*

75. *Una pietra sopra* 41.

76. *Una pietra sopra* 45.

77. Carter 59. Carter refers to Mircea Eliade's *Myth and Reality,* whose thesis is that the nature of the past can be discovered from myth.

78. The Italian original is much more dramatic: "Dovrò considerare pari a me questo scudiero, Gurdulù, che non sa neppure se c'è o se non c'è?—Imparerà anche lui . . . Neppure noi sapevamo d'essere al mondo . . . Anche ad essere si impara."

79. Prefazione xviii.

CHAPTER FIVE

The Speculating Intellectual at the Crossroads: Four Novellas

One could say that in Italy being an intellectual is regarded as something damaging, as an unredeeming negative condition.[1]

What Calvino's long stories or novelettes—*La formica argentina*, 1952 (*The Argentine Ant*), *La speculazione edilizia*, 1957 (*A Plunge into Real Estate*), *La nuvola di smog*, 1958 (*Smog*), and *La giornata d'uno scrutatore*, 1963 (*The Watcher*) have in common is the plight of the rational, progressive, and committed individual in contemporary Italian society, undergoing rapid and radical transformation due to political, industrial, and economic pressures. What is the role of such an individual, and can he safeguard his intellectual integrity, his freedom of thought and action, if he chooses to get involved in the struggle for a safer and better world? In an interview with Maria Corti in 1985 Calvino characterized this condition as the "reaction of the intellectual versus the negativity of reality."[2] In an earlier interview with Mario Boselli in 1964, Calvino revealed that he wrote the four long stories as if they were essays—he calls it "the essayistic dimension"—whose essence, however, has been entirely purged, and "there remain only shadows of bits and pieces of quasi philosophic dialogues."[3]

The Argentine Ant

In his writings Calvino often makes reference to the presence of ants, most notably in *The Cloven Viscount*, where in describing Pamela's small cottage, he adds: "The subsoil was so full of ants that a hand put down anywhere came up all black and swarming with them" (195). Calvino's ant phobia can be traced back to when, as a teenager, he witnessed an infestation of Argentinian ants in the San Remo region and in the gardens of Villa Meridiana. In his riveting and elusive *The Argentine Ant*, written between 1949 and 1952, the insects dramatically become the main subject of the novelette.

A young couple and child take up residency in a Ligurian coast country house that seems to be pleasant enough, although unbeknown to them it is infested with ants. When the landlady shows them the dwelling, she distracts them from the swarming walls. They put the baby to bed and take a stroll outside their home, where they meet their neighbor, Signor Reginaudo, who is spraying his garden with insecticide. "Oh . . . the ants" (145), he tells them casually, as if they were of no consequence. When they return to the house they find it crawling with ants, including the baby's crib. The father suddenly remembers that the region was known for these ants, which had originated in South America, and that in fact his Uncle Augusto, who had suggested they move into this region where jobs are more plentiful, had casually mentioned the presence of the insects. In their vain attempts to control the infestation they are as unsuccessful as all the others in the valley who have tried with various chemicals, poisons, and fantastic contraptions. Even the Argentine Control Corporation and their field representative, Signor Baudino, who has begun to look and act like an ant, have failed with their control method of dispensing molasses to the ants, ostensibly to destroy them, but actually to nourish them, as many believe. The corporation, in fact, is more interested in its own continued existence than in its responsibility to rid the region of the pests. The troubled parents are told by the landlady that ants do not come to well-kept houses, but from the way she squirms in her chair they know that the insects are crawling all over her body. They come to the inevitable realization that it is impossible to eliminate the ants, or to even forget them with a good glass of wine, as many try to do in the local tavern.

In spite of the surrealistically haunting quality of the narrative—very much evocative of Kafka's stories—it contains much humor pertaining to the various methods and, above all, the determination with which the region's inhabitants fight against the pestilent ants. The couple's next-door neighbors, Signore and Signora Reginaudo, not only minimize the ant problem, but actually laugh at the ants. The other neighbor, Captain Brauni, has invented fantastic devices and contraptions that kill ants, but not in sufficient quantities, despite the "pyramids of sacks" of dead ants he keeps in the kitchen. He is truly comical in the way in which he is described by the narrator:

> I saw a head covered with a shapeless white linen beach hat, pulled forward to a wavy brim above a pair of steel-framed glasses on a spongy nose, and then a sharp flashing smile of false teeth, also made of steel. He was a thin, shriveled man in a pullover, with trousers clamped at the ankles by bicycle clips, and sandals on his feet. (156)

When the protagonist's almost hysterical wife (the members of the family do not have a name) throws herself on Baudino and berates him for his inefficiency in controlling ants— "The ants are eating us alive. . . . Ants in

69

the bed, ants in the dishes, ants every day, ants every night'' (179)—the women of the surrounding hovels, who have incited her to do so fail to take part in the protest. From this incident the narrator/protagonist understands that although no one has been able so far to find a solution to the ants, he and his family must fend for themselves, because "this was their new home" (179). *The Argentine Ant* concludes with an open ending, as the narrator and his family go down to the nearby shore where there are no ants and it is pleasant:

> The sea rose and fell against the rocks of the mole, making the fishing boats sway, and dark-skinned men were filling them with red nets and lobster pots for the evening's fishing. The water was calm, with just a slight continual change of color, blue and black, darker farthest away. I thought of the expanses of water like this, of the infinite grains of soft sand down there at the bottom of the sea where the currents leave white shells washed clean by the waves. (181)

What does the story's concluding paragraph signify, besides the obvious catharsis and the analogy between the sea's sand and the infinite multitude of Argentine ants? Is Calvino suggesting—as Francesco Guicciardini had done in his *I Ricordi* (*Maxims and Reflections of a Renaissance Statesman*)—that one must adapt to circumstances, learn how to live in difficult times, and navigate in treacherous waters to survive? Is he intimating that Italy cannot find a solution to its colossal problems in actual rebellion; that most members of the Italian Communist Party, in the words of Luigi Barzini, "want to enjoy the privileged status of revolutionaries in a frightened capitalistic society," without a violent revolution,[4] and that a Marxist state would not remedy the social injustices of the country? And the ants: are they similar to the flies in Sartre's play *The Flies* (1943), where the repulsive insects become symbolic of France's moral dilemma during the German occupation as well as the avenging spirits of those who collaborated with the enemy? Like the flies, do Calvino's ants symbolize conscious acceptance of the consequences of one's acts?

Because of their overwhelming numbers and indestructibility in their labyrinthian paths, the ants bear an ominous symbolic significance and dramatize modern society's fragile character and impotence. Calvino's emphasis seems to focus on the persistence and endurance of the region's inhabitants, who, no matter how much harm has been done to them by the ever-present multitude of ants, refuse to throw in the towel, and continue to combat the infestation with all possible means. The young couple do not even contemplate moving out of the infested house. In fact, when they confront their rich landlady, it is to "remonstrate" with her for having rented the house without warning them about the infestation, and "chiefly" to find out how she "defended herself against this scourge" (171). The placid sea, with "shells washed clean by the waves," presages a better future, a land free of physical, social, or ethical problems. In Calvino's important essay "La sfida al labirinto" (Challenge to the Labyrinth), the labyrinth has become the archetype of the world's literary images due to the multiple and complex representations—like Guicciardini's treacherous waters—that contemporary society offers of the world. Calvino proposes that the best way to find a way out of our modern dilemma, especially for the writer, is to pass from one labyrinth into another, since one cannot defeat the labyrinths by running away from their inherent predicament:

> What literature ought to do is to define the best stance for a way out, even if this way out will entail going from one labyrinth to another. It is the *challenge* of the labyrinth that we want to save, it is a literature of *challenge to the labyrinth* that we want to enucleate and distinguish from the literature of *surrender to the labyrinth*.[5]

It is precisely this need to save the *challenge* and defeat *surrender* that is reflected in the attitude of the region's inhabitants, who are besieged by ants whose meandering paths create infinite terrene and subterranean labyrinths. According to Calvino, for the intellectual writer and for all concerned, survival is a matter of decoding the labyrinths and then preparing "the most detailed map" possible. This may explain why the uncle had suggested that they settle in this region despite the infestation. After all, the narrator/protagonist muses, "This had been Uncle Augusto's ideal countryside" (163).

Having grown up in a household where both parents were scientists interested in plants and insects, Calvino was certainly familiar with the important role that ants play in the balance of nature, and no doubt would have agreed with Holldober and Wilson's recent findings that ants are "the little creatures who run the world" because they are essential for the survival of many species of plants and animals.[6] Indeed, although worried about the menacing presence of the ants, the narrator of *The Argentine Ant* can't help but be in awe of their resilience, industry, social nature, and ability to carry out complex tasks. Unlike human beings, they cooperate and act in the interest of the whole, even sacrificing themselves in order to maintain their colony.

Gore Vidal, among the first in the United States to promote Calvino's writings, suggests that if *The Argentine Ant* "is not a masterpiece of twentieth-century prose writing, I cannot think of anything better. Certainly it is minatory and strange as anything by Kafka." Calvino, he goes on to say, "gives us the human condition *today.* Or the dilemma of modern man. Or the disrupted environment. Or nature's revenge. Or an allegory of grace. Whatever. . . . But a story is, finally, what it tells and no more."[7] Indeed, because of Calvino's wit, clarity of depiction, attention to significant detail, and the aura of incontrovertible actuality, no allegorical interpretation is necessary to show its greatness. Calvino offers us no solution because the task of the intellectual in our modern society is limited to looking into the roots of problems, without having the opportunity to find a cure for them. However, in a world of absurdity, aimlessness, and futility, there is always the occasional faint hope that allows Calvino's protagonists to go on and to be indestructible, just like the ants. The prospect of transcendence—going from one labyrinth to another—is the redeeming inspiration which endures in this incomprehensible world.

A Plunge into Real Estate

Quinto Anfossi, the protagonist of *A Plunge into Real Estate* written in 1956 and 1957, is a Communist intellectual who, on a whim, embarks on a building venture that is doomed to fail. Although the locality is not identified by Calvino, the story is clearly set in San Remo and perhaps even in Villa Meridiana (suggested by the presence of professoressa Anfossi and her exotic garden).[8] Quinto has no steady job or income, although he first collaborates in the founding of a literary magazine (Vittorini's *Menabò*?) and then works briefly in the cinema industry. Whenever he returns to his hometown to visit his mother, he is disturbed by the "sight of a town that was his, but was vanishing under cement."[9]

Clearly the backdrop of this story is Italy's difficult but rapid economic comeback after World War II. As a result of the Marshall Plan, the 1947–52 European recovery plan created to rebuild the war-ravished economies of Western Europe, Italy was finally recovering, during the late 1950s, from the war's devastation.[10] In fact, many in the industrialized North, primarily those belonging to the middle class, were at last enjoying a general prosperity. One consequence of this affluence was that the *nouveaux riches* felt compelled to have a place at the shore not only for comfort and relaxation, but mainly as a social imperative. This resulted in an inordinate amount of unregulated construction on the Italian Riviera, especially in the San Remo region, where the old stately villas and gardens were replaced by ugly apartment complexes and perennial traffic congestion.[11] Furthermore, the massive influx of these well-to-do tourists and part-time residents corrupted the social fiber of the longstanding residents of the area:

The town had become rich though it no longer knew the pleasures gotten by the older people from their modest earnings at the mill or at the store, or that obtained from fierce recreational activities such as hunting. . . . Now, instead, the local residents were concerned with the tourist way of enjoying life, the Milanese and impermanent way, there on the narrow Aurelia crowded with convertibles and camping trailers; and they were always in their midst as fake tourists or as congenitally ill-mannered "hotel industry" workers (82).

Yet, the third-person narrator tells us, in spite of this "tourism civilization" one could still discern "a strong defense of the ancestral moral stamina, made up of sobriety, roughness, and *understatement,* a defense that consisted primarily in the shrugging of one's shoulders, a repudiation" (83).

After the death of his father, Quinto, his brother Ampelio, an unpaid university teaching assistant, and their mother find themselves in financial difficulty on account of the steep inheritance tax they must pay. Quinto, still a Communist but now with a bourgeois consciousness, convinces them first to sell part of their land to a builder, Caisotti, in spite of his unsavory reputation, and then to become partners in his building venture. Thus, they too become accomplices of the speculators who gnaw into the last remaining tracts of green and who turn some of the loveliest land in the world into a cement jungle, irretrievably fouled: "No hint of tradition," writes William H. Whyte concerning high-rise apartments, "nothing native in the architecture is allowed to interrupt their vast redundancy."[12] This concern for the protection of Italy's diminishing natural resources appears in many of Calvino's writings. In a 1962 essay, "I beatniks e il 'sistema' " (The Beatniks and the System), he discusses the "new barbaric invasion" experienced by modern society; we have become slaves to our possessions, to the modern system of production, to forced consumption, to the mass media, etc.—including "the building fever which is imposing a monstrous face on all the places dear to us."[13] Similarly, in another critical essay written in the same year, "The Challenge to the Labyrinth," in which he deals with the problems brought about by the "second industrial revolution" and automation, he declares that not only can we not keep up with this technological progress, but that we are also "unable to prevent the building jungle from turning Italy into a monstrous country."[14]

As one might expect, Quinto's venture is fraught with mishaps and broken promises, given that the Anfossi are no match against Caisotti, a shrewd and unscrupulous conniver who toys with them and always gets away with it. At the end, they are forced to make all sorts of concessions to him, without ever seeing a penny for their property and with no promise that they will ever do so. Caisotti represents the unscrupulous entrepreneur who, in spite of his humble background, has managed to make something of himself through hard work, determination, and sheer drive. He stands also for "the newly minted equivocal and antiaesthetic bourgeoise, very much like the antiaesthetic and amoral true face of the times" (37). Quinto, who constantly falls victim to Caisotti's dishonesty, still takes his side in spite of repeated warnings. He actually feels admiration for the man, whom he regards as a victim of society, struggling against the system the way the proletariat does for its own ends: "The contractor seemed to him a defenseless hero in a hostile world, totally alone in his struggle against everyone" (96). In Giuseppe Bonura's view, Quinto's odd attitude toward Caisotti allows Calvino to better present to us the class enemy, and to not reject him a priori. Through Caisotti we understand better the "social, psychological, and moral forces" that give rise to such an individual, "a new man" who totally embodies the reality of the building industry.[15]

In addition to Calvino's concern for the unscrupulous destruction of Italy's irreplaceable natural resources, the role of the intellectual in modern society seems to be the essence of this quasi-essay/narrative. It examines the nature of Italian intellectuals of the left who, by and large, do not come from a proletariat background, but rather from an extremely bourgeois conditioning: "To venture into an economic initiative, to manage land and money, was also a duty, perhaps a less epic duty, a middle-class duty; and Quinto, definitely bourgeois, how could he ever have thought that he could be something else?" (33). In fact, these intellectuals "are neither bourgeois nor proletarians" (42), muses Quinto. Calvino questions here one's faith in the intellectual's ability to understand the reality of his time and change it. In this regard, Gian Carlo Ferretti points out the coexistence of contradictory themes in Calvino's 1956–59 writings, as well as a "substantial attitudinal duplicity." Calvino moves from "a pragmatic version of commitment (engagé literature and culture seen as *breeder* of a new leadership nucleus for a functional and modern society) to its criticism."[16] He alternates between feeling impotent and being renewed by hope. In essence, *A Plunge into Real Estate* dramatizes the plight of the intellectual and his inability to escape from it.

Another social and political commentary concerns the labyrinthian intricacies of the Italian legal and bureaucratic systems, hampered by callousness, by ambiguous and contradictory laws, and by a tangle of statutes, procedures, regulations, and traditions that paralyze virtually all activities; and the courts do almost nothing to unravel the confusion. This explains why Caisotti exceeds the building's height limitation, reduces the size of the rooms and thereby increases their number, and manages a continuous juggling of prom- issory notes, all with impunity and always one step ahead of the bailiff. "If we get involved in a legal suit," remarks Ampelio, "we'll lose our shirts" (121). And when the Anfossi finally do press charges against the builder for contractual nonfulfillment and damages, he in turn sues them for libel, vio- lation of contract, and theft. Their final realization is that "Caisotti does not have a reputation to lose" and "one can never catch him because he never does the logical thing. . . . And yet, with this type of a system, he keeps afloat; he is someone with whom one always has to reckon" (133). Caisotti defeats the Anfossi, and ironically everyone accepts this as something quite normal and even acceptable.

Calvino is not interested in giving us a clear resolution to his narrative. What does concern him is the clash between the uncultured builder and the new intellectual entrepreneur. Ironically, the two men share common traits: both fought in the same underground unit, and both want to get rich. The dif- ference is that Caisotti is a man of action, totally committed to his occupa- tion, and has no qualms about his way of doing business—his trickery, the nonaesthetic appearance of his buildings, etc.—as long as there is a profit for him. He is openly dishonest, but there is no duplicity in him. Quinto, instead, neither proletarian nor bourgeois, is an antiheroic weakling who lacks the same certainty of purpose; if he were truly committed as an intellectual of the left, then his task would be to build a new and better society. Bonura thinks that there is a "sort of a glass panel that separates the Italian intel- lectual from the world he represents. Calvino shatters this panel and enters into that world, he becomes compromised, even if he has to do violence to his own nature."[17]

Smog

In *The Argentine Ant* the *mal de vivre* is caused by nature. However, in *Smog*, as in *A Plunge into Real Estate*, it is caused primarily by the abuses of society: by the pollution resulting from the ever-growing need to have all sorts of goods and services, necessary and unnecessary, to which we have become slaves. Worse still, as Calvino pointed out in 1962, looms the ever- present nuclear danger:

> It is clear that the list of these barbarian and subjugating things can only cul-
> minate with the evocation of the one thing which includes, symbolizes, and ren-
> ders useless all the others, that barbarian and controlling thing *par excellence*, the
> bomb that can terminate the history of humanity.[18]

In *Smog*, the first-person narrator comes to a northern Italian industrial city—very likely Turin—where he has been offered a position as managing editor of an environmental periodical, *Purification*. The publication is the official organ of IPUAIC (the Institute for the Purification of the Urban Atmosphere in Industrial Centers). What immediately strikes the unnamed narrator is the pervasive soot that seems to cover everything in the city, indoors as well as outdoors. At first he settles in at his new job, but he soon finds out that IPUAIC is subsidized and run by the very same industrial enterprises whose excesses it is supposed to curb. Indeed, Commendatore Cordà, the director of the institute and editor-in-chief of *Purification*, is also the chairman of the board of a number of industries which are the principal polluters of the city's atmosphere. The narrator quickly learns to play the game by underscoring in his articles Cordà's hypocritical conviction that although their "foggy industrial city" has a most serious problem of air pollution, it is nevertheless a city "where most is being done to counteract the situation! At the same time, you understand?" (95). In other words, his task as managing editor of *Purification* is to create the impression that the institute is actively pursuing its environmental activities, thus giving the public a false sense of security. The narrator conforms to Cordà's wishes until one day, having taken his lover, Claudia, to a hill overlooking the dirty city, he is shocked by the presence of a cloud quite different from the others:

> It was, in short, a shadow of dirt, soiling everything and changing—and in this too it was different from the other clouds—its very consistency, because it was heavy, not clearly dispelled from the earth, from the speckled expanse of the city over which it flowed slowly, gradually erasing it on one side and revealing it on the other, but trailing a wake, like slightly dirty strands, which had no end.
> "It's smog!" I shouted at Claudia. "You see that? It's a cloud of smog!" (110–11)

When he visits Cordà's factory and notices the pollutants it is releasing, he realizes firsthand that the director of the institute

> was the smog's master; it was he who blew it out constantly over the city, and the IPUAIC was a creature of the smog, born of the need to give those working to produce the smog some hope of a life that was not all smog, and yet, at the same time, to celebrate its power. (117)

The narrator now starts to slip into the pages of *Purification* information regarding atomic radiation in the atmosphere, realizing that the cloud of smog, was "a tiny little puff, a cirrus, compared to the looming atomic mushroom"

(130). Yet the effect is nil because the people have become so accustomed to such news that "even if you wrote that the end of the human race was at hand nobody paid any attention" (132–33).

Similar to *The Argentine Ant*, *Smog* closes with an open-ended, cathartic, and redeeming experience. The narrator becomes aware of the presence each Monday of mule-drawn laundry carts on the residential streets of the city. He also notices that when he sees the laundrymen, "bringing back the clean laundry and taking away the dirty," he feels "happier, more confident" (134), and everyone is "happy to give away the clothes soiled by the smoke and to wear again the whiteness of fresh linen, even if only for a short while" (135). One day he follows the laundry carts to Barca Bertulla, a little village of laundries. Here the laundry of the whole city is being done by washerwomen with red faces "who laughed and chattered," and where others, "with baskets as if harvesting grapes . . . picked the dry linen from the lines, and the countryside in the sun gave forth its greenness amid that white, and the water flowed away swollen with bluish bubbles" (137). He feels somewhat cleansed and relieved to be away from the gray city and to see the clean air, the clear water of the river, the country green and the contrasting clean white linen under the bright sun, as well as the accompanying *joie de vivre* of the washers. This may not totally solve the protagonist's anguish, but for him it is nevertheless a new realization filled with hope. "It wasn't much," he notes with understatement, "but for me, seeking only images to retain in my eyes, perhaps it was enough" (137).

The anxiety about the city's pollution manifests itself further with the narrator's own phobia concerning the soot that seems to cover everything—his clothes, his books, his papers, his desk—to the extent that he suffers from an obsessive compulsion to constantly wash his hands, almost as if he were, psychologically speaking, expressing feelings of personal guilt. Even when he admires Claudia's breasts, "still those of a young girl, the pink, pointed tips," he is "seized with torment at the thought" that some dust may have fallen on them. He extends his hand "to touch them lightly in a gesture resembling a caress but intended, really, to remove from them the bit of dust." Eventually, he throws himself upon the woman mainly to cover her rather than to make love to her, and to take "all the dust" upon himself "so that she would be safe from it" (113). The fashionable Claudia, on the other hand, is totally oblivious to the pervasive pollution and is unsoiled by it, and where he finds misery and filth, she finds adventure and romance.

The narrator feels totally isolated and alienated from the other city dwellers—he never speaks to the other men in his boarding house—even from

Claudia, with whom he has little in common save the sexual aspect of the relationship. He is a typical product of what sociologist David Riesman called *The Lonely Crowd:* he is alone, lost in the crowd, and a stranger to those with whom he comes in contact, both at work and where he lives; no mention is ever made of his family. The only individual he befriends is Omar, a union organizer who has lost his job in one of Cordà's factories. However, Omar is more interested in changing society than in the problem of pollution. For him, "It's a question of social structure. . . . If we manage to change that, we will also solve the smog problem. We, not they" (121). His landlady, who is hard of hearing, compounds this sense of isolation. A microcosm of society as a whole, she represents the institute's hypocritical efficiency regarding environmental matters. Although she hardly cleans her boarders' rooms and spends all of her time keeping her private rooms spotless, the kitchen where she spends most of her time is never cleaned. Ironically, by cultivating the "perfection of those rooms she was self-condemned not to live in them, never to enter them as mistress of the house, but only as cleaning woman, spending the rest of her day amid grease and dust" (90). Unlike her, the narrator refuses to elude his responsibilities vis-à-vis the ever-increasing man-made atmospheric poisons. "If he expects something, it comes only from what he sees, an image to set against another image; and the story ends without any assurance that he has found it, without excluding however the possibility of finding it."[19]

The tone of the novel and the narrator's existentialistic angst—being alienated from life and even from himself as he faces desperate choices—are reminiscent of Elio Vittorini's *Conversation in Sicily,* particularly of the novel's opening paragraph, noteworthy for the "abstract furies" and "quiet hopelessness" that afflict the despondent Silvestro, who believes that mankind is doomed. Similarly, at the very beginning of *Smog,* we read: "That was a time I didn't give a damn about anything. . . . I wanted everything around me to remain flowing, temporary, because I felt it was the only way to save my inner stability, though what that consisted of, I couldn't have said" (77). Shortly after, the ambitionless narrator tells us that he walks the noisy streets in the poor section of town, "because all that wear, that exterior clashing kept me from attaching too much importance to the wear, the clash that I carried within myself" (79). Like his mentor Vittorini, Calvino reveals with poignancy the conflict between the individual who struggles to choose his own path in life and the power of the system as it seeks to entrap him. In *Smog,* however, the "abstract furies" do not stem from Fascist tyrannies, but rather from an industrial materialism that has alienated the individual from society, from nature, and from the self. As in Sartre's play *Dirty Hands*, the implication of the story seems to be that in order to accomplish anything, the narrator must be willing to have "dirty hands," must be willing to continue to collaborate in the publication of *Purification*. In essence, Calvino presents the ultimate negative from which, he hopes, the positives of existence can grow.

When Calvino wrote *Smog*, he considered it to be unlike his other stories because he had written it "in a different key of transformed experience." However, he associated the story with *The Argentine Ant*, finding "structural and conceptual affinities" in the narratives.[20] Both have a first-person narrator who is unnamed, and neither story is highly structured; nor does either have a clear resolution. According to Carter, they "are like sketches that have a surprising shift in the last few pages, an epiphanic vision of perfection."[21] Like Sisyphus, whom Camus considered "the epitome of the absurd hero," the protagonists of both stories are condemned to roll symbolically a large stone to the top of a hill, again and again. But they ultimately attain "heroic proportions by rebelling" against their "torment and by demonstrating that the struggle itself gives definition and joy" to their existence.[22]

The Watcher

Alessandro Manzoni's great novel *I promessi sposi* (*The Betrothed*) is renowned for the author's artistry in depicting the 1630 plague in Milan as well as for his impassioned description of the city's lazaretto bursting with the multitudes doomed to die and the fortunate few destined to survive. Like Manzoni, Calvino makes use of a historical event by placing the story of *The Watcher* in a different sort of lazaretto: Turin's Cottolengo Hospital for Incurables, a shelter for the mentally and physically afflicted. Manzoni's intent was partly to show the harmful excesses of the nobility and church, the abuses of foreign and local rulers, and the resulting chaotic conditions prevalent in Milan under Spanish rule. In Calvino's case, although the original purpose for writing this short novel may have been politically motivated—the protagonist is a leftist intellectual intent on showing the abuses of religious institutions in the politics of the nation—the focus soon shifted to a series of moral and ethical questions triggered by gruesome presentations of what Giuseppe Bonura calls Cottolengo's "degraded humanity."[23] In the narrative, the main character first focuses on the deplorable conditions of the inmates, and then he transcends the walls of the asylum by scrutinizing his own conflicts as an intellectual Communist Party worker. He also considers the quality of human life and the problems facing the nation and the world. As has been properly noted by Giorgio Pullini, with *The Watcher* Calvino reverted back to his realistic phase, touching upon certain "moral interrogatives" that had been only implicit in his trilogy; but in this narrative the author "felt the need to set foot again on the ground" and make us fully aware of these questions.[24]

The Watcher is based on Calvino's firsthand experiences as a poll watcher in 1961 at a voting place situated in the Cottolengo Hospital for Incurables, otherwise known as the Piccola Casa della Divina Provvidenza (The Small House of Divine Providence).[25] In the narrative Amerigo Ormea, representing the Communist Party, is similarly assigned to be poll watcher during the controversial election of 7 June 1953.[26] As he sees it, his task is not only to make sure that the inmates of the asylum are qualified and competent to vote, but to prevent them from being manipulated by the clergy to cast their ballot in favor of the Christian Democratic Party.

Although Amerigo Ormea is familiar with the underhanded way the Cottolengo complex of hospitals, asylums, and even convents has become a reservoir of votes for the Christian Democrats, he nonetheless feels optimistic about his role as he undertakes his electoral duties. He acknowledges to himself that, in politics, change is a slow and long process, and that "there are two important principles for a man of sense; don't cherish too many illusions, and never stop believing that every little bit helps" (4). As he checks the voters' identification papers, he is somewhat detached from the proceedings and unconcerned about minor irregularities. Amerigo knows that he and the other leftist poll watcher can easily be outvoted by their conservative counterparts.

From the very beginning the reader learns that the action of the novel occurs on two levels: the external, whereby the mechanical aspect of the voting process is presented, including the Goyalike grotesque descriptions of the inmates; and the internal, manifest by an introspective stream of consciousness, constantly triggered by the appearance of new voters. It is at this second level, indicated in the text by the use of parentheses, that Calvino probes Amerigo's mind and conscience, posing political, philosophical, ethical, and religious questions concerning the nature of democracy, religion, the church, and the significance of personal involvement over theory. As the people of Cottolengo become "less alien to him," things become clear to Amerigo concerning "what should be demanded of society" and what "couldn't be asked of society"; but above all, he fully realizes that one has to achieve this awareness "in person, otherwise it was useless" (65). In essence, Amerigo spells out Calvino's own *summa politica* to the extent that even the character's personal profile is almost identical to that of the author: relationship to the party, ambivalent political ideas and activities, timidity, introspective qualities, and aloofness.

Although Calvino is interested in personal questions, he is constantly drawn to consider universal ones as well. Yet Amerigo's desperate attempt to formulate a cohesive system of political and ethical thought, by relentlessly raising questions, remains inconclusive. Indeed, the story's entire reasoning follows Hegelian dialectic, whereby a thesis generates its opposite, or antithesis, and from the interaction of the two a synthesis arises. For example, when Amerigo first enters the Cottolengo world, he expects to find the "presence of a contrary force, an antithesis" (12) that would stand against his thesis concerning the struggle between state and church. But instead of arriving at an understanding, a synthesis, he "could grasp nothing" (12). What occurs in *The Watcher,* always following the Hegelian process, is that each synthesis forms a different thesis for a new cycle. This is especially so when Amerigo considers the dialectical materialism of Marx and that of the Italian Communist Party, which, he fears, is doomed to failure because "to be right is not enough" (39). Like all other institutions, Cottolengo has outlived its usefulness and perverted its fundamental purpose by becoming more interested in survival than in fulfilling its original ideals. The same is true for the Communist Party, which, by becoming elitist with a double personality—"an intransigent revolutionary and an Olympian liberal" (26)—was perpetuating the "old gap between managers and the managed" (13). Furthermore, the larger the movement, the more the individual members lose their inner richness and feel compelled to "conform to the compact, cast-iron block" (26).

The protagonist also analyzes his qualified participation in the Communist movement and his tendency to accept only small assignments from the party. He concludes his musings by noting the "hereditary optimism" required to belong to the Communist movement because, as a minority party, it thinks "it has won each time it loses; in short, the optimism and the pessimism were, if not the same thing, then opposite sides of the same artichoke leaf" (8). What he means to say is that, historically, Italians have been able to survive by being skeptics and by adapting to circumstances, as has already been pointed out in *The Argentine Ant.* Amerigo Ormea (whose first name is a clear reminder of the famous explorer who understood that Columbus had discovered a new continent) and Calvino appear to have embraced Marxism more out of a psychological need for discipline and commitment than out of a sheer political conviction. This explains Amerigo's modest participation in the Communist movement and Calvino's continuing but ambivalent sympathies for it, even after his resignation in 1957.

While the voting proceeds, Amerigo considers the true meaning of democracy, and the merits of universal suffrage which grants the right to vote to all sorts of people, even if they are unable to make proper and logical distinctions. Moreover, he calls into question the degenerative process undergone by political parties and other institutions, and yearns for the goodwill that had permeated Italy's postwar period when these rights were first instituted. He assumes that even in Cottolengo, when it was first founded, "there must have been warmth in the piety that filled the people"; that at one time, "between the outcasts and their benefactors there must have been created the image of a different society, where life, and not self-interest, was what mattered" (14). But now, in spite of all the progress, the "gray shadow of the bureaucratic State," so pervasive under fascism, had taken over again. And Cottolengo, besides offering its services to the indigents, "had become productive, in a way no one could have imagined at the time of its foundation: it produced votes" (14).

As Amerigo comes in contact with the inmates disfigured by crippling physical and mental diseases, he notices the excitement among the "inhabitants of a hidden world . . . as if their existence has finally been recognized" (17). Gradually, he feels drawn by this human vortex "where beauty no longer existed" (20) and is overcome by a "sense of human history's vanity" (42). To escape from the realities that are becoming a nightmare and this sense of depression, "from those drab, colorless people" (21), he thinks of his girlfriend, Lia, and her beauty. He wonders why one feels the need for beauty and inquires into its physical nature. He theorizes that if human evolution had reacted differently, or if it were to suffer mutations caused by atomic radiation, the misshapen idiots of Cottolengo would be regarded as normal and beautiful "in a world that was totally deformed" (22). To society they would be monsters, but to themselves they would be "human beings in the only way that beings are human" (23). As he struggles not to be swallowed by the presence of inmates giving off "a hypnotic fluid, as if it made him prisoner of a different world" (20), Amerigo inevitably feels more and more overcome by the prospect that Cottolengo might be the *only* possible world. Still, he never fears that he will sink into its depths.

During lunch break Amerigo goes home and reads a passage from Karl Marx's *Youthful Writings* on the relationship between man and nature; Amerigo's interpretation is that even the handicapped of Cottolengo are restored to the rights of the human race by participating in the electoral process. As he wonders if communism could do a better job in restoring the crippled and the maimed, his reflections are interrupted by a telephone call from Lia. They argue about silly things; she hangs up; he calls her back; they argue again; and Lia finally tells him she is pregnant. When he recommends an abortion, she becomes very angry and hangs up once more. At this point Amerigo reflects on the problems of overpopulation and the urgency for birth control; it is ironic, he thinks, that both his party and the church have always been in agreement about the need to multiply the human species, without any concern for feeding the hungry, "all that India of people born to unhappiness, that silent question, an accusation of all those who procreate" (53). And yet, however irritated he may be by Lia's emotional behavior, he feels reassured by her resilience and constancy in being irrational and unpredictable. At the same time, he is disappointed by their inability to communicate better but heartened by her humanity and by the fact that she never changes.

Upon his return to Cottolengo he is assigned to officiate at the bedside of immobilized inmates. When his colleagues are inclined to allow the vote of a patient who is totally paralyzed, disturbed, and incapable of expressing himself, a "hairless, swollen face, stiff, with opened, twisted mouth, the eyeballs sticking out of the lids without lashes" (58), Amerigo finally objects to this travesty. But much to his surprise, the other poll watchers agree with him, including the priest who has been taking them around the ward. For the first time Amerigo prevails, and all the other bedridden patients of the same ward are not allowed to vote—actually, the accompanying nun is prevented from voting for them. Among these wretched outcasts from society Amerigo notices a peasant father seated next to his idiot son who is intent on eating the walnuts handed to him. In vain the parent "stares into his son's eyes to be recognized, to keep from losing him, from losing that little, poor thing that was his, his son" (59). This sad scene allows Amerigo to consider "the quality of love" and to contrast the dedication of the mother superior, devoted to her work, with no recognition except the good she derives from her wards, to that of the father's true love. He understands that the peasant and his son "are necessary to each other" and that "humanity reaches as far as love reaches; it has no frontiers except those we give it" (64). Unlike the nun, who offers her care and love partly because of a possible heavenly reward, the father's love is totally spontaneous, selfless, natural, pure, and with no expectations. This awareness makes Amerigo understand that he truly loves Lia, that she relieves the barrenness of his existence, and that he cannot do without her;

and gradually it allows him to escape the depression he has been experiencing all day.

As the protagonist works his way into the chasm of Cottolengo's complexes, where human suffering and depravity prevail in a steady crescendo, he is shocked by the nightmarish scenes he has to confront and by the horrible guttural sounds coming from a wretched creature:

> A boy, sitting in bed in a white shirt, or rather not sitting, but emerging, trunk and head, from the bed's opening as a plant peeps up in a pot, like a plant's stalk that ended (there was no sign of arms) in that fishlike head, and this boy-plant-fish (At what point can a human being be called human? Amerigo asked himself) moved up and down, bending forward at each "gee . . . gee . . ." And the "gaa! gaa!" that answered him came from another boy who seemed even more shapeless, though a head stuck out in his bed, greedy, flushed, a large mouth, and it must have had arms—or fins—which moved beneath the sheets where it seemed sheathed (to what degree can a creature be called a creature of whatever species?), and other voices echoed, making more sounds, excited perhaps by the appearance of people in the ward, and there was also a panting and moaning, like a shout ready to burst forth but promptly stifled. (56)

The horrifying scene—it has a poetic quality even when translated into English—makes Amerigo aware of the insignificance of his political role as a poll watcher and member of the party compared to the momentous question pertaining to "the boundary of the human" (57). What makes us human and at what point can a human being be called human? Is it more humane to help Cottolengo's unfortunates "live or help them die?" (61), he asks, without arriving at an answer because he is incapable of giving replies or finding solutions.

In his writings Calvino has generally shown a greater propensity for expressing ideas, philosophies, and geometrical patterns, as well as for being a lucid rationalist who objectively views reality, than for expressing emotion and intimate feelings. But according to Pullini, Calvino expresses in *The Watcher* "an anguish which opens up a new dimension: the dimension of feelings, besides that of ideas."[27] Yet an alienated vision of man, referred to by Cesare Cases as "the pathos of distance,"[28] is quite visible in Amerigo's imperfect relationship with Lia, who remains distant, unseen, and inapproachable. Nonetheless, Calvino's haunting and at the same time poetic portrayal of Cottolengo proves the "definite existence of a natural reality that cannot be penetrated or fathomed by reason" alone.[29]

Amerigo is additionally disturbed by his contradictory position vis-à-vis the inmates' right to vote. Ideologically, he considers himself a Communist as well as a "final, anonymous heir of eighteenth-century rationalism" (8). As such, his principles on human equality demand that suffrage should be granted to all, with no exception. However, as a partisan poll watcher interested in checking the opposition, he feels compelled to restrict the rights of some inmates on the grounds that they are not sufficiently human to cast a ballot.

The dialectics of *The Watcher*, as well as the dialectics of the other narratives considered in this chapter, could easily lead the reader to label the novella ambiguous, particularly since it lacks a clear dénouement. The drama (it has the quality of drama found in Peter Weiss's play *Marat/Sade*) contains a bleak statement about old and new institutions, and about the insane quarrels of contemporary Italy as best exemplified by Cottolengo, its staff, and inmates. The story begins with a civic optimism tempered by the electoral abuses practiced by the ruling party in collaboration with the church; however, it is quickly overcome by the gruesome reality of Cottolengo. But then, from the depths of despair, the poll watcher gradually begins to see certain truths—the nature of love and the essence of humanity—that were not visible to him in the outside world, in his familiar setting. Yet nothing is ever crystal clear throughout the whole day, and the open-ended conclusion sheds no light on the entire story. In fact, as has been well put by Claudio Milanini, "The end does not reveal more than the beginning."[30]

When the polls are about to close, the protagonist encounters a fifty-year-old man who has lived his entire life in Cottolengo. He has no hands but manages to overcome his handicap by skillfully using his stumps. Amerigo is encouraged by this encounter, which prompts his last observation of the day, one of encouragement and hope: "Man triumphs even over malign biological mutations" (71). The armless man—the *homo faber* (man the maker) as he defines him—represents the "working humanity" which, in its own way, is also deprived; and Cottolengo, an allegory of existence and symbolic of cities, should therefore not be regarded exclusively as an impersonal institution, but primarily for its human qualities and for the human determination and ingenuity that has created it: "*Homo faber's* city always runs the risk of mistaking its institutions for the secret fire without which cities are not founded and machinery's wheels aren't set in motion; and in defending institutions, unawares, you can let the fire die out" (72).

The story ends as Amerigo looks out the window and notices a group of dwarfed women who are happily engaged in their daily tasks. He concludes that "even the ultimate city of imperfection has its perfect hour . . . the hour, the moment, when every city is the City" (73).

In the vein of Bertold Brecht's epic theater, *The Watcher* contains elements of the absurd and the grotesque; it is experimental in form, violent in imagery, poetic in style, and reflects diverse trends ranging from the expressionists to the Peter Weiss play. By presenting life as strange and grotesque, Calvino makes us more vividly aware of its essence. As in Brecht's case, by means of distancing, we are reminded that we are only watching Amerigo's experiences (like in a play), instead of becoming emotionally involved in them (stage action), thus remaining dispassionate observers and judges. Calvino's aim is to make readers step back from the picture in order to see it better, to make them think, and to urge them into action against apathy and social injustice. He accomplishes this by observing Brecht's rules for *Verfremdungseffekte* (distancing)—the use of the third person, the past tense, and the spoken stage directions which are achieved via the use of numerous parentheses. By drawing us into the unfamiliar and haunting recesses of Cottolengo, a microcosm of society and of us as individuals, Calvino makes us ever more aware of our moral uneasiness as he compels us to recognize the integrity of other moralities and philosophies.

If Italo Calvino's writings share a theme, it is loneliness. All his narratives pit the individual against the group as well as against nature, and probe the solitude of an individual who always remains somewhat inscrutable despite the author's patient observation. This is certainly so in *La giornata d'uno scrutatore*, where the term *scrutatore*, from the verb *scrutare* (to scrutinize, to probe, to examine, to delve into difficult or hidden things), implies more than being a mere poll watcher. The interest of the novelette and its scope are evident in Calvino's skill at showing us the uncertain and unforeseen ways in which the human lives in the Cottolengo world touch one another, including Amerigo Ormea, his alter ego.[31]

NOTES

1. "Il midollo del leone," *Una pietra sopra* (Turin: Einaudi, 1980) 7.

2. Maria Corti, "Intervista: Italo Calvino," *Autografo* 2 (Oct. 1985): 49. In this interview, given shortly before his death, Calvino informs us that "*La speculazione edilizia, La giornata d'uno scrutatore,* and a third story of which I wrote only a few pages, *Che spavento l'estate,* were all conceived around 1955 as a set of three stories *Cronache degli anni Cinquanta,* based on the reaction of the intellectual versus the negativity of reality." Since he did not complete *La giornata d'uno scrutatore* until the 60s, a period when he "felt a need to find new forms," the series was left unfinished. Eventually *La formica argentina, La speculazione edilizia,* and *La nuvola di smog* appeared in *I racconti* (1958) under the heading "La vita difficile" (Difficult Life). The English version of *The Watcher, Smog,* and *The Argentine Ant* is available in *The Watcher and Other Stories* (New York: Harcourt Brace, 1971). The first two stories are translated by William Weaver and the last by Archibald Colquhoun. Page numbers in parentheses refer to this edition.

3. "Italo Calvino a Mario Boselli," *Nuova Corrente* 9 (Spring-Summer 1964): 102–16.

4. Luigi Barzini, "Realism and Guicciardini," *The Italians* (New York: Bantam, 1972) 173.

5. "La sfida al labirinto," *Una pietra sopra* 96. In this essay Calvino also discusses Robbe-Grillet's 1959 book *Dans le labyrinthe* (*In the Labyrinth*).

6. Bert Holldobler and Edward O. Wilson, *The Ants* (Cambridge: Belknap Press, 1990).

7. Gore Vidal, "Fabulous Calvino," *New York Review of Books* (30 May, 1974): 14.

8. As we have already noted in chapter 1, Calvino was very much aware of the role San Remo played in his writings. See Corti, 51.

9. *La speculazione edilizia* (Turin: Einaudi, 1958) 11. Numbers in parentheses refer to this Einaudi edition.

10. In 1949 Italy joined NATO, and, starting with 1956, it participated in the creation of the EEC, of which it became a member in 1958.

11. After leaving his San Remo home at nineteen, Calvino used to return occasionally to visit his mother. When Eva Mameli-Calvino died, Villa Meridiana remained his only tie to San Remo. In 1979 he sold the villa and was glad to get rid of it, since it was "besieged by cement." A condominium was eventually built there. See Stefano Malatesta, "La vigna di Calvino," *La Repubblica* (30 Nov. 1986): 17.

12. William H. Whyte Jr., "Are Cities Un-American?" in *The Exploding Metropolis* (Garden City: Doubleday, 1958) 41.

13. *Una pietra sopra* 75.

14. *Una pietra sopra* 83.

15. Giuseppe Bonura, *Invito alla lettura di Italo Calvino* (Milan: Mursia, 1987) 63.

16. Gian Carlo Ferretti, *Le capre di Bikini: Calvino giornalista e saggista 1945–1985* (Rome: Editori Riuniti, 1989) 56.

17. Bonura 65.

18. *Un pietra sopra* 75–76.

19. Back page of *La nuvola di smog e La formica argentina* (Turin: Einaudi, 1958). The blurb most likely was written by Calvino, who was an editor at Einaudi.

20. Corti 49. Because of the "affinities," Calvino published the two stories in one volume.

21. A. H. Carter III, *Italo Calvino: Metamorphoses of Fantasy* (Ann Arbor: UMI Research Press, 1987) 66.

22. George R. McMurray, *Jorge Luis Borges* (New York: Ungar, 1980) 2–3.

23. Bonura 77.

24. Giorgio Pullini, *Volti e risvolti del romanzo italiano contemporaneo* (Milan: Mursia, 1971) 155.

25. In 1953 Calvino first visited Cottolengo as a political candidate running on the Communist ticket; he returned there in 1961 as a poll watcher, still representing the party, though no longer a card-carrying member.

26. Dubbed by the opposition as the "swindle law," the defeated proposition would have allowed the coalition two-thirds of the seats in Parliament if it were to get more than 50 percent of the vote. The effect of such legislation would clearly have diminished the power of the Communist Party and that of other minority parties.

27. Pullini 155.

28. Cesare Cases, "Calvino e il 'pathos della distanza!' " in *I metodi attuali della critica*, ed. Maria Corti and Cesare Segre (Turin: Edizioni RAI, 1970) 53–59.

29. Ferretti 92.

30. Claudio Milanini, *L'utopia discontinua: Saggio su Italo Calvino* (Milan: Garzanti, 1990) 75.

31. For an earlier discussion of this novella, see my "Cottolengo: Calvino's Living Hell," *Italian Culture* 9 (1991).

CHAPTER SIX

Calvino's Co[s]mic Mosaic

What interests me is the whole mosaic in which man is set, the interplay of relationships, the design that emerges from the squiggles on the carpet. . . . The stories I write come into being within a human brain, by means of a combination of signs worked out by the human cultures that have gone before me.[1]

The French Connection

In 1964 Calvino, now over forty years of age, moved to Paris and finally married. There he intensified his contacts with the latest innovative literary trends, ranging from the antinovel or *nouveau roman*, structuralism, and semiotics, to Oulipo, the sensational Parisian literary workshop dominated by the writer Raymond Queneau (1903–76). Drawn to these provocative, diverse, but rarefied experimental movements and ideas, and at the same time stimulated by a lifelong interest in genetic, astronomic, and cosmologic theories, Calvino was inspired to create an intriguing genre of fantastic narratives in Italy: *Le Cosmicomiche* (*Cosmicomics*) in 1965, *Ti con zero* (*t zero*) in 1967, and *La memoria del mondo e altre storie cosmicomiche* (Memory of the World and More Cosmicomic Stories) in 1968.[2] Yet, no matter how rooted these narratives may be in scientific epistemological theories and speculations, Calvino always manages to present them on a human scale, colored with a subtle comical, ironic, albeit disheartening patina.

The antinovel, with its repudiation of established conventions such as character and plot, was characterized by experimentation with fragmentation and dislocation, and by an exacting concentration on the exterior description of objects and events without any social or ethical judgments. The movement's most prominent exponents were the French novelists Alain Robbe-Grillet, renowned for *For a New Novel: Essays on Fiction* and his exemplary antinovel *The Voyeur*, and Nathalie Sarraute, Michel Butor, and Claude Simon. At the same time the structuralists were gaining eminence with their theory that by using culturally interconnected signs one can reconstruct systems of relationships, but that no single element has meaning except as part of a structural connection. As we shall see later in this study, Calvino experimented with fragmentation and deemphasis on traditional characterization not only in his series of *Cosmicomics* tales, but also in subsequent writings, such as *The Castle of Crossed Destinies, Invisible Cities,* and *If on a winter's night a traveler.* In 1968 Calvino stated that as a writer he was not drawn to either psychology, analysis of emotions, or introspection. But nonetheless he was convinced that new horizons are opening up, "no less broad than those dominated by characters with clear-cut personalities, or those revealed to people who explore the depths of the human mind."[3]

Having parodied man's awareness of living in *una civiltà segnica* (a civilization dominated by signs) through Marcovaldo's experiences in "Luna e Gnac" ("Moon and GNAC"), Calvino felt a particular interest in the ideas of Roland Barthes, the semiologist who not only systemized the study of signs already proposed by the structuralist Ferdinand de Saussure, but also distinguished what he called *écriture,* the act of writing, from conventional forms of language and style. Of course Calvino was already familiar with the nineteenth-century writings of Edward Lear and his nonsense drawings and verses, Lewis Carroll's works of fantasy, mathematical puzzles, and complex patterns of logical play, and Alfred Jarry's surrealist, audacious, and keen-witted vision of the functioning society seen as an absurd and evil force in the universe.

Jarry's plays and novels were interpreted by the surrealists and the dadaists as precursors of their own artistic principles. In his farcical drama (*King Ubu,* 1896), considered the first work of the Theater of the Absurd, Jarry coined the term *'pataphysique,* which, generally speaking, refers to a logic of the absurd whereby one can give a logical demonstration of an impossible proposition; that is to say, "he presents his sense of the irrationality of the human condition in the form of highly lucid and logically constructed reasoning."[4] He toys, according to Roger Shattuck, "with the arrangement of things and their significance until we see the improbable hypothesis as real." Unlike the Cartesian principle of noncontradiction, with 'pataphysics Jarry not only pokes fun at revered traditions, but he also intentionally violates logical analysis by relying "on the truth of contradictions and exceptions."[5]

Jarry's influence on Calvino's evolving artistic formation is due primarily to Jarry's demonstration that reality resides not only in observable, physical laws, but in exceptions to these laws. He is important too not only for showing Calvino the combinatory potentials of language and text, and that 'pataphysics is the "science of imaginary solutions," but also for being among the first "to reject chronological time sequence" in favor of the "spatialization of time," and for dismantling "standards of perception generally presumed adequate to measure and represent reality."[6] But above all, Jarry's works demonstrate, according to Linda Klieger Stillman, that science has "a rigorous method whereby one could imagine, and consequently create, a World." That is precisely the world that Calvino envisions in his pseudo–science fiction *Cosmicomics* and *t zero*.

Jarry's ideas were revitalized in Paris by a committed group of followers who founded the Collège de 'Pataphysique in 1948. This mock-serious secret society consisted of a group of artists, mathematicians, and writers who called themselves the "transcendent satraps." One of these was Raymond Queneau, who in 1960 cofounded with the mathematician François Le Lionnais an offshoot organization *'Ouvroir de littérature potentielle'* (Workshop of Potential Literature), commonly known as Oulipo. In addition to its continued adherence to 'pataphysics, the workshop explored the "infinite potential of language for new forms" in order to "determine how arbitrary limitations work as aesthetic principles, how, for example, restraints generate innovations."[7] Both 'pataphysics with its antimetaphysical implications and Oulipo with its mathematical, geometrical, whimsical, and playful linguistic experimentations are reflected in Queneau's prolific writings in prose and poetry.

Although Queneau, who has been called the Rabelais of the twentieth century and the Joyce and Borges of France, had been one of the pioneers of surrealism and a contributor to various surrealist manifestos, he eventually broke with the movement, repudiating many of his former positions. He was primarily fascinated with language, its combinatory qualities, and the ability to play with it; and as a prominent mathematician, he applied mathematical concepts to language and literature. In a 1967 article he stated that since 1960, Oulipo

> has been working towards the discovery of new or revived literary forms, this research being inspired by an interest in mathematics. Its aim could be described as the foundation of a new kind of rhetoric, a new rhetoric which, nowadays, could not possibly do without mathematics.

In addition to literature's need for mathematics, he believed that "linguists, psychologists, and sociologists can no longer remain ignorant of mathematics. Psychologists and ethnologists can no longer remain ignorant of biology. Criticism and literary history have followed suit." As editor of Gallimard's prestigious *Encyclopédie de la Pleiade*, Queneau combined his literary culture with a vast scientific erudition. He was convinced of the need to renew contact between science and literature given that "science" now included also the social sciences:

Literature, if it survives, cannot ignore this fact; even less can it remain indifferent to it. . . . It is all the time becoming more evident that the system that comprises the sciences is not linear (Mathematics—Physics—Biology—Anthropology), but that it is indeed circular, and that the social sciences are intimately linked to math. It is quite clear, therefore, that there is nothing to stop Poetry taking its place in the centre, without thereby losing anything of its specificity.[8]

Since Calvino's post–1963 approach to literature can be traced in significant measure to Queneau's models—his interest in science and its effect on our way of thinking, the application of science and mathematical concepts to literature, the search for new literary forms, the combinatory and playful nature of writing,—it may be useful to discuss briefly some of his most influential works.[9]

Le Chiendent, 1933 (*The Bark Tree*): Queneau's first novel, considered a commentary on Descartes, deals with the Platonic, Cartesian, and Pirandellian question about what is real beyond appearances. This antinovel is replete with events, situations, characters, and plots that are all held together by a structure based on numbers: seven chapters of thirteen sections each—seven being the number of letters in the author's first and last names; thirteen is considered a beneficent number; the total comes to ninety-one, the sum of the first thirteen numbers. The entire work is circular and full of repetitions and permutations. In his autobiographical novel in verse, *Chê et chien* (1937), Queneau again uses his proper name to show the potential for how words have plural meaning.[10] The narrative deals with his childhood and youth as well as his first experiences with psychoanalysis which, following the example of Joyce's *Finnegans Wake*, he jokingly refers to as *psychanasouillis*. In the novel the author becomes aware of the disparity between language and experience. In *Exercises de style*, 1947 (*Exercises in Style*), Queneau relates the same episode, dealing with two characters meeting first on a bus and then at the railroad station, in ninety-nine different ways, by means of substitutions, permutation of letters, and metatheses. Calvino will do something similar with an ingenious use of tarot cards to tell a series of fantastic tales in both *The Castle of Crossed Destinies* and in *The Tavern of Crossed Destinies*. Very much like a musical composition where the theme is explored and developed to the fullest,[11] Queneau shows the potential language has for transformation and renewal. In his poem of 1,396 lines, *Petite cosmogonie portative* (A Small Portable Cosmogony, 1950), Queneau tried to invent a formula for a cosmogony by tracing the history of the universe from the beginnings, to the creations of the galaxies—very much as in *Cosmicomics*—and finally to the invention of computers. The work, written in a syntactically irregular way, conveys the chaotic transformations in the physical universe: the earth gives birth to itself; life occurs spontaneously; a crystal produces a virus; and the universe evolves from a single atom to mechanical intelligence. He reveals, thus, that man is only a small part of a much larger universe.

His most important and complex novel is *Le fleurs bleues* (*The Blue Flowers,* 1965) which Calvino translated into Italian in 1965. This is how Queneau summarized it:

> I focus on a person who goes back in time—and one who emerges from some past era. In other words, modern and ancient. My historical character lived in the thirteenth century and reappears every one hundred and seventy-five years until he meets the other protagonist and becomes his contemporary. There is a Chinese saying in this connection: ''I dream that I am a butterfly and pray there is a butterfly dreaming he is me.'' The same can be said of the characters in my novel—those who live in the past dream of those who live in the modern era—and those who live in the modern era dream of those who live in the past.[12]

Because both protagonists dream each other's actions and thoughts, it is difficult to tell whether we are confronting one or two characters. Like the primordial experiences of the timeless Qfwfq in *Cosmicomics* and *t zero,* the events in *Les fleurs bleues* are at first remote (the thirteenth century), but eventually meet the modern era. Thus the contrasting spatial and temporal dimensions (both linear and cyclical time) in Queneau and in Calvino bring about a constant shifting in perspective, a continuous circularity and perpetual regression. Their writings, very much like those of Borges's recursive labyrinths, suggest clarity and symmetry but inevitably become tropological, in that they convey something other than what we anticipated. Whereas the absurd is present in the works of Borges, it is much rarer in Calvino the fabulist, in whose ''poetic world,'' according to Geno Pampaloni, ''the marvellous exists,'' and precisely by virtue of a creative symbiosis between reason and fantasy it ''may cross over into the ineffable, or the metaphysical, but it never disregards the rules of reason.''[13]

As in the case of Calvino, two related themes stand out in Queneau's thinking: the importance of artistic creation and the human value of knowledge. In his essay ''Qu'est-ce que l'art?'' (What Is Art?) he argues that all artistic activity gets its true value from being an integral part of other aspects of life—that ''art, poetry, literature express natural realities (cosmic, universal) and social realities (anthropological, human) and they transform both natural and social realities.''[14] Queneau was convinced that scientific work must be related to its human context because ''science is *also* a human activity, a social and historic phenomenon."[15] Notwithstanding the obvious distinctions between art and science, he saw a fundamental affinity between the two: "Science taken in a strict sense as knowledge finds itself in the same situation as Art which some also have tried to turn into a kind of knowledge."[16] Calvino, who considered this passage to contain the essence of Queneau, wrote in 1981:

> His working method is always situated within two simultaneous dimensions, that of art (as technique) and that of play, grounded in radical gnostic pessimism. Convinced that this paradigm is suited to literature as well as to science, he shifts easily from one to the other and is able to unite them in the same discourse.[17]

From these discerning observations it is apparent that Calvino was a great admirer of Queneau and his writings, and that he followed closely the Frenchman's career, starting in 1947 with a review of *Pierrot mon ami*, continuing with the translation into Italian of *Les fleurs bleues* in 1967, and ending in 1985 with Calvino's Italian version of the poem "Le Chant du Styrène" (The Song of Styrene), perhaps Calvino's last literary composition.[18] Commenting on the relationship between science and literature, Calvino stated in 1968 that for Roland Barthes literature was more scientific than science, and that "the idea of language given by science is that of a neutral utensil that is used to say something else, to mean something foreign to it." Queneau the mathematician, on the other hand, regarded science in a very different way, because

> he stresses the place that mathematical thought, through the increasing "mathematization" of the human sciences, is now acquiring in humanistic culture, and therefore in literature as well. . . . [In Oulipo] the dominant feature here is play, and the acrobatics of the intellect and the imagination.[19]

Calvino revealed that he himself swayed between these two positions, fully aware of the attractions and the limitations of each of them: he viewed Barthes as being antagonistic to science even though he thinks and expresses himself with scientific precision; but he clearly favored Queneau as a friend of science, as someone who thinks and talks "in terms of caprice and somersaults of language and thought."[20] In 1981, in the preface to the Italian version of *Bâtons, chiffres et lettres* (Sticks, Figures, and Letters) Calvino further expressed his appreciation for Queneau, because the latter's attitude was that of an "explorer of imaginary universes, ready to capture the most paradoxical details with an amused and "pataphysic" eye, but this does not preclude the possibility of perceiving there a glimmer of true poetry or true knowledge."[21] Had we not known that he was commenting on Queneau, we would conclude that Calvino was referring to his own *écriture*, imaginary universes, and the pataphysic eye combined with poetry and knowledge.

With reference to Queneau's philosophical itinerary, Calvino found it interesting that the Frenchman's point of departure was Hegel's philosophy of nature and particularly his mathematical formalizations. "Queneau," he wrote, "directs the beginning of history toward a point of arrival proclaimed by him: the overcoming of history, the beyond history." Further, Queneau's principal objective is to "introduce a little order, a little logic, in a universe which is totally the opposite. How to accomplish it if not by 'breaking free from history'?"[22]

At this juncture in his literary career in Paris, less than two years after the publication of *Marcovaldo* and *The Watcher*, works which were innovative but still written according to traditional narrative conventions, Calvino felt the need to change his approach to writing, to "change route," and find new and different ways of expressing his literary inspiration "in order to say something I would not have been able to express with a previous conceptualization."[23] As has been pointed out by Pier Vincenzo Mengaldo, Calvino's *Cosmicomics* marks a "fundamental turning-point" not only in form and content, but also in style, and all his successive works will retain clear traces of his cosmicomic language.[24] Indeed, it was in part due to the impact of Queneau and Oulipo, of which he became an active member, that Calvino found a new conceptualization that prompted him to reject all limitations of formal realism and radically veer course toward a new quasi fantastic literary world. The artist, characterized by Pavese as the squirrel with a pen, is no longer perched on a tree where he astutely observes contemporary Italy, but rather is a sort of scientific-literary cosmonaut who, with his imaginative fantasy, voyages in both time and space through the vast, infinite, and still largely inscrutable universe. It is useful to recall once more how the narrator of *The Baron in the Trees* explains to Voltaire Cosimo's determination to live in the trees: because "anyone who wants to see the earth properly must keep himself at a necessary distance from it." Voltaire, who likes the explanation, replies: "Once it was Nature which produced living phenomena. Now 'tis Reason" (144). We, can add modern science to Calvino's formula. Indeed, in a 1967 article written for *The Times Literary Supplement* on the relationship between philosophy and literature, Calvino suggested a *ménage à trois* with the addition of science, because the latter

is faced with problems not dissimilar to those of literature; it constructs models of the world which are continually being challenged, it alternates the inductive and the deductive method, and has always to take care not to mistake its own linguistic conventions for objective laws. A culture that is equal to the situation will exist only when the problems of science, those of philosophy and those of literature are continually challenging each other.[25]

Cosmicomics

In 1964, three years after Gagarin's first flight into space and five years before Armstrong's walk on the moon, Calvino's first four cosmicomic tales appeared in the journal *il Caffè*. They were accompanied by a prefatory note in which the author explained that the inspiration had come from renewed contacts with George De Santillana, the philosopher of science, who, while lecturing in Italy in 1963, had restated the theory that a scientific hypothesis precedes the formulation of a myth.[26] This is exactly how Calvino structures all his cosmicomic stories inasmuch as each tale is preceded by such a hypothesis. The first story, "The Distance of the Moon," begins with George H. Darwin's theory that at one time the moon was very close to the earth, but *"then the tides gradually pushed her far away: the tides that the Moon herself causes in the Earth's waters, where the Earth slowly loses energy"* (3). All the other stories in *Cosmicomics* are preceded by principles taken from modern science: the length of time it takes the sun to make a complete revolution of the galaxy; Edwin P. Hubble's calculations on the galaxies' velocity of recession; speculations concerning the extinction of the dinosaurs; the application of cybernetics to demonstrate how the creation of the galaxies, the solar system, the earth, and cellular life was inevitable; the theory that the more distant a galaxy is, the faster it moves away from us. Each tale is self-contained and each cosmogonic theory finds an eager witness in the ageless Qfwfq, "ready to verify with his youthful memories contradictory and even opposing hypotheses."[27]

Calvino was an avid follower of contemporary scientific discoveries and hypotheses in the fields of astrophysics, the nature of time and the universe, biology, mathematics, cybernetics, artificial intelligence, as well as literary and linguistic theories. Although he was a man of letters and not a scientist, he had the ability of singling out a stimulating scientific principle or phenomenon upon which he could create a story. He named these narratives *cosmicomics* because "by combining in one word the two adjectives *cosmic* and *comic,* I have tried to bring together various things that are of great concern to me."[28] For him the *cosmic* element did not necessarily evoke the latest space discoveries, but, more importantly, it allowed him to "get in touch with something far more ancient." Calvino believed that the cosmic sense was the most natural attitude for primitive man as well as for classical literature. However, when we moderns have to confront great and lofty things, "we require a shield, a filter, and this is the function of the *comic*." He was convinced that the beginning of the cosmos, Earth, life, and their possible demise were of such great importance that one could deal with these concepts only by pretending to joke—the only way of thinking "on a cosmic scale."[29]

Calvino's cosmicomic narrator, a polymorphous immortal creature bearing the unpronounceable, palindromic name Qfwfq, is as old as the universe.[30] He creates a different and much older genealogy of man (and universe) than the one found in *I nostri antenati*. Since the point of origin for Calvino's cosmicomic narratives is never traditional character or plot, but instead a theory, an idea—as it is for Borges[31]—Qfwfq is never described physically, and we are led to assume that he started out as a primitive living organism that finally evolved into a man. Having witnessed the creation of the solar system, the galaxies, and the birth of cellular life, Qfwfq describes his experiences of many million years ago in time, space, and during the various stages of evolution (including the contemporary era) as though they were all part of everyday life. At times he is "a voice, a point of view, a human eye (or a wink) projected on the reality of a world which seems ever more refractory to word and image."[32] He travels freely in the cosmos as a presence, a biological cell, a dinosaur, or an unspecified life form in the evolutionary chain link, or just as an unidentified observer who simply *was there*. "We are never told," says Calvino, "who he was or what he was, only that he was, that he was there."[33] By his own admission Calvino followed in the footsteps of Galileo in using throughout *Cosmicomics* and *t zero* a precise prose, "scientific-poetic imagination," and the continuous "posing of conjectures" in trying to create "an image of the universe by means of the written word." He also notes that this has been a long-standing tradition in Italian letters, started by Dante and continued by Galileo: "the notion of the literary work as a map of the world and of the knowable, of writing driven on by a thirst for knowledge that may by turns be theological, speculative, magical, encyclopedic, or may be concerned with natural philosophy or with transfiguring, visionary observation."[34]

Although the stories of *Cosmicomics* draw on modern theories in astronomy, physics, chemistry, biology, and computer science, among others, they do not follow the norms of traditional science fiction, as Calvino himself tells in his introduction. Normally, science fiction narrative deals with existent or futuristic scientific phenomena which are presented as fantastic predictions of potential scientific achievements. Although the genre may deal occasionally with highly improbable events—alien beings, monstrous creatures, etc.—more often than not it is grounded in solid scientific hypotheses and speculations. Typically it is the scientific hypothesis that allows the writer to create a highly fantastic story. In Calvino, however, it is an established thesis that lies at the base of his narrative, and not a hypothesis. In other words, Calvino's starting point is an accepted scientific principle—expanding galaxies, the big bang theory, mitosis; then he works his way back to the origin of the universe in order to render it concrete by relating imaginary cosmic occurrences. Calvino is not interested in anticipating the future of the universe, but rather in reconstructing its past, in a kind of science fiction in reverse, which he defines as a narrative resulting from mere deductive reasoning.[35] Indeed, however informed we may be about the past, our knowledge is incomplete, and much still remains shrouded in speculation. Calvino's fertile imagination, propelled by his profound scientific knowledge, conjures up our distant past, the myths of origin, instead of our future, allowing the reader to bridge the chronological and spatial chasms and recognize the similarity between the ancient and the modern universe.[36]

"The Distance of the Moon," "A Sign in Space," "All at One Point," "The Dinosaurs," "The Form of Space," and "The Spiral" are perhaps the most interesting and intriguing of the twelve stories of *Cosmicomics*. In the first one, Qfwfq describes the fun he used to have when the moon was so close to the earth that he and his companions would be able to climb to it during high tides: "All you had to do was row out to it in a boat and, when you were underneath, prop a ladder against her and scramble up" (3). The reentry consisted in jumping high in the air, arms upraised, similar to the movements of a swimmer jumping off a diving board. When the body would come within reach of the boat, the people on board would help pull it down. The best part for Qfwfq was during reentry, when he used to "seize one of Mrs. Vhd Vhd's breasts, which were round and firm, and the contact was good and secure and had an attraction as strong as the Moon's or even stronger" (9). Unfortunately, the boat captain's wife was more interested in Qfwfq's deaf cousin who was as oblivious—or deaf in more than one way— to her attentions as the captain was to her indiscretions.

Once during a visit to the moon its orbit suddenly began to widen, making it impossible for Qfwfq and Mrs. Vhd Vhd to return to the boat and forcing them to spend an entire month there waiting for the moon to circle the planet. Yet instead of being happy about the anticipated intimacy with the woman— "Up there, wrested from the Earth," explains Qfwfq, "it was as if I were no longer that I, nor she the She, for me"—he was eager to return to Earth, fearing to have lost forever "a where, a surrounding, a before, an after" (14). When the two globes were once again near each other, Qfwfq saw his friends in boats who had come to rescue them with long poles which, however, turned out to be not long enough to reach the moon. Suddenly one of the longer poles, handled by his deaf cousin, seemed to be touching the moon, actually trying to drive it away from Earth.[37] Qfwfq clutched the pole and managed to return to Earth; but Mrs. Vhd Vhd, thinking that the cousin "loved the distant Moon, then she too would remain distant, on The Moon," stubbornly refused to return to Earth. From the boat Qfwfq continued to see the woman all alone on the lunar surface:

> I could distinguish the shape of her bosom, her arms, her thighs, just as I remember them now, just as now the Moon has become that flat, remote circle, I still look for her as soon as the first sliver appears in the sky, and the more it waxes, the more clearly I imagine I can see her, her or something of her, but only her, in a hundred, a thousand different vistas, she who makes the moon the Moon and, whenever she is full, sets the dogs to howling all night long, and me with them. (16)

Like the mythical Endymion, Qfwfq is endowed with perpetual life that allows him to prolong forever his dream of lunar bliss, but which does not grant him the realization of his desire.

Although Calvino at the beginning of the story describes the astral body in strictly scientific terms, he ends up portraying the moon according to ancient myths and traditions which ascribed to it magic powers and regarded it as the representative of the stereotypically volatile feminine element. Thus, the moon's gravity controls not only the earth's tides and climate but also our moods and romantic inclinations. Gravity, which has an effect on both moon and earth, also exerts its influence on the interpersonal relationships of the story's characters, causing, according to Kathryn Hume, the "attractions and repulsions generated within the group by their intrigues, loves and jealousies." Furthermore, concludes Hume, the "moon's forces guide their outer lives; the loves and jealousies control their inner, and manage to keep the social group functioning" even after the separation.[38]

Curiously, although the narrator tells us very little about the earth during those primordial times—as he also fails to provide details about his own nature—he does give us a detailed description of the moon and its composition. He informs us that he and his companions used to go to the moon in order to collect "Moon-milk,"[39] a sort of ricotta cheese, with a large spoon and a bucket. The milk, found in the moon's crevices, was formed through fermentation of various bodies and substances of terrestrial origin which had flown up from the prairies and forests and lakes, as the Moon sailed over them. It was composed chiefly of vegetal juices, tadpoles, bitumen, lentils, honey, starch crystals, sturgeon eggs, molds, pollens, gelatinous matter, worms, resins, pepper, mineral salts, combustion residue. (6)

Throughout "The Distance of the Moon" Calvino shows off both his scientific erudition and his jocular 'pataphysical disposition, which, in this instance, turns into a tour de force. In the vein of Jarry and Queneau, Calvino amuses himself and the reader with a blending of fact and fancy, he validates but at the same time mocks the belief that at the very early stage in the history of the solar system, when the earth had not yet completely solidified, the moon broke away from the planet carrying with it "various bodies" and "substances of terrestrial origin," including, of course, Mrs. Vhd Vhd. In any event Calvino pokes fun at arguable theories by violating logic, by showing off the playful nature of writing, by toying with the language and with it creating his own lunar geological evidence.

In "A Sign in Space," Qfwfq describes how while circling the galaxy he once decided to create a point of reference by drawing "a sign at a point in space," so that he could find it again two hundred million years later—the time it takes the sun to make a complete revolution of the galaxy—when he would be passing by again. He recalls a time when there were no signs at all in the Milky Way; there was only space. Although his sign could not be seen because eyes had not yet been developed, it was recognizable because "all other points in space were the same, indistinguishable, and instead, this one had the sign on it" (32). The sign is significant because it allows Qfwfq to initiate his thinking process, to establish a point of reference that will generate independent and interdependent ideas. It is the first time that he thinks of something, which had not been possible before,

> first because there were no things to think about, and second because signs to think of them by were lacking, but from the moment there was that sign, it was possible for someone thinking to think of a sign, and therefore that one, in the sense that the sign was the thing you could think about and also the sign of the think thought, namely, itself. (32)

Besides the obvious allusion to the structuralist/semiotic meaning of signs— *signifier* = Qfwfq's sign; *signified* = the idea in mind when it is perceived— Calvino wishes to show how combinatory the entire process can become with the addition of new signs. In fact, Qfwfq's sign is first erased and then copied by a certain Kgwgk, "a spiteful type, consumed with envy" (36), who comes from another planetary system. Qfwfq, about seven hundred million years after the first sign, now creates a new sign, but then he regrets it because he understands that everything is changing and that his sign will no longer be valid in the future. And so he erases it. Only the original sign, erased by Kgwgk, will remain beyond the attacks of time and its changes, because it was only a sign and in relation to no other. Unable to make true signs, Qfwfq starts to make false ones, which are all erased by his rival. But then he notices that his erased signs are reappearing together with the signs of others who have joined in making signs, to the extent that he can no longer recognize his own signs.

The story ends with the narrator's unexplained presence on the docks of Melbourne, where signs have multiplied in series of signs, in a universe where it is no longer possible to establish a point of reference, because there is "no longer a container and a thing contained, but only a general thickness of signs superimposed and coagulated, occupying the whole volume of space" (39). Not only does Calvino exclude from this gargantuan agglomeration of signs the fundamentally *auditory* nature of language, but he also brings Qfwfq to a point in contemporary society that is totally devoid of "logocentrism," a center of meaning[40] in which the structural and conceptual relationship between *signifier* (container) and *signified* (things contained) is lost in an utter chaos of meaningless signs.

Calvino looks into the origin of language (signs) and questions its nature, as well as the reliability of our perceptions. He seems to be anticipating ideas he would develop more clearly years later. In a lecture given in New York City in 1983, Calvino applied phenomenology[41] to counteract two contemporary prevailing philosophies: one, that the world is unspeakable; the other, that only language exists. Although drawn to both views, Calvino offered a third philosophical approach as a solution to this paradox. He explained that "the phenomenological approach in philosophy, the estrangement effect in literature, urges us to break through the screen of words and concepts and see the world as if it appeared for the first time to our sight." He added that in a work in progress (*Palomar*), the character "thinks only insofar as he sees, and mistrusts every thought coming to him by any other means."[42] Indeed, Qfwfq the protagonist, and not the narrator living in modern times, is devoid of any presuppositions and focuses solely on phenomena whose meaning he elucidates through intuition and not reasoning. Only phenomena perceived by his consciousness are considered by him; all else is excluded.

The notion of logocentrism is taken up again in "All at One Point," which is based on Edwin P. Hubble's calculations on the galaxies' velocity of recession that can "establish the instant when all the universe's matter was concentrated in a single point, before it began to expand in space" (43).[43] Qfwfq remembers that before that moment he and the others did not know that space and time were possible because they were "packed like sardines" and "every point of each of us coincided with every point of each of the others in a single point, which was where we all were" (43). Now that the universe has expanded into space, as have all his former companions, and no longer functions as referent, Qfwfq laments the separation from Mrs. Ph(i)Nk$_o$, who used to go to bed with Mr. De Xuaeau, and consequently, because they were all in a single point, she was also in bed with each one of them. What he still continues to admire in her the most is that she "contained and was contained with equal happiness, and she welcomed us and loved and inhabited all equally" (46). The logocentrism of "A Sign in Space" and "All at One Point" reminds us of "The Aleph," one of Borges's most intriguing *ficciones,* in which the Aleph represents a point in space containing all points, a locus where all loci in the world come together and are visible from every angle.

"The Form of Space" begins with the scientific statement: *"The equations of the gravitational field which relate the curve of space to the distribution of matter are already becoming common knowledge"* (115). The equations Calvino has in mind refer to Einstein's theory that "the gravitational field is represented by curved space-time: particles try to follow the nearest thing to a straight path in a curved space, but because space-time is not flat, their paths appear to be bent, as if by a gravitational field."[44] In the narrative— clearly a parable of alienation—Qfwfq tells us that as a lovelorn young man he was unable to communicate with Ursula H'x, who, like him, was falling unceasingly in void. The earth, or anything else solid, did not yet exist, and there was no celestial body able to attract them into its orbit. As he recalls these early experiences, he is no longer certain whether he was falling quickly or slowly, or in what direction, given that there was no such thing as above or below. He even wonders if he was really falling or if he was motionless in space. The fact remains that he, Ursula H'x, and Lieutenant Fenimore were falling at the same speed and rate of acceleration, which made it impossible for him to reach the object of his desire:

> She was very beautiful to see, and in falling she had an easy, relaxed attitude. I
> hoped I would be able sometimes to catch her eye, but as she fell, Ursula H'x was

always intent on filing and polishing her nails or running her comb through her long, smooth hair, and she never glanced toward me. Nor toward Lieutenant Fenimore. (115)

Jealous of the dapper lieutenant and frustrated by his inability to ever get close to Ursula—she shows no interest in either of them—Qfwfq fantasizes a battle with his rival. But just when he is about to strangle him, their paths separate again.

As Qfwfq continues his reverie, the parallel lines on which they are traveling become similar to

lines of handwriting made on a white page by a pen that shifts words and fragments of sentences from one line to another, with insertions and cross-references, in the haste to finish an exposition which has gone through successive, approximate drafts, always unsatisfactory. (123)

Despite the ability of this pen (word processor?) to arrange and rearrange text, if we were to take the letters and words of text, which are perceived by Qfwfq as the letters of a handwritten script, and draw them out "in their black thread and unwound in continuous, parallel, straight lines," they would never meet, just as he and Ursula are prevented from meeting. What Calvino is trying to demonstrate, according to Benussi, is that "as long as *écriture* continues to be more or less an exercise of positioning signs, it will inevitably be displaced vis-à-vis its objective."[45] This may explain why Qfwfq is unable to ever reach Ursula or to complete the story whose trajectory is unique and unparalleled. Indeed, the lines of his handwritten text become a series of letters that make up "the script of a cowboy shoot-out scenario,"[46] very much like a TV children's cartoon, in which the two men fight for possession of Ursula:

And so we pursued each other, Lieutenant Fenimore and I, hiding behind the loops of the *l*'s, especially the *l*'s of the word "parallel," in order to shoot and take cover from the bullets and pretend to be dead and wait, say, till Fenimore went past in order to trip him up and drag him by his feet, slamming his chin against the bottoms of the *v*'s and the *u*'s and the *m*'s and the *n*'s. (123)

In his essay "Quickness," Calvino explains that throughout his career he felt more at ease writing short narratives because of the difficulty of sustaining the "inner energy" and "motion of the mind" as well as keeping up tension in very long works. For him, writing prose was not different from writing poetry, since both require the *mot juste*, the unique expression that is "concise, concentrated, and memorable." Indeed, when he wrote *Cosmi-*

comics and *t zero*—"giving narrative form to abstract ideas of space and time"—Calvino realized that he could succeed only within the brief span of a short story.[47] This drew him to Borges, whom he called the master of the short form. Calvino admired the Argentinian's "crystalline, sober, and airy style," his synthetic manner of narration, his concrete and precise language and its inventiveness, his literature "that is like the extraction of the square root of itself." And since Borges and Bioy Cásares had already published an anthology of short stories (*Cuentos breves y extraordinarios,* 1955), Calvino contemplated preparing a collection of stories made up of one sentence only, or one line. The most perfect he could find in this regard was the one-line story by the contemporary Guatemalan writer Augusto Monterroso, "El dinosaurio" (The Dinosaur): "Cuando despertó, el dinosaurio todavía estaba allí" (When he awakened, the dinosaur was still there).[48] In fact it may very well have been this mystifyingly hermetic narrative, which conjures up various possible interpretations, that inspired Calvino to write his cosmicomic "The Dinosaurs," which starts with the usual scientific pronouncement:

> *The causes of the rapid extinction of the Dinosaur remain mysterious; the species had evolved and grown throughout the Trissic and the Jurassic, and for 150 million years the Dinosaur had been the undisputed master of the continents. Perhaps the species was unable to adapt to the great changes of climate and vegetation which took place in the Cretaceous period. By its end all the Dinosaurs were dead.* (97)

In "The Dinosaurs," unlike the previous stories, Qfwfq does reach a momentary sense of clarity and perspective, as well as a physically satisfying union with the opposite sex. Since he goes through the entire evolutionary scale, it is not surprising that during his long life our protagonist should also have been a dinosaur for fifty million years. His existence spans the beginning and the end of the universe as proposed by the scientific theory that the end of the universe, implosion or big crunch, will be caused by the same conditions that created it, explosion or big bang.

Unlike his extinct species, however, Qfwfq survived "the great death" and is still proud of his past experiences because "if you were a Dinosaur in those days, you were sure you were in the right, and you made everyone look up to you" (97). Although for millennia he had struck terror among the other living creatures, when the world changed he was no longer feared or recognized as a dinosaur by the new inhabitants. Nonetheless, the "New Ones, small specimens, but strong" (98), continued to tell terrifying stories about dinosaurs and were even able to recognize the skeletons of his dead counterparts for what they were. And so he began to live with them, earning his keep by carrying tree trunks, nobody suspecting who he might be. They simply called him the Ugly One because he was different from them. Fern-flower, the only one who took a special interest in him, confided in him a dream she had about a dinosaur who carried her away wanting to eat her alive. Oddly, she told him, "I wasn't the least frightened. No, I don't know how to say it. . . . I liked him" (101). Although he knew that Fern-flower wanted him to "assault her," he failed to do so because the dinosaur she imagined was too different from the dinosaur he was. Finally, when he tried to convince the New Ones that *he* was a dinosaur, general snickering broke out among them. But when a dinosaur skeleton was found, Qfwfq identified with it, recognizing his limbs, his lineaments carved in the stone, everything his species had been, their majesty, their faults and ruin. At night he secretly buried the bones.

When a band of vagabonds stopped at his village, he alone recognized that a young female was a "Half-breed, a Dinosaur Half-breed," but she was not aware of it, being "unrecognizable to the others, and to herself" (110). She was a pretty and cheerful female, and he was smitten by her charm, mostly by "the familiar and yet unusual form of the Half-breed which made me desire a natural, direct relationship, without secret thoughts, without memories" (111). And so the dinosaur carried the half-breed off and spent the night with her. The following day she left the village.

As time went by, people only told sad stories about dinosaurs, and Qfwfq came to realize that the more the dinosaurs disappear, the more they extend their dominion "in the labyrinth of the survivor's thoughts" (111). When he left the village forever, he observed along the way that the trees, rivers, and mountains were no longer the same as those that existed during the era of the dinosaurs. He met a band of vagabonds, and among them he recognized the half-breed, followed by a little son, "a little Dinosaur, so perfect, so full of his own Dinosaur essence, and so unaware of what the word 'Dinosaur' meant" (112). When Qfwfq approached his son and asked him if he knew who he was, the youngster replied: "What a question! Everybody knows that: I'm a New One!" (112). The father, who had expected this reply, patted him on the head and went off. And then suddenly the story concludes with: "I traveled through valleys and plains. I came to a station, caught the first train, and was lost in the crowd" (112).

In "The Dinosaurs," Calvino travels in time from the Trissic and the Jurassic ages to a crowded modern railroad station. He presents a parable concerning contemporary society that is no longer capable of expressing or recognizing the human qualities of its species; modern civilization is becoming lost, and will inevitably become extinct like the dinosaurs if it does not change. Whereas the causes of the sudden extinction of the dinosaurs remain mysterious, the causes of humanity's potential extinction are well known, and certainly still preventable. We are very much like old Qfwfq, who "amidst the events that slip out of his hand . . . like the snail which is sizzling on the fire, seems to be laughing, but meanwhile it is dying."[49]

In "The Spiral," the final story in *Cosmicomics,* Qfwfq narrates how as a primitive mollusk he clung to a rock and grew at random but "in radial symmetry" (141). He had no eyes, no head, and all parts of his body were the same except two cavities, the mouth and the anus. He recalls that occasionally he would have odd fantasies, such as scratching his armpit, crossings his legs, "or even growing a mustache" (141). Since he did not yet have a shell or form, he felt "all possible forms" in himself; there were no limitations to his "thoughts, which weren't thoughts," after all, because he had "no brain to think them; every cell on its own thought every thinkable thing all at once" (142). Life was beautiful then, with no limitations, given that all evolution lay before him. Water, which provided Qfwfq with nutrients, was his only source of information. With practice he learned to discriminate among the various stimuli transmitted by the water, and he realized that he was not alone, that there were "the *others,*" and some of them were females who "transmitted a special vibration" (143). As a consequence of his sexual awakening, he began to respond to the females' vibration "with a personal vibration of his own." When one, who "corresponded best" to his "taste," emitted her eggs, he fertilized them. For by then, he had learned to distinguish,

> to isolate the signs of one of those from the others, in fact I waited for these signs I had begun to recognize, I sought them, responded to those signs I awaited with other signs I made myself, or rather it was I who aroused them, these signs from her, which I answered with other signs of my own, I mean I was in love with her and she with me, so what more could I want from life? (144)

Though unable to see her or even touch her, through the water he was able to perceive essential information which he then developed at length in his imagination. Eventually he became jealous of her, fearing that she might be practicing "collective ecstasy" (145) because of her likely inability to distinguish him from the others. It was then that he decided to mark his presence "in an unmistakable fashion," "simply to express" himself, by secreting the calcareous matter that would result in a shell twisted into a spiral:

> At regular intervals the calcareous matter I was secreting came out colored, so a number of lovely stripes were formed running straight through the spirals, and this shell was a thing different from me but also the truest part of me, the

explanation of who I was, my portrait translated into a rhythmic system of volumes and stripes and colors and hard matter. (146–47)

Qfwfq explains that although mollusks cannot see each other, this did not prevent them from having colored stripes; that the shell was able to "create visual images of shells" which exist on a retina. "An image therefore presupposes a retina, which in turn presupposes a complex system stemming from an encephalon. So, in producing the shell, I also produced its image." The important thing for him was first to form visual images, "and the eyes would come later in consequence" (150). Now, five hundred million years later, as he observes contemporary life—including a Dutch girl on the sand being courted by a beach boy, tourists, an ice cream wagon, a truck loaded with paperback encyclopedia volumes, a passenger on a train reading Herodotus in a bilingual edition, the queen bee swarming, and the daughter of an observatory keeper reading a film magazine—he realizes his ancient mistake in thinking that sight would come to mollusks, "that the eyes that finally opened to see us didn't belong to us but to others" (151). Yet, he knows that in creating his colored shell—indicative of other biological evolutions—and by providing the image, he had played an active part in making sight possible in other species. He observes: "I see all this and I feel no amazement because making the shell implied also making the honey in the wax comb and the coal and the telescopes. . . . And so I feel as if, in making the shell, I had also made the rest" (148). Kathryn Hume comments that the "whole story is a philosophical pun on the meaning of vision."[50] Indeed, as creator of images he has made possible this colorful and varied world. Nonetheless, though now endowed with vision, for five hundred million years Qfwfq has been searching in vain for his beloved. He is in love with all the women he meets, and at the same time he is "sure of being in love always with her alone" (149).

From several of his writings it would appear that Calvino's favorite extended metaphor was the spiral, just as the labyrinth was for Borges, to whom it meant "being baffled and suffering terror and anguish in the mysterious universe that makes no sense."[51] In the cosmicomic "The Form of Space," Qfwfq describes Ursula's fall as being "like a winding and unwinding in a sort of spiral that tightened and then loosened" (121). And in "The Spiral" the sinuous image refers to a mollusk's shell, "all twisted into a spiral" (146), which, though lacking vision, still has a vague perception of other individuals of his species and of their surroundings. No doubt Calvino knew that the Milky Way appears visually as a spiral galaxy; and he was very familiar with Dante's spiraling journey downward in Hell and its unwinding in the opposite direction when he ascends into Purgatory. But most significantly, Calvino also knew that the symbol of 'pataphysics is the *gidouville*, a spiral indicating the giant gut of Ubu, Jarry's ubiquitous farcical character, a "symbol of eternal consciousness circling forever around itself."[52] In Klieger Stillman's view, Ubu's gut, or spiral, "symbolizes the processes of assimilation and rejection, construction and destruction, upon which all life depends."[53] For the ancient Egyptians the spiral denoted "cosmic forms in motion, or the relationship between unity and multiplicity."[54] In fact, according to traditional interpretation, the "creative" spiral, as it unwinds around a point while moving ever further from the point, is a symbol of growth and represents the evolution of the universe and the unfolding of creation. The immortal Qfwfq, who has evolved from this spiral form, is indeed a symbol of eternal consciousness as he recounts his vast experiences, usually concentrated more in gaining awareness than in deeds. And since the spiral symbolizes both expansion and regression, he circles from one stage of development to another. He moves at will, in space and time, in a spiraling direction that permits him to show the relationship between his own unity (his sign or unique expression) and that of multiple other forms belonging to the cosmos and to other species. Indeed, although the dominant feature of Calvino's cosmicomic tales is typically play, the essence of "The Spiral" is the idea of self-creation, the realization of the self, and the consolidation of Qfwfq's inner being, which will be continued in *t zero*, the sequel to *Cosmicomics*.

NOTES

1. Calvino, "Two Interviews on Science and Literature," *The Uses of Literature* (New York: Harcourt Brace, 1986) 34.

2. *Le Cosmicomiche* (Turin: Einaudi, 1965) and *Ti con zero* (Turin: Einaudi, 1967). The English editions are: *Cosmicomics* (New York: Harcourt Brace, 1968) and *t zero* (Harcourt Brace, 1969); page numbers referring to these editions are shown in parentheses.

Cosmicomics includes "The Distance of the Moon," "At Daybreak," "A Sign in Space," "All at One Point," "Without Colors," "Games without End," "The Aquatic Uncle," "How Much Shall We Bet?" "The Dinosaurs," "The Form of Space," "The Light-Years," and "The Spiral."

t zero is divided into three parts: More of Qfwfq ("The Soft Moon," "The Origin of Birds," "Crystals," "Blood, Sea"); Priscilla ("Mitosis," "Meiosis," "Death"); t zero ("t zero," "The Chase," "The Night Driver," "The Count of Monte Cristo").

La memoria del mondo e altre storie cosmicomiche (Milan: Club degli Editori, 1968), which has not yet been published in English, consists of six narratives taken from *Cosmicomics*, six from *t zero*, and eight new stories: "La Luna come fungo" (The Moon as a Mushroom), "Le figlie della Luna" (The Daughters of the Moon), "I meteoriti" (Meteorites), "Il cielo di pietra"

(The Sky of Stone), "Fino a che dura il Sole" (As Long as the Sun Exists), "Tempesta solare" (Solar Storm), "Le conchiglie e il tempo" (Conches and Time), and "La memoria del mondo" (The Memory of the World). Except for the last two narratives, all of Calvino's short stories found in the above anthologies are now collected in, *Cosmicomiche vecchie e nuove* (Old and New Cosmicomics; Milan: Garzanti, 1984).

3. "Two Interviews" 34.

4. Martin Esslin, *The Theatre of the Absurd* (Garden City, NY: Anchor Books, 1969) 5–6. Although a precursor, Jarry differs from the actual Theater of the Absurd, which "expresses its sense of the senselessness of the human condition and the inadequacy of the rational approach by the open abandonment of rational devices and discursive thought" (6). Calvino and Jarry rely heavily on rational devices and discursive thought processes.

5. Quoted from Suzanne Chamier, " 'Pataphysics and Poetry," in Raymond Queneau, *Pataphysical Poems*, trans. Teo Savory (Greensboro: Unicorn Press, 1985) ii.

6. Linda Klieger Stillman, *Alfred Jarry* (Boston: Twayne, 1983) 18, 133, 20.

7. Chamier ii–iii.

8. Raymond Queneau, "Science and Literature," *Times Literary Supplement* (28 Sept. 1967): 864.

9. For a thorough discussion of Queneau's influence on Calvino, see Carlo Ossola, "L'invisibile e il suo 'dove': 'geografia interiore' di Italo Calvino," *Lettere Italiane* 39 (Apr.-June 1987): 220–51.

10. Accented on the first syllable, Queneau comes from *quêne* or *quenne*, Norman for oak, but when accented on the second the name derives from *quenet or quenot*, Norman for *chien* (dog). Queneau wants the reader to pronounce his name both ways and be aware of the two meanings. In *Le Chiendent* there is a similar pun on his surname.

11. Michel Leiris shows that Queneau was inspired by Bach's musical fugues (Leiris, *Brisées* [Paris: Mercure de Paris, 1966] 244).

12. Quoted from *Dictionary of Literary Biography* 72, ed. C. S. Brosman (Detroit: Gale Research, 1988) 311.

13. Geno Pampaloni, "Il lavoro dello scrittore," *Italo Calvino: Atti del Convegno internazionale (Firenze, Palazzo Medici-Riccardi 26–28 febbraio 1987)*, ed. Giovanni Falaschi (Milan: Garzanti, 1988) 19–20.

14. Queneau, *Le voyage en Grèce* (Paris: Gallimard, 1973) 94–95.

15. *Le voyage*, 22.

16. Queneau, *Bords: Mathématiciens, précurseurs, encyclopédistes* (Paris: Hermann, 1963) 127.

17. "Qui est Raymond Queneau," *Les Amis de Valentin Brû* 15 (1981): 14.

18. Following is a tentative listing of Calvino's writings on Queneau and his own contributions to Oulipo: (1) "*Pierrot amico mio*," in *l'Unità* (1 June, 1947): 3 (review of Italian translation of *Pierrot mon ami*). (2) "Introduzione a Raymond Queneau," in *Suburbio e fuga* (introduction to Italian translation of *Loin de Rueil* [Turin: Einaudi, 1970]). (3) "Lippogrammi," *L'Europeo* (23 Aug., 1979) 39. (4) Introduzione, *Segni, cifre e lettere e altri saggi* (introduction to Italian edition of *Bâtons, chiffres et lettres* [Turin: Einaudi, 1981]). (5) "Qui est Raymond Queneau?" (6) "Prefazione," *Piccola cosmogonia portatile* (Italian edition of *Petite cosmogonie portative* [Turino: Einaudi, 1982]); the volume includes "Piccola guida alla Piccola cosmogonia di Italo Calvino." (7) "Dal fango sbocciano i fiori blu di Raymond Queneau," (From the mud blossom the blue flowers of Raymond Queneau [*la Repubblica* (25 Feb. 1984), 20]. (8) "Piccolo sillabario illustrato," in *Oulipo la letteratura potenziale (Creazioni Ri-creazioni Ricreazioni)*, ed. R. Campagnoli and Yves Hersant (Bologna: Clueb, 1985) 224–31. (9) *La canzone del polistirene* (Milan: Libri, Scheiwiller, 1985) 13–16; the volume includes Calvino's translation of Queneau's "Le chant du Styrène." (10) "Prose and Anticombinatorics," in *Oulipo: A Primer of Potential Literature*, trans. and ed. Warren F. Motte Jr. (Lincoln: University of Nebraska Press, 1986) 143–52; the essay appeared originally in *Atlas de littérature potentielle* (Paris: Gallimard, 1981).

19. "Two Interviews" 29–30.
20. "Two Interviews" 31.
21. Introduzione, Queneau, *Segni, cifre e lettere e altri saggi*, xviii.
22. Introduzione xviii, xix.
23. Maria Corti, "Intervista: Italo Calvino," *Autografo* 2 (Oct. 1985): 48.
24. Pier Vincenzo Mengaldo, "La lingua dello scrittore," *Italo Calvino: Atti del Convegno internazionale*, 221–22.
25. "Philosophy and Literature," *Times Literary Supplement* (28 Sept., 1967): 871–72.
26. Calvino's first four cosmicomic tales, "The Distance of the Moon," "At Daybreak," "A Sign in Space," and "All at One Point," appeared in *il Caffè politico e letterario* 12 (1964): 3–33. In an accompanying note, Calvino explains: "Contemporary science no longer gives us images that can be represented; the world it opens up for us is beyond the realm of any possible image. And yet, for the profane reader of scientific books (written either for a sophisticated readership, or as encyclopedic entries, as in my own case, given that I am fascinated by cosmogony and cosmology), occasionally a sentence awakens an image. I have tried to make a note of some, and to develop them into a story; into a special type of "comicosmic" (or "cosmicomic") tale. The *Cosmicomics* have as a basis above all else Leopardi, Popeye's comics, Samuel Beckett, Giordano Bruno, Lewis Carroll, the paintings of Matta and in certain instances Landolfi, Immanuel Kant, Borges, as well as the engravings of Grandville.
27. *Le Cosmicomiche* back cover.
28. *La memoria del mondo e altre storie cosmicomiche* (Turin: Einaudi, 1968) 210.
29. *La memoria del mondo* 210–11.
30. One can only speculate concerning the origin of this name: does the letter Q come from Queneau? In addition to mathematical formulas or algebraic symbols, the idea may have come from Borges's "Tlön, Uqbar, Orbis Tertius"; or perhaps from Jarry's palyndromic Ubu. The protagonist of the cosmicomic *t zero* is named Q.
31. Ronald J. Christ, *The Narrow Act: Borges' Art of Illusion* (New York: New York University Press) 1969.
32. *Cosmicomiche* back cover.
33. *Cosmicomiche* back cover.
34. "Two Interviews" 32.
35. "Two Interviews" 34.
36. In 1969, two years after the publication of *t zero*, the Italian film director Federico Fellini attempted something similar in his film *Fellini Satyricon* by using Petronius's Latin text to make a commentary on modern society. Bondanella observes that "the fragmentary, incomplete nature of Petronius's masterpiece appealed to Fellini, since its very incompleteness forced his work into the realm of fantasy. Since he felt that pre-Christian Rome was as unfamiliar as a distant planet or a dream world, everything had to be reconstructed in his imagination." (Peter Bondanella, *Italian Cinema from Neorealism to the Present* [New York: Continuum, 1990] 234).
37. One could say that the pole of the deaf cousin, which is the longest and is used to drive the moon away as if he were "juggling with it," represents the phallus, and perhaps even impotence. Qfwfq is clearly jealous of him because he has the captain's wife's love.
38. Kathryn Hume, "Science and Imagination in Calvino's *Cosmicomics*," *Mosaic* 15 (Dec. 1982): 50–51.
39. The milk represents the moon's feminine nature.
40. Jacques Derrida argues that the notion of structure presupposes a center of meaning; that we need a center because it assures "being" as "presence." The mental and physical perception of ourselves is centered on a subjective *I* and everything else is perceived from such a perspective. Derrida calls this desire for a center *logocentrism* (Derrida, *On Grammatology* [Baltimore: Johns Hopkins University Press, 1976]).
41. Phenomenology was originated by Edmund Husserl (1859–1938). To phenomenologists any object acquires meaning only through the active use of a consciousness in which the object

109

registers. Hence phenomenology "examines a phenomenon in the consciousness by excluding presuppositions of both objective reality and subjective response. . . . Imaginary phenomena have equal status with those taken from the physical world. One realizes the presence of the mental phenomenon, then describes and elucidates its meaning intuitively, eschewing both the empirical analysis of science and that rational deduction of logic" (Northrop Frye, Sheridan Baker, George Perkins, *The Harper Handbook to Literature* [New York: Harper, 1985] 345–46).

42. "The Written and the Unwritten Word," *The New York Review of Books* 12 May 1983: 38–39.

43. Edwin Hubble found that ours was not the only galaxy, that distant galaxies are moving rapidly away from us, and that the universe is expanding. It was from his observations that the "big bang" theory resulted.

44. Stephen W. Hawking, *A Brief History of Time: From the Big Bang to Black Holes* (New York: Bantam, 1988) 135.

45. Benussi, *Introduzione a Calvino* (Rome: Laterza, 1989) 107.

46. Hume 50.

47. Calvino, "Quickness," *Six Memos for the Next Millennium* (Cambridge: Harvard University Press, 1988) 48–49.

48. Augusto Monterroso, *Obras Completas* (*y otros cuentos*) (Ciudad de México: Imprenta Universitaria, 1960) 69. Monterroso's hauntingly mysterious and yet illuminating narrative is reminiscent of Ungaretti's famous two-line poem, "Mattina" (Morning) ("M'illumino/ d'immenso" [I am filled with light of immensity]), in which the poet senses the presence of the infinite in the sea and in the sky.

49. Benussi 101.

50. Hume 54.

51. George R. McMurray, *Jorge Luis Borges* (New York: Frederick Ungar, 1980) 160–61.

52. Roger Shattuck, quoted Jacques Guicharnaud, *Raymond Queneau* (New York: Columbia University Press, 1965) 44.

53. Klieger Stillman 46.

54. J. E. Cirlot, *A Dictionary of Symbols* (New York: Philosophical Library, 1962) 290–92.

CHAPTER SEVEN

An Intellectually Playful Artifice: *t zero*

What are you doing, moon, there in the sky?
Tell me, what are you doing, silent moon?
You rise in the evening, and go, contemplating deserts: then you rest.
Are you not sated with going over the everlasting paths?
Do you not feel a loathing, are you still eager to look upon these valleys?
The shepherd's life is like yours.[1]

Like other writers, and in particular Giacomo Leopardi (1798–1837), Calvino was fascinated by the moon, from a scientific as well as a poetic perspective. Leopardi, one of Calvino's favorite writers of prose and verse, had repeatedly turned to the moon (and to cosmic space) in order to wrench from her the secret of life and the reason for man's suffering. Calvino identified with the Leopardian attraction to the moon, and indeed was impressed by the fact that the poet, when he was only fifteen years old, had written a very erudite *History of Astronomy,* in which, among other issues, he summed up Newton's theories. In "Lightness," one of the "memos" prepared for the undelivered 1985 Charles Eliot Norton Lectures at Harvard, Calvino wrote: "The gazing at the night skies that inspires Leopardi's most beautiful lines was not simply a lyrical theme: when he spoke about the moon, Leopardi knew exactly what he was talking about."[2] Furthermore, Calvino appreciated the fact that Leopardi, the artist of the vague and the indefinite, could "also be the poet of exactitude, who is able to grasp the subtlest sensations with eyes and ears and quick, unerring hands."[3]

In 1967, in response to the novelist Anna Maria Ortese, who had questioned the superpowers' space explorations that were destroying her idyllic and poetic ideas about space, and had predicted that outer space would soon become a construction site, a new hunting ground, a place of competition and terror, Calvino replied that he too was against such a dangerous race for space supremacy. Nonetheless, he felt that one could no longer find consolation from man's suffering by merely contemplating the skies; that what truly interested him, was

everything that concerns the authentic appropriation of space and of celestial bodies, that is to say, *knowledge:* a way out from our limited and certainly misleading framework, the definition of a relationship between ourselves and the extrahuman universe. Since antiquity, the moon has represented for mankind this desire, and this explains the devotion poets have for her. But does the poets' moon have anything to do with the lactiferous and porous images that are being transmitted today by spaceships? Perhaps not yet; but the fact that we are compelled to *rethink* the moon in a new way will cause us to rethink so many other things as well.

He concluded by stating that those who truly love the moon want to enter into a closer relationship with her, "want to see *more* in the moon, want the moon to *tell us more.*"[4]

It is not surprising, therefore, that Calvino wrote four cosmicomic tales about the moon, eventually grouped together in *Cosmicomiche vecchie e nuove* (Old and New Cosmicomics, 1984) under the heading "Storie sulla Luna" (Moon Stories): "La molle Luna" ("The Soft Moon"), "Le figlie della Luna" (The Daughters of the Moon), "La distanza della Luna" ("The Distance of the Moon") and "La Luna come un fungo" (The Moon as a Mushroom).

In *t zero*, which is divided into three parts ("More of Qfwfq," "Priscilla," and "t zero"), Calvino picks up where its forerunner, *Cosmicomics*, left off. Very much like Borges's *ficciones*, the new stories continue to be inventive, erudite, combinatory, problematic, highly imaginative, fantastic, at times geometric, and, always intellectually stimulating and playful.[5]

"More of Qfwfq"

Once again a lunar story, "The Soft Moon," ushers in these tales. However, the situation is contrary to that in "The Distance of the Moon," where the distance separating the earth and the moon was expanding. In "The Soft Moon" we find instead that the two bodies are getting closer again. In fact, the scientific basis for this theory, as indicated in an epigraph that precedes the story, stems from calculations of H. Gerstenkorn and H. Alfven which show that the terrestrial continents are simply fragments of the moon that fell upon the earth. Originally the moon gravitated around the sun, until its proximity to our planet caused it to change orbit. Captured by the earth's gravity, the moon moved closer to it, reducing its orbit around it. Eventually the reciprocal attraction altered the surface of the two bodies and lunar matter fell upon the earth. Later, through the influence of our tides, the moon moved away again, until it settled in its present orbit, "but part of the lunar mass, perhaps half of it, had remained on Earth, forming the continents."[6]

In "The Soft Moon" Qfwfq remembers his irritation when the moon began to take shape and get closer to the earth. One evening, in Manhattan, as he was driving home from work, he noticed that the moon was much brighter than usual and that it was "approaching as if it were going to slip between the skyscrapers of Madison Avenue" (5). He quickly drove to the observatory, where he found his companion Sibyl observing it through a telescope. She tried to reassure him, telling him that the phenomenon was foreseen and that the moon was no longer a planet; that eventually the earth, since it was much stronger than the soft moon, would cause it to shift from its orbit around the sun and make it revolve around the earth, thus becoming its satellite. Nonetheless, Qfwfq became more anguished when he learned that the moon was supposed to come even closer. Later, from the porch of their suburban cottage, they observed that the moon was starting to disintegrate, to melt down onto the earth, depositing "a matter composed of gelatin and hair and mold and slaver" (9). Finally the earth started to vibrate and things began to rise in the direction of the moon: "unbreakable glass and plates of steel and sheets of nonconducting material, drawn up by the Moon's attraction as in an eddy of grains of sand" (10). Sibyl—the scientist who resembles Dr. Strangelove, or even better a star-wars general intent on conquering satellites from outer space—was fascinated by these phenomenal changes and totally oblivious to their human consequences. She explained that the damage was only minimal, that it was only "logical that the capture of a satellite should cost us some losses: but it's worth it, there's simply no comparison" (11). But then soft meteorites began to fall upon the earth, followed by "something like a mud of acid mucus which penetrated into the terrestrial strata, or rather a kind of vegetal parasite that absorbed everything" (11). Suddenly another large lunar fragment submerged their cottage as well as most of the region in which they lived. At dawn it was all over. The earth was no longer recognizable, covered by "a deep layer of mud, a paste of green proliferations and slippery organisms" (12). And the moon was moving off in the sky, also unrecognizable.

As Qfwfq brings us back to the "as I am writing" present, he tells us that hundreds of thousands of centuries have passed since the change in the lunar orbit, and the earth is still trying to regain its former natural appearance; that "we are reconstructing the primitive terrestrial crust of plastic and cement and metal and glass and enamel and imitation leather" (12). We still have a long way to go and much to do until we erase "the alien and hostile additions" fallen from the moon (13). We are hampered in this task by the quality of today's materials, and the products of a "corrupt Earth" are inferior to those lost to the moon. That is why some say that it would be worthwhile going to the moon to recover them. But Qfwfq thinks that we will be disappointed because even the materials of old days—"the great reason and proof of terrestrial superiority''—have disintegrated by now; they were "inferior goods, not made to last, which can no longer be used even as scrap" (13). There was a time when he would not have dared to say such things to Sibyl, but now he is no longer afraid because "she's fat, disheveled, lazy, greedily eating cream puffs, what can Sibyl say to me now?" (13).

As usual, Qfwfq, the narrator of his own experiences, stands within and outside the story. In this case, however, he narrates not only what occurred in the distant *and* recent pasts, but also what is happening in the present, and provides in each instance a different perspective in time and space. To a degree, he has done this before in other tales, notably in "The Spiral." What is different in "The Soft Moon" is that at first we erroneously assume that the cataclysmic events described occurred when there was not yet life upon the earth. But we soon learn that they actually took place in a highly developed civilization that first was destroyed by the lunar bombardment and then rebuilt and replaced by an exact replica of itself: our modern society. Since then, having inherited the ills of our precursor, civilization has not advanced, and no changes for the better have occurred. In trying to achieve the same standards of the former society by imitating its prime substances—"which cannot be equalled"—we waste natural resources, use a preponderance of synthetic materials, intentionally produce goods with the same built-in obsolescence as before, and introduce "hostile additions" to the earth's environment (12, 13). We, like Sibyl, have become spoiled by our materialistic way of life, too self-indulgent, fat, and greedy. We have not learned from our past mistakes and are bound to repeat them. The difference is that the moon is no longer as distant as before its change in orbit, and the earth has turned out to be neither more powerful nor superior to its satellite. But the immortal Qfwfq has become wiser and more cynical because of his greater experience. He has also emerged stronger than Sibyl, who, like the rest of humanity, is degenerating and is destined to become extinct. The theme of "The Soft Moon" may be metaphysical, speculative, or fantastic—as in Borges' *ficciones*—but the effect is distressingly close to reality.

"Priscilla"

The three stories concerning Qfwfq's love for the elusive Priscilla—"Mitosis," "Meiosis," and "Death"—are preceded by a series of scientific quotations from Georges Bataille, Jean-Paul Sartre, James D. Watson, Jacques-Bénigne Bossuet, John von Neumann, Galileo, and from the *Encyclopaedia Britannica* concerning cellular biology, genetics, DNA, and philosophy. We have already seen how Calvino was interested in cosmogonic theories regarding the creation of the universe as well as in the cosmologic ones dealing with the character of the universe. Likewise, he seems to have been fascinated with the mystery of life, and in particular with the cell, the smallest unit of every living organism: the molecular events that initiate and then control cell division, the intricate behavior of the cell as it awakens from its normal state and then proceeds to replicate its chromosomes and distribute them to two progeny cells. All these biological phenomena are regarded by Calvino from not only a scientific perspective but a figurative one as well. In fact, because of their constant division, multiplication—each day more than a trillion cells divide in a sound human body—transmission of coded information, aggression and defense in the immune system, etc., cells represent for the author archetypal figures that illustrate ontological situations. And finally they are metaphors that serve to show that human behavior depends on phenomena far too numerous and complex to be fully understood.

In the first story, "Mitosis," Qfwfq recalls humorously the time when he was a one-cell organism and fell in love with himself rather than with someone else:

And when I say "Dying of love,"—*Qfwfq went on,*—I mean something you have no idea of, because you think falling in love has to signify falling in love with another person, or thing, or what have you, in other words I'm here and what I'm in love with is there, in short a relationship connected to the life of relationships, whereas I'm talking about the times before I had established any relationships between myself and anything else, there was a cell and the cell was me, and that was that. (59)

Being self-sufficient, he did not yet distinguish between time and space, between this mental and physical functioning, nor between himself and other organisms: "As language I had all those specks or twigs called chromosomes, and therefore all I had to do was to repeat those specks or twigs and I was repeating myself in so far as language" (68). Eventually, very much like the mollusk in "The Spiral," Qfwfq felt a strong urge to expand himself. Thus, he gave birth to two new cells by means of mitosis, but in doing so he destroyed his individuality with the elimination of the parent cell. It is apparent that his expansion from the nucleus of a single concentrated cell parallels the expansion of the universe. Indeed, as already reflected in the cosmicomic "All at One Point," Hubble's theory asserts that at the beginning of the universe, before it began to expand in space, all its matter was concentrated in a single point; that before the "cosmic big bang," the universe was "infinitesimally small and infinitely dense,"[7] and all objects were close together at the same place—just like the single cell embodied by Qfwfq. Once again, as in the case of "All at One Point" and "A Sign in Space," this reminds us of Borges's *Aleph*, as representative of a point in space containing all points: a locus where all loci in the world come together and are visible from every angle. The implication for both Borges and Calvino is that this center is symbolic of the author's state of mind, his artistic intuition, as he sets out to express it by constructing and developing his story. Thus, as McMurray has pointed out, "The Aleph compresses the world into a small sphere, which becomes a metaphor of esthetic unity and divine perfection."[8]

Qfwfq depicts the notion of dying for love as ironical because the somatic cell in effect does so in the process of its nuclear division, which results in the creation of two new cells. Thus, each cell formed receives chromosomes that are identical in composition and equal in number to those of Qfwfq, the parent cell. This leads him to engage in a satirical consideration of cytoplasma, protoplasma, chromosomes, and the nature of the cell's erotic desire. At the end of "Mitosis," we are finally told tongue in cheek that the other cell—presumably one that has evolved—with whom Qfwfq has fallen in love, is "the otherwise with first and last name address red coat little black boots bangs freckles: Priscilla Langwood, chez Madame Lebras, cent-quatre-vingt-treize Rue Vaugirard, Paris quinzième" (74).

In "Meiosis" the continuing love story is at first not between two individuals, but between two proteins whose relationship is difficult to describe, because cells are constantly changing. Qfwfq explains that "from one moment to the next I am no longer the same I nor is Priscilla any longer the same Priscilla because of the continuous renewal of protein molecules in our cells through, for example, digestion or also respiration which fixes the oxygen in the bloodstream" (76–77).

Therefore, cellular activity—which is synonymous with life—and the resulting changes in composition are like the cosmic universe, where nothing ever stands still and everything is in flux either by moving away (expanding) or by getting closer (contracting).

After a long disquisition on cellular reproduction, and on the possibilities and probabilities of the genetic reproduction code, Qfwfq turns the genetic issue into a complicated combinatory game of RNA and DNA. The conclusion is that if the individual cell questions its identity, then we humans, as far more evolved biological organisms composed of countless cells, certainly confront an untenable situation. Who are we? Who is the lovelorn Qfwfq? Biologically, our parents have programmed us to be what we are, and in *their* genetic instructions are contained the instructions of *their* parents: "What each of us really is and has is the past; all we are and have is the catalogue of the possibilities that didn't fail, of the experiences that are ready to be repeated. A present does not exist" (80). Therefore, what leads Qfwfq and Priscilla to seek each other is "the final action of the past that is fulfilled through" them (80–81)—although, despite their encounter and their embraces, the two will always remain distant and apart. Likewise, the meeting of two cells—sperm and egg—also fails to lead to cohesion, because we are born "not from fusion but from a juxtaposition of distinct bodies" (81). Finally, biological meiosis does not balance between the father's and mother's genetic influence because the characteristics that determine the individual's interior and exterior form are selective. Indeed, they "are orders denied in the depth of cells, counterbalanced by different orders which have remained latent, sapped by the suspicion that perhaps the other orders were better" (82).

After having proclaimed the genetic tyranny of the past, disposed of the possibility for individuality, destroyed the notion of being in love, and proven the impossibility of fusion between two bodies—all done with subtle humor—we are suddenly surprised to find, at the end of "Meiosis," that the emancipated Priscilla and Qfwfq no longer live in Paris but in the sandy desert: they are two camels in love, whose erotic fusion is possible and veritable after all. The narrator concludes:

> This is in itself enough, Priscilla, to cheer me, when I bend my outstretched neck over yours and I give you a little nip on your yellow fur and you dilate your nostrils, bare your teeth, and kneel on the sand, lowering your hump to the level of my breast so that I can lean on it and press you from behind, bearing down on my rear legs, oh how sweet those sunsets in the oasis. (86)

In the end, Qfwfq's scientific musings may be feasible in theory, but not necessarily in practice.

In "Death," the last story of the triptych, the narrator—we assume he is still Qfwfq—expresses the wish of all matter, physical or biological, to live forever, in spite of the destructive implications for the earth if this were to occur. The narrator distinguishes between the biological part that determines the reproductive genetic code and the part that executes such a program. He first describes the dramatic universal urge for continuity and self-perpetuation, and then transcends into the sphere of human language, or communication, considered from a semiotic perspective:

> a collection of sounds, ideograms, morphemes, numbers, punched cards, magnetic tapes, tattoos, a system of communication that includes social relations,

kinship, institutions, merchandise, advertising posters, napalm bombs, namely everything that is language, in the broad sense. (91)

This implies that our survival or our destruction is no longer limited to mitosis or meiosis but depends on the ability to live harmoniously together, as well as on some form of human communication. At the end of the narrative Qfwfq finally eclipses to the level of *écriture*. As the biological reproduction of cells sets in motion a constant chain reaction, the multiplication of written words and thoughts in turn creates a similar response, where the elements of language "can also acquire speech, where machines can speak, exchange the words by which they are constructed" (92).[9] And as chromosomes provide the cells with an indelible genetic imprint, so language is similarly determined by a code, as when a "circuit of vital information that runs from the nucleic acids to writing is prolonged in the punched tapes of the automata, children of other automata" (92). In the future, he concludes, new families of machines will go on living and speaking the lives and ideas that were once ours; and "electronically, the word 'I' and the word 'Priscilla' will meet again" (92). Once more, the notion of circularity of time and space—the "will meet again"—takes us back to Borges, particularly his story "Death and the Compass." In it, detective Lönnrot, who is about to be shot by a murderer, tells him of a labyrinth composed of a single straight line and entreats him to kill him at a designated point on that line in a future incarnation. The killer promises that the next time he kills him it will be in such a labyrinthian line. But then he moves back and shoots him. In Borges's world there exist a number of combinations which eventually are bound to be repeated, just as Calvino's Qfwfq and Priscilla are destined to meet again in "a ritualistic repetition of an endless cosmic charade."[10]

If meiosis implies a sexual act, so does the act of writing which, in this case, however, is no longer limited to pen, ink, and paper (Freudian erotic icons); it now includes generations of machines that keep procreating totally oblivious to the biological exigencies of death. This circularity or self-referentiality of language that operates almost independently of the author is very similar to Queneau's *Petite cosmogonie portative,* where, like a machine that is stuck, the same line is repeated over and over again: "compter parler soigner" (counting speaking dreaming). The final conclusion one could come to as to the meaning (message) of this cosmicomic is that death is meaningless because it does not exist as such; there is no end, but a constant rearrangement—Qfwfq refers to it as "birth-death"[11]—on the cosmic and the biological levels, including the existential one.

When Calvino was asked in an interview why he seemed to show more interest in the cell than in mankind, mathematical calculation than sentiment, mental impulses rather than ideas, the author replied: "Because my cosmicomic stories might easily be reproached for exactly the opposite; that is, for making cells talk as if they were people, for inventing human figures and language in the primeval void, and, in short, of [sic] playing the old game of anthropomorphism."[12]

"t zero"

In the last part of *t zero*, Qfwfq is no longer present and the human narrator is not identified—except for Q in the first story and Dantès in the last.[13] Moreover, all four stories no longer deal with either biological or cosmological phenomena, but rather they reflect both Queneau's and Borges's playful geometric and mathematical dialectics: an infinite search for reality; an overriding concern for the nature of literature and the process of creating it; a deep interest in language (communication) as a way to verbalize, systematize, and de-form the real world; the creation of an ambience of abstract unreality based on concrete reality. Indeed, Calvino tells us that in the concluding stories of *t zero* he has attempted to "make narrative out of a mere process of deductive reasoning," and that he has departed from the anthropomorphism that characterized most of his other cosmicomic stories, since "these human presences defined only by a system of relationships, by a function, are the very ones that populate the world around us in our everyday lives, good or bad as this situation might appear to us."[14]

In the title story Calvino portrays a hunter as he tries to determine, according to the laws of physics, whether the arrow he has shot in the direction of a leaping lion is going to hit the target and save his life. The coincidence of the arrow's trajectory with that of the suspended lion, or better the absolute moment of truth and the beginning of time, is denoted by the formula t (time) sub zero (t_0). The hunter Q, explains that each second is a universe for him: "The second I live is the second I live in, la seconde que je vis c'est la seconde où je demeure, I must get used to conceiving my speech simultaneously in all possible languages if I want to live my universe-instant extensively" (108).[15] The image he is trying to evoke with speaking simultaneously in different languages is akin to playing the same musical motif on a multikeyboard electronic synthesizer, or having the melody played by a full symphony orchestra. Eventually, the narrative becomes so complex and abstract that the reader becomes lost in Calvino's virtuoso performance:

Through the combination of all contemporaneous data I could achieve an objective knowledge of the universe-instant t_0 in all its spatial extension, me included, since inside $t_0 I$, Q_0, am not in the least determined by my past Q_{-1} Q_{-2} Q_{-3} et cetera but by the system composed of all the toucans T_0, bullets B_0, viruses V_0, without which the fact that I am Q_0 could not be established. (108)

Clearly Calvino is not interested in explaining the anguish of the hunter, frozen in that moment of fear and not knowing if the arrow is going to save his life. He is more interested in the game of speculation, in patterns, formulas, and in the theoretical sequences of the event. In fact, replying to a question posed to him on the occasion of Tzvetan Todorov's publication of *Introduction à la littérature fantastique (The Fantastic: A Structural Approach to a Literary Genre)*, Calvino commented:

For me the main thing in a narrative is not the explanation of an extraordinary event, but the order of things that this extraordinary event produces in itself and around it; the pattern, the symmetry, the network of images deposited around it, as in the formation of a crystal.[16]

"t zero" evokes Zeno of Elea, the inventor of dialectics, who taught by paradoxes. The assumption of the Eleatic school was that the universe is static, that there is no motion or change, and that we need to distinguish appearance from reality. Zeno's paradoxes postulate the infinite divisibility of space and time, raising problems about the nature of space, time, and motion. One paradox postulates that it is impossible to cross an infinite number of points within finite time because in order to go from point A to point B we would have to pass all the intermediate points; since the distance from A to B can be divided into an infinite number of intermediate points, it is impossible to travel an infinite number of spaces within the limited time, and arrive at point B. It is in this infinite number of intermediate spatial and temporal points that Calvino's hunter becomes entwined, unable to bring to a resolution the dilemma of life and death: Is he going to be killed, or is the lion? Frozen in "each second" that is in itself "a universe," he is compelled to suspend the narrative with a series of ellipses.

In "The Count of Montecristo," the concluding story and perhaps the best of the *t zero* collection, Calvino once again displays Borgesian influences, in particular those revolving around the labyrinth. The narrative is based on the Alexandre Dumas novel *The Count of Monte Cristo*. In this work Edmond Dantès has been condemned to life imprisonment in the Château d'If, a prison on an island in the harbor of Marseilles. There he befriends another prisoner, the Abbé Faria, an Italian priest whom the authorities consider insane because he tries to bribe his way out of prison by promising them a fortune in a buried treasure. Faria becomes Dantès's mentor and convinces him that the secret treasure really exists on the Island of Monte Cristo. The abbé promises that if the two escape together, they will share the fortune. However, when the abbé dies, Dantès places the body in his own bed, and then slips into the sack in which the cadaver had been laid out for burial at sea. When the sack is thrown into the water, Dantès swims to freedom. Eventually he makes his way to the Island of Monte Cristo, where he unearths the treasure which makes him a rich and powerful man. He becomes the Count of Monte Cristo, and, finally, all who had persecuted him suffer his revenge.

In Calvino's story the abbé Faria is trying to escape by tunneling through the walls of the fortress, in order to retrieve the treasure on Monte Cristo and use it to liberate Napoleon, held prisoner on the island of Elba. But something always goes wrong: his excavations lead him inexorably deeper into the interior of the fortress. Unlike the abbé, whose plans are based on the conviction that escape is possible, Dantès hypothesizes that the topography of the fortress is such that escape is impossible. And whereas the abbé's explorations are all physical and centripetal, those of Dantès are mental, hypothetical, and centrifugal. The latter listens carefully to the sounds made by his jailers' movements, which allow him to fix them in a succession of points in time, but not in space. But working with hypotheses he can construct a detailed picture of the fortress. Faria nonetheless is a necessary complement for Dantès's own escape plans, not because he is going to show him a way out, but because his failures provide Dantès with the only information about the prison. But the abbé loses his sense of orientation and his itineraries take him constantly through Dantès' cell: "He walks across the ceiling and the walls like a fly, he sinks his pick into a certain spot, a hole appears; he disappears" in the "labyrinth of the fortress" which has "no favored points: it repeats in space and time always the same combination of figures" (141–42). Dantès, too, loses his ability to distinguish between sound and fantasy, to the extent that in his hypotheses of escape he tries to imagine Faria as the protagonist who allows him mentally to envision his own escape, "dreaming it in the first person." But now he can no longer distinguish between the sounds made by the real Faria and those made by the hypothetical one; in any case, "it is the fortress that wins" (143).

According to Dantès, Faria's escape plans are doomed because they rely on planning and carrying out the perfect escape. He, however, has an opposite premise:

> There exists a perfect fortress, from which one cannot escape; escape is possible only if in the planning or building of the fortress some error or oversight was made. While Faria continues taking the fortress apart, sounding out its weak points, I continue putting it back together, conjecturing more and more insuperable barriers. (144)

With time, the two images of the prison become ever more different, and the fortress, envisioned via the abbé's explorations, seems to grow with the speed of time, to the extent that one would have to move faster and retrace time in order to escape to the outside. In fact, Dantès' mental explorations and calculations bring him to the realization that the outside represents his past, from which he cannot escape, and the future represents the "innermost point of the island of If, in other words the avenue of escape is an avenue toward the inside" (146). Eventually, the speculations for escape inside-outside, past-future, become reversible and lead to relations between an island one cannot leave (If) to an island one cannot enter (Monte Cristo), and finally, because of Napoleon's role in the story, to the extended relation If–Monte Cristo–Elba–Saint Helena.

These insular "intersections" of "various hypothetical lines" permit Dantès to have Faria go through a wall, enter Alexandre Dumas's study, and read the discarded pages of the novel he is writing, thus discovering the life he, Dantès, might have had. Dumas is seen as a manipulator of hypotheses since his two assistants furnish him with the outline of "all the possible variants of an enormous supernovel" from which he "selects, rejects, cuts, pastes, interposes" (149). Faria's and Dantès's escape diagrams resemble those made by Dumas on his papers to establish "the order of the chosen variants" (149) for his novel. In one version Dantès escapes to Monte Cristo and finds the treasure. But Faria cannot find the "page without which all the possible continuations of the novel outside the fortress become impossible" (150). Indeed, his true confinement is in the "concentric fortress, If–Monte Cristo–Dumas' desk" (150).

Since Edmond Dantès's hypotheses are reversible, one can easily make a comparison between Calvino's tale and Franz Kafka's "The Castle," where, however, unlike "The Count of Monte Cristo," the protagonist meets with obstacles that prevent him from entering a structure, not from escaping it. In theory there are many ways out of the Château d'If, as there are many roads that lead to Kafka's castle. In practice, however, no way leads in or out. In either situation one can see signs of desire, privation, and quest that lead to endless reflection.[17] Since Dantès conceives his prison as a place that is valid "even if instead of 'outside' I say 'inside' and vice versa" (146), then the effort to enter or escape becomes a frustrated attempt to transcend his dilemma and frustrations, and achieve a rational perspective which would let him penetrate the secrets of the fortress and explain the meaning of his existence. This, however, cannot be done in actuality but only in the sphere of the hypothetical.

On an artistic level, an author's planning of a book, its plot and structure, are like a prison with all its hidden passageways, tunnels, and corridors into which the author and his characters must venture. As the narrator in "The Count of Monte Cristo" informs us, "to plan a book—or an escape—the first thing to know is what to exclude" (151). Just as Alexandre Dumas discards possible solutions for his novel, so does Dantès eliminate all the unsuccessful routes taken by Faria. In both cases, observes Calvino, the labyrinthine narratives evoke "the image of a world in which it is easy to lose oneself, to get disoriented—a world in which the effort of regaining one's orientation acquires a particular value, almost that of a training for survival." He concludes by quoting from an essay by German poet and critic Hans Magnus Enzensberger on labyrinths: "Every orientation presupposes a disorientation" and only someone who has suffered bewilderment can free himself.[18]

In order to understand this puzzling tale of "disorientation," as well as other cosmicomics such as "t zero" and "The Chase"—all so typical of Borges's *ficciones*—one should bear in mind that for Calvino literature was an enthralling game, as it was for Queneau and the members of Oulipo. Moreover, Calvino frequently reminds the readers of "The Count of Monte Cristo"—albeit indirectly—that they are being led into a world of fiction, extremely removed from reality. We notice this in particular at the very beginning of the story, when Faria, in a surrealistic scene comparable to a Chagall or Bosch painting, walks upside down in Dantès's cell and across the ceiling and the walls. One could say that the two antithetical characters constitute Calvino's total self: the daring and impulsive Faria creates the plot of the story, while Dantès, the logical geometrical thinker, analyzes all its ramifications and points out its weaknesses.

The labyrinth, inherent in the infinite and invisible passages running through the fortress, emerges not only as the story's major setting but also as its aesthetic form and its theme. The prisoners' journeys—one physical and the other intellectual—to the center of Château d'If represent metaphorically Calvino's state of mind, as well as his meandering creative process while developing his narrative, very much as Dumas had done with his novel. The story's resolution, however, is left to the readers, who, in their imagination, have to consider that Faria comes close to achieving the perfect escape while Dantès imagines the perfect prison from which there is no escape. They must understand that Edmond Dantès's and the Abbé Faria's plans and maps for escape represent, in a Borgesian reading, the clash between reality and a diagram of reality, the way the mirror faithfully duplicates appearances in Borges's "The Library of Babel." Indeed, the readers must participate in the combinatorial mathematical game and find a solution independently of the author's intentions. In 1967, with reference to Enzensberger's essay "Topological Structures in Modern Literature," Calvino commented concerning combinatorial mathematical games:

> The game can work as a challenge to understand the world or as a dissuasion from understanding it. Literature can work in a critical vein or to confirm things as they are and as we know them to be. The boundary is not always clearly marked, and I would say that on this score the spirit in which one reads is decisive: it is up to the reader to see to it that literature exerts its critical force, and this can occur independently of the author's intentions.
>
> I think this is the meaning one might give to my most recent story, which comes at the end of my book *Ti con zero.*[19]

Edmond Dantès, like the protagonist in Borges's "The House of Asterion," lives in a labyrinth constituted by his prison, but in the end, we hope, he will succeed in creating for himself a more comprehensible labyrinth. This may explain why Calvino concludes his essay "Cybernetics and Ghosts" by writing: "And this is the most optimistic finale that I have managed to give to my story, to my book."[20] Indeed, as we have already seen in chapter 5, Calvino proposes that since one cannot defeat the labyrinth—that is, it is impossible to find a way out of life's dilemma—the best way out is to pass from one labyrinth to another. This, he asserts, is particularly true for the writer.

According to semiotics, since no text can be completely free of other texts, it follows that all texts are involved in the intertextuality of all writing given that any text makes reference not only to itself but also to other texts. Thus, as has been pointed out by Terence Hawkes, "Books finally appear to portray or reflect, not the real physical world but a world reduced to other dimensions; to the shape and structures of the activity of writing; the world as a text."[21] While the intertextuality of virtually all the other cosmicomic tales involves scientific texts, in the case of "The Count of Monte Cristo" it concerns a Dumas literary text. Additionally, the novel is deconstructed by

Calvino, who disrupts the traditional notions of author and his work and undermines the conventional practices of reading a story, so that meaning is never clear. In short, Calvino takes Dumas's text, changes it, eliminates the author's prerogatives, and finally promotes the role of the reader over that of the author. This literary game is best summed up by Claudio Milanini, who sees "The Count of Monte Cristo" as a "Borgesian *pastiche* in whose heart there takes shape a spiral of both the positive print and negative print of a hyper-novel; a spiral of conjectures and potentialities that are able to combine or cancel each other out, within a vertiginous game of variants and combinations of variants."[22]

The Memory of The World

When Calvino published *La memoria del mondo e altre storie cosmicomiche* (The Memory of the World and More Cosmicomic Stories) in 1968, he fell back on his trick of recycling old material in new packaging. Indeed, out of the twenty stories, only eight are new. The collection is arranged thematically into five parts—"stories about" the moon; the earth; the sun, stars, and galaxies; evolution; and time and space. Qfwfq continues to be present in the first three parts, but is totally absent from the last. His disappearance suggests that Calvino's cosmicomic phase was over. As in the case of "The Count of Monte Cristo," cosmogony, cosmology, and biology are supplanted by deductive reasoning, logic, mathematical speculation, and narrative discourse. Indeed, in the last part of *La memoria del mondo* the dominant feature is no longer playfulness in the ludic sense, but rather in acrobatics of the intellect and imagination, as well as toying with language and the nature of writing. Qfwfq's optimistic 'pataphysic eye gives way to pessimism, cynicism, and despair.

In her interesting article "Calvino's *La memoria del mondo:* The Forgotten Record of Lost Worlds," Kathryn Hume points out the differences between the three cosmicomic collections. *Cosmicomics* is seen as being cheerful and mythographic; *t zero* is bleaker and "focussed on paradox, on the mind caught in a web of words." *La memoria del mondo,* which includes more stories set in contemporary life with all its evils, contradictions, and disorder, indicates that Calvino "had evidently relinquished hope for social renewal" and that "his artistic engagement with social problems does not lead to answers." Thus, according to Hume, the last collection moves even further away from emotions and more toward intellectual responses. The stories are "more specifically concerned with how contemporary humanity can relate to a cosmos that includes not just reality scientifically defined, but society as well."[23]

In the title story, "La memoria del mondo," a nameless director of the largest data base center for documentation ever conceived is about to resign. He discusses with his designated successor, Müller, the function of the institute's data gathering and history writing:

> a file that will include and arrange all that is known about any subject, any individual, any animal, as a prelude of a general inventory of not only the present but also of the past, of everything that has existed since the origins, in short a general history of everything all at once, or better a catalog of everything moment by moment.[24]

The reason for this monumental task is that the institute is resolved to leave a record of the terrestrial world because it is foreseen that life on Earth is coming to an end sooner than expected. Given that in millions of unknown planets there must be beings similar to us, the important thing is to communicate to them our "memory" of the world. And by burying this legacy in a sort of capsule, it is hoped that eventually some extragalactic archaeologists will discover it. The new director's task will be to make sure that this work is done properly and to selectively exclude misleading information from the data bank, since by "withholding certain information one provides more details than one would otherwise do by revealing everything. . . . Our organization controls only the negative side of things, a frame around the void of insignificance" (170). The director then justifies why certain data should be falsified, explaining that a lie can be far more revealing to a psychoanalyst than the truth.[25] In fact, he has done precisely so concerning his missing wife, Angela, in order to record their love as if it had been perfect and unmarred by her infidelities. To do so he has falsified many entries and he has killed her, so that the image of the "living Angela" would not superimpose itself on the computerized image of "Angela-information." Moreover, the director has also eliminated all but one of his wife's possible lovers, of whom no trace will be left in the computer's memory; now he is about to eliminate his last remaining rival. After explaining that we change reality in order to make it look better in our history books, he pulls out a gun, aims it at Müller, and kills him.

It is interesting to note that here for the first time—and to the best of my knowledge, the only time—Calvino makes reference to psychoanalysis in presenting the utilitarian aspects of mendacity. Obviously there is a semiotic connection between truth and lies, between actual history and revisionist history. I think that Calvino, like Derrida, cautions us to reject the notion of the primacy of the signified (meaning over word) and to subvert the logocentric theory of the sign (language). In modern society, unfortunately, rather than presenting the truth, we employ the sign whose meaning can be perverted. Thus we are surrounded by a multitude of subverting signs, icons, that distort completely the truth and ultimately condition our self-image as well as every conceivable aspect of our life: TV advertisements selling deodorants that lead us to believe that our bodies are constantly emitting malodorous exhalations; an automobile sales pitch that promises romance if we buy the machine; political pronouncements that do not resemble even remotely the real situation; and even the revisionist historians who now claim that the Holocaust never took place.

Derrida has constructed a concept which he calls *différance* and which expresses two distinct ideas: to "differ," to be different in quality or structure, and to "defer," to postpone. In French the verb *différer* has both meanings, which are only recognizable in written form *(-ance* and *-ence)* and not in oral form. Therefore, language is an endless combinatorial play of signifiers (word over meaning) where the meaning is constantly deferred because one signifier refers to another signifier which refers yet to another, etc., etc. "Thus, as Saussure pointed out, language is a system of differences rather than a collection of independently meaningful units. . . . As soon as there is meaning, there is difference."[26] Calvino, however, disqualifies writing in the traditional sense as well as in the cybernetic sense. The premeditated *différance* practiced by the director in "La memoria del mondo" reflects the ominous presence of secret CIA and FBI computerized files—in Italy the Secret Intelligence Services—which have been compiled on unsuspecting citizens whose careers may be destroyed on the basis of false and unverified information over which they have absolutely no control. Worst of all, such data banks—another Calvino labyrinthian image—deprive the individual of privacy and anticipate the verification of George Orwell's novel *1984:* a society where there is no place for truth, because historical records are destroyed and propaganda replaces factual information; a society where there is no privacy, because "Big Brother is watching you."

Finally, "La memoria del mondo," written with a Borgesian haunting power,[27] is unique in its distinction from all the other cosmicomic tales. It is closer to a bizarre Rod Serling *Twilight Zone* TV story of the fantastic and the imagination, or, even better, to a thriller by Alfred Hitchcock, the master of suspense and unforeseen dramatic twists. Like these film directors, Calvino creates in the readers a state of intense anxiety and uncertainty as we confront out own potentialities for horror and violence.

NOTES

1. Giacomo Leopardi, "Nocturne of a Wandering Shepherd in Asia," *The Penguin Book of Italian Verse*, ed. George Kay (Baltimore: Penguin, 1958) 279.

2. "Lightness," *Six Memos for the Next Millennium* (Cambridge: Harvard University Press, 1988) 24.

3. *Six Memos* 60.

4. Anna Maria Ortese and Italo Calvino, "Filo diretto Calvino-Ortese: Occhi al cielo," *Corriere della sera* 24 Dec. 1967: 11. Ortese is best known for her *Il mare non bagna Napoli (The Bay is not Naples*, 1953).

5. Although the term *ficciones* (fictions) is widely used today, it is difficult to define with precision. What Borges meant was a short untraditional narrative that is a blending of reality and fiction rather than strict fiction and that typically presents problems of interpretative levels. It is of some significance that Borges titled part of his original *Ficciones* "artificios" (artifices).

6. *t zero* (New York: Harcourt, Brace, 1969) 4. Page numbers referring to this edition are shown in parentheses.

7. Stephen W. Hawking, *A Brief History of Time*, 8.

8. George R. McMurray, *Jorge Luis Borges* (New York: Frederick Ungar, 1980) 31.

9. "Cybernetics and Ghosts," *The Uses of Literature* (New York: Harcourt Brace, 1986) 13.

10. McMurray 222.

11. In "Mitosis," Qfwfq muses about the consequences of his own mitosis: "I understood that this picking up and moving out of oneself which is birth-death would make the circuit, would be transformed from strangling and fracture into interpenetration and mingling of asymmetrical cells that add the messages repeated through trillions of trillions of mortal loves" (73).

12. "Two Interviews on Science and Literature," *Uses of Literature*, 33.

13. Very likely, Q is derivative of Qfwfq.

14. "Two Interviews" 34.

15. In the original, Calvino does not intermingle Italian and French, but rather Italian and English: "Ogni secondo è un universo, il secondo che io vivo è il secondo in cui io abito, the second I live is the second I live in, bisogna che mi abitui a pensare" (*Ti con zero* [Milan: Garzanti, 1988] 109–10).

16. "Definition of Territories: Fantasy," *Uses of Literature* 73. Originally in *Le Monde* 15 Aug. 1970.

17. Calvino uses these terms with reference to Kafka's short story "Der Kübelreiter" ["The Knight of the Bucket"] ("Lightness" 28).

18. "Cybernetics and Ghosts" 25.

19. "Cybernetics" 26.

20. "Cybernetics" 26.

21. Terence Hawkes, *Structuralism and Semiotics* (Berkeley: University of California Press, 1977) 144.

22. Claudio Milanini, *L'utopia discontinua* (Milan: Garzanti, 1990) 100.

23. Kathryn Hume, "Calvino's *La memoria del mondo:* The Forgotten Record of Lost Worlds," *Calvino Revisited*, ed. Franco Ricci (Toronto: Dovehouse, 1989) 97, 98.

24. *La memoria del mondo e altre storie cosmicomiche* (Turin: Einaudi, 1968) 167. Page numbers referring to this edition are shown in parentheses.

25. This recalls Dante's famous lines: "Sempre a quel ver ch'ha faccia di menzogna/de'l'uom chiuder le labbra fin ch'el pote,/però che sanza colpa fa vergogna/ma qui tacer nol posso" [A man should always close his lips, as far as he can, to the truth that has the face of a lie, since without fault it brings him shame, but here I cannot be silent] (*Inferno* 16. 124–27, trans. John D. Sinclair).

26. That is to say, *différance* between "signifier" and "signified." See Barbara Johnson, translator's introduction, Jacques Derrida, *Dissemination* (Chicago: University of Chicago Press, 1981) ix.

27. As in Calvino's story, in Borges's *ficción* "The Garden of Forking Paths," the readers also assist when a crime is committed whose purpose does not become clear until the last moment.

CHAPTER EIGHT

The Combinatorial Play of Narrative Possibilities: *The Castle of Crossed Destinies* and *Invisible Cities*

Once we have dismantled and reassembled the process of literary composition, the decisive moment of literary life will be that of reading.[1]

In "Cybernetics and Ghosts," a lecture delivered in several Italian cities in 1967—the publication year of *t zero*—Calvino analyzes the impact of structuralism and semiotics, as well as the problems facing writers of modern fiction. What is the role of the reader, and how important is the author when text is considered? How should narrative be analyzed and how is it constructed? To what extent does the text offer combinations of interpretative possibilities? At the core of these questions and observations was the structuralist/semiotic notion that the relation between words (signifiers) and things/ideas in mind when words are used (signifieds) is vague and circumstantial. This uncertainty creates a "play" of language that readers are compelled to confront. Consequently, meaning, which is neither constant nor precise, is to be found not in words but between words; not in things but between things. Meaning therefore results from differential relations, from signifying relations. Signs, things, and ideas are meaningful only in relation to each other because in language there is only difference.

Calvino sympathized with those who in the literary magazine *Tel Quel* were expressing the need for radical changes, for whom the act of writing was "no longer in narrating but in saying that one is narrating, and what one says becomes identified with the very act of saying."[2] He was clearly echoing Roland Barthes's ideas pertaining to the new role of writing. Calvino felt that literature is a self-contained system of codes; that it calls the attention of the reader to these codes and discloses how they work. According to Barthes, for some writers the act of writing is transitive because it leads to other things. But there is also another kind of author—such as Borges and Calvino, among others—for whom the act is intransitive. According to Hawkes, such a writer's central concern

> is not to take us "through" his writing to a world beyond it, but to produce Writing. He is an author: what Barthes terms *écrivain*. Unlike the writer (*scripteur*,

écrivant), who writes for an ulterior purpose in a *transitive* mode, and who intends us to move from his writing to the world beyond it.[3]

The *écrivain*'s only concern, according to Barthes, is "nothing but writing itself, not as the pure 'form' conceived by an aesthetic of art for art's sake, but much more radically, as the only area for the one who writes."[4] As Hawkes points out, Barthes is distinguishing between *writer* and *author.* The former "writes *something*" and the latter "just *writes,*" not to take us "*beyond*" his writing, but to draw our attention *to* the activity itself."[5] In other words, according to Barthes, modern authors offer their writing as an end in itself, just as some modern painters or musicians want us to appreciate their artistic expressions without expecting us to go beyond the moment's pleasure.

These Barthesian structuralist notions led Calvino to envision a computer that would be able to create the perfect literary text:

> The true literature machine will be one that itself feels the need to produce disorder, as a reaction against its preceding production of order: a machine that will produce avant-garde work to free its circuits when they are choked by too long a production of classicism. In fact, given [the] developments in cybernetics . . . nothing prevents us from foreseeing a literature machine that at a certain point feels unsatisfied with its own traditionalism and starts to propose new ways of writing, turning its own codes completely upside down.[6]

The consequence of such a machine capable of dismantling and reassembling the process of literary composition would be the displacement or elimination of the author, and the emphasis placed upon "the text-reader axis over the author-text and author-reader relationship."[7] Given this repudiation of the author, Calvino concludes,

> the decisive moment of literary life will be that of reading. In this sense though entrusted to machines, literature will continue to be a "place" of privilege within the human consciousness, a way of exercising the potentialities contained in the system of signs belonging to all societies at all times. The work will continue to be born, to be judged, to be destroyed or constantly renewed on contact with the eye of the reader. What will vanish is the figure of the author . . . that anachronistic personage, the bearer of messages, the director of consciences.[8]

Here Calvino is pointing to Barthes's distinction between a readerly (*lisible*) text and a writerly (*scriptible*) text. In the first, the transition between signifier and signified is obvious and predetermined. In the second, however, readers must participate and be aware of the interrelationship writing/

reading; furthermore, they must also be aware of the nature of language itself and the interplay of signs. That is to say, one has to learn how to dismantle and put back together what Calvino considers "the most complex and unpredictable" of all machines: "language."[9] "The writerly texts," comments Hawkes, "presume nothing, admit no easy passage from signifier to signified, are open to the 'play' of the codes that we use to determine them."[10] Barthes, in his *Le plaisir du texte,* referred to the readerly text as one of "pleasure" and the writerly text as one of "bliss" (*juissant*). Unlike the former, which is "linked to a *comfortable* practice of reading," the latter "imposes a state of loss and discomfort"; it "unsettles" many of the reader's historical, cultural, psychological assumptions, "the consistency of his tastes, values, memories," bringing to a "crisis his relation with language."[11]

It is on the basis of the writerly text that Calvino sees the modern author as being similar to a machine that can easily be replaced and which can also replace him—a deconstructionist tendency, recently referred to as "the Age of Death of the Author."[12] What does not change, however, is how the reader perceives the text. Thus, he predicts that the author shall vanish to "give place to a more thoughtful person [reader], a person who will know that the author is a machine, and will know how this machine works."[13] In fact, virtually all of Calvino's post–mid-60s writings, especially *The Castle of Crossed Destinies* (1969), *Invisible Cities* (1972), and *If on a winter's night a traveler* (1979), reflect the centrality of the text vis-à-vis the author and, above all, the primacy of the reader. They also reflect Barthes's view that texts can be devised not only as the result of linguistic combinatorial games, but also that the notion of author must yield to that of "scriptor," the mediator through whom language deploys its textual virtualities.[14]

As we shall see in this and the following chapters, Calvino, very much influenced by the Zeitgeist of narratological games, demonstrates in these three works how the "endless variety" of forms can be reduced "to the combination of certain finite quantities" and that "the struggle" of literature is to evade the confines of language. Just as in *Cosmicomics* and *t zero* Calvino had made use of the concept of defamiliarization by stripping Qfwfq of any egocentrism, so now the writer is diminished and loses his central narrative role, a role which had always been a privileged domain. It is now the interactive reader's function to make sure that "literature exerts its critical force, and this can occur independently of the author's intentions."[15] Calvino recognizes the reader's creative participation in what he reads as well as his explicatory role. One could say that, like Borges, he arrives at the conclusion—

especially in *If on a winter's night a traveler*—that the reader more than the writer is the real author of books; the author is replaceable, the reader is not. Calvino is convinced that a narrative text is rewritten every time it is read and that "one literature differs from another, past or future, less because of the text than for the way it is read."[16]

Calvino had previously explored the combinatorial play of narrative possibilities in *The Nonexistent Knight* and in his cosmicomic tales, where he played with the text's self-referentiality as well as with the artifices of writing that cause the text to comment on itself and eventually become its own subject. Indeed, his 1967 lecture shows that he seemed determined to proceed in this particular direction with his writings; and that under the influence of his French fellow writers (including Oulipo) and, in particular, semioticians, he endeavored to show that narrative could be reduced to a combination of a certain number of "logico-linguistic (or better, syntactical-rhetorical) operations, in such a way as to be reducible to formulas."[17]

Of course, the magisterial Borges continued to impress Calvino's combinatorial propensities, as he himself was to state several years later:

> The last great invention of a new literary genre in our time was achieved by a master of the short form, Jorge Luis Borges. It was the invention of himself as narrator. . . . The idea that came to Borges was to pretend that the book he wanted to write had already been written by someone else, some unknown hypothetical author—an author in a different language, of a different culture—and that his task was to describe and review this invented book. . . . In the same way, critics of Borges feel bound to observe that each of his texts doubles or multiplies its own space through the medium of other books belonging to a real or imaginary library, whether they be classical, erudite, or merely invented.[18]

As already mentioned, Calvino was fascinated with the image of the labyrinth, the challenges it poses and the various means of escaping from it. He saw it as representative of the multiple aspects of literature. In fact, he cites Hans Magnus Enzensberger to support his position:

> The labyrinth is made so that whoever enters it will stray and get lost. But the labyrinth also poses the visitor a challenge: that he reconstruct the plan of it and dissolve its power. If he succeeds, he will have destroyed the labyrinth; for one who passes through it, no labyrinth exists.[19]

The labyrinth represents Calvino's fictional world, namely the chaotic and bewildering conditions imposed on modern society by industry and technology. To Borges it represents "being baffled," "terror and anguish in the mysterious universe that makes no sense," and the "epistemological and ontological" difficulties man faces trying to make sense out of a world he no longer understands.[20] At the same time, it serves as a healing force against the "simplistic views" of traditional writers who still use outmoded, anachronistic instruments. Nonetheless, unlike Borges, Calvino suggests that reading may be the key for escaping the labyrinth. Consequently, he challenges literature to find a way out of the labyrinth, and to explore the relationship between signs and the purported realities they try to represent. Thus, wittingly or unwittingly, Calvino joins, slowly but resolutely, the difficult-to-define *coterie* of postmodern writers whose common set of concerns is the production of "open, discontinuous, improvisational, indeterminate, or aleatory structures."[21] In short, as for the kindred poststructuralists, the postmodern experience stems from a deep sense of ontological uncertainty. In Calvino's case, the absence of a center in terms of narrative structure, theme, and language becomes ever more manifest in his post-70s writings, where he creates a playful convergence between fiction and the latest critical theories emanating from Paris and New Haven.

The Castle and the Tavern

The poststructuralist Calvino, who, like Derrida, felt that no text is stable and that "all texts are haunted by self-referential aporia and intertextual openness,"[22] compels us to deal with him on his own inexorable terms as we deal with no other prominent contemporary Italian writer except, perhaps, Umberto Eco. Starting with *Cosmicomics,* each new Calvino work creates unusual and different challenges for the reader, none more so than *The Castle of Crossed Destinies,* narrated by means of the ingenious use of tarot cards. "This book," writes Calvino in an accompanying note, "is made first of pictures—the tarot playing cards—and secondly of written words. Through the sequence of the pictures, stories are told, which the written word tries to reconstruct and interpret."[23]

It is axiomatic that the games and sports of a nation often reflect a particular way of perceiving life. After all, "life is a game that each one of us has play," observed Juan Luis Vives, the Spanish Renaissance humanist and philosopher; "children play, the young and old alike play: talent, dignity, old age, prudence, are nothing but games. And, finally, what is mortal life if you take away virtue, but rotten game or useless tale?"[24] And as Louis C. Pérez writes, "All games mean something, and like art they cannot be separated from their cultural climate." It is quite possible, therefore, that Calvino's preference for the game of cards resulted from the fact that "it reflects more accurately than chess, the political changes, philosophical, psychological, historical and cultural of the new age."[25]

Individual tarot cards look different, and like words signify differently in different contexts. They have no real existence until they are played and read, and their meaning is only gleaned by the reader's ability to apply codes that have conditioned him. According to Wolfgang Iser, all texts contain blanks, and the reader must fill them.[26] That is to say, the act of interpretation requires that the reader act upon the text (cards) in order to produce meaning. Umberto Eco, in his essay "The Role of the Reader," argues that some texts are open and others are closed.[27] The open text, such as Joyce's *Finnegans Wake*, invites the reader's collaboration in the production of meaning; the closed text—comics, detective stories—predetermines the reader's responses. In writing *The Castle of Crossed Destinies* Calvino sets out both to present the reader with an open text containing all the baffling and challenging elements found in Joyce's novel, and to allow a variety of possible readings; in Iser's terms, he seeks to provide "the chance to formulate the unformulated."[28]

The Castle of Crossed Destinies includes two novellas, *The Castle of Crossed Destinies* and *The Tavern of Crossed Destinies*. The first makes use of tarots painted by Bonifacio Bembo around the middle of the fifteenth century for the Dukes of Milan. The second is based on a popular reproduction of the eighteenth-century *Ancien Tarot de Marseille*, printed in 1761 and still readily available in France today. Both tarot decks consist of seventy-eight cards, but are very different in appearance and in name.

The inspiration to use tarot cards as "a narrative combinatorial machine" first came to Calvino in 1968 while listening to a lecture given by Paolo Fabbri. After consulting other writings on the narrative function of fortune-telling cards, he came to the conclusion that the meaning of each card depends on the position that it holds in the sequence of cards that precede or follow it. From this starting idea, Calvino set out to write *The Tavern* using the popular *L'Ancien Tarot* cards of Marseilles. Like the structuralists, by using interconnected signs (cards), Calvino creates a system of relationships that allows him to tell his stories; but no single element has meaning except as part of a structural connection consisting of the other tarot cards. He tried to arrange the cards so that they would create successive scenes of a pictorial narrative. Whenever the randomly placed cards presented a story that made sense, he would write it down. In this way he composed a great part of *The Tavern*. Still, dissatisfied with the results the cards were giving him, he kept changing the rules, the structure, and narrative solution in an attempt to achieve a sequence that "contained and determined the plurality of the stories."[29]

Just when Calvino was about to give up the project, the publisher Franco Maria Ricci asked him to prepare a text for a projected volume containing reproductions of the fifteenth-century cards painted by Bonifacio Bembo and now housed in the Pierpont Morgan Library in New York and the Accademia Carrara in Bergamo.[30] At first Calvino thought of making use of the material already written for the Marseilles cards, but he quickly came to the realization that certain *Arcana* cards were not the same and that the world depicted in Bembo's highly refined miniatures was very different from that of the other, less elegant deck. He knew instinctively that the Bembo cards "could well represent the visual world in which Ariosto's fantasy had been formed."[31] And so he began to compose certain sequences inspired by Ariosto's epic poem *Orlando Furioso*, one of the greatest works of the Italian Renaissance, creating a kind of crossword puzzle made of designs instead of words, in which each sequence could be read in both senses: textually and iconographically. In one week the text for *The Castle* was ready for publication. The volume, *Tarocchi, Il mazzo visconteo di Bergamo e New York*, came out in 1969, in an exclusive edition; each right-hand page displays a full-size color reproduction of an individual card, while on the left side, in addition to Calvino's text, there are comments by the art historian Sergio Samek Ludovici.[32]

After receiving considerable praise for this publication, Calvino felt sufficiently encouraged to publish *The Castle* in a lower-priced Einaudi edition without the color plates. But first he was determined to finish *The Tavern*, because the Marseilles cards were extremely suggestive to him. Unable to obtain a "coherent significance" with them, he kept taking apart and putting back together various puzzles, constantly trying out new rules for the game. The resulting pattern became so complicated that he was soon entrapped by the game. He gave up previous patterns, and rewrote the stories determined that the game would have meaning only if he followed strict rules within a framework of construction that would condition "the insertion of one story into the others, otherwise the whole thing would be gratuitous." The work was further complicated by the fact that although some stories were visually successful, they failed to be so when put into writing. Some lacking impetus were eliminated; others, however, immediately acquired the "cohesive strength of the written word which, once written, cannot be changed." Problems of "stylistic orchestration" kept coming up since each novella was set in a different period and presented in distinct art forms—Bembo's elegant Renaissance miniatures vis-à-vis the rough carvings of the Marseilles tarots—which required different modes of expression. After a long period of time during which he felt "trapped in this labyrinthine maniacal obsession" and was tempted to give up the entire project, he often would suddenly get an idea to try displaying the cards in a different way, "more simple and rapid," with guaranteed success. Though not fully satisfied, he published the work in 1973 in order to be free of it and of the obsession that plagued him even when he was correcting the proofs, taking them apart and rewriting them. He knew that only with the publication of the book he would "be outside it once for all."[33]

In addition to *The Castle* and *The Tavern*, Calvino also toyed with the idea of writing a third part entitled "The Motel of Crossed Destinies," narrated by people, who, having survived a horrible catastrophe, find refuge in a half-destroyed motel where only a burnt comics page is left from a newspaper. The survivors, who like those of the other two parts have lost the power of speech because of fright, tell their stories by pointing to the comics without following any precise order, shifting from one strip to another. Calvino never went further than the formulation of the idea; his interests moved on in other directions: "My theoretical and expressive interest for this sort of experiment is gone," he concludes in his *nota*. "It's about time (from every point of view) to move on to something else."[34]

The Castle and *The Tavern* are composed of a series of narratives enclosed within conventional frames similar to those in Chaucer's *Canterbury Tales,* Boccaccio's *Decameron* and Basile's *Pentameron*. In Calvino's work, however, the various narrators are participants in the narrated stories very much like Dante in the *Divine Comedy,* who is both actor and narrator. Additionally, the main narrator is both author and reader insofar as he interprets the cards played by the pilgrims. Each of the many *racconteurs* identifies with and resembles one of the picture cards of the deck with which he initiates his narrative. The action takes place in a solitary castle and in a tavern, both at the edge of a dark forest.[35] The travelers, who are strangers to one another (we don't know where they come from) and have magically lost their power of speech because of some shocking ordeal in crossing the forest, feel tormented by their inability to exchange the many experiences each of them wants to communicate.

After dinner the lord of the castle—and later on the innkeeper—sets a pack of tarot cards on a table. The guests, who are "lords and ladies, royalty and their retinue, humble wayfarers" (3), spread out the cards; but instead of using them for playing games or reading fortunes, they see something else in the "gilded pieces of that mosaic":

> One of the guests drew the scattered cards to himself, leaving a large part of the table clear; but he did not gather them into a pack nor did he shuffle them; he took one card and placed it in front of himself. We all noticed the resemblance between his face and the face on the card, and we thought we understood that, with the card, he wanted to say "I" and that he was preparing to tell his story. (6)

In *The Tavern,* the mute guests around the table are "men and women, dressed well or poorly, frightened, indeed frightful to see, all with white hair, young and old." They all try to "explain something to the others with gestures, grimaces . . . like monkeys (52). When they notice the Marseilles tarots, the narrator writes:

> We all grab for the cards at once, some of the pictures aligned with other pictures recall to me the story that has brought me here, I try to recognize what happened to me and to show it to the others, who meanwhile are also hunting there among the cards, pointing a finger at one card or another, and nothing fits properly with anything, and we snatch the cards away from one another, and we scatter them over the table. (52–53)

The basic need to communicate their stories inspires the narrators to make use of the cards as a system of signs similar to language. But in lieu of a linguistic code, observes De Lauretis, "the tales are told by means of a substitute code or system, namely, the tarot deck."[36] Each figure has a multiple meaning just as all words do, and exact meaning is inferred from the context in which it is uttered or perceived. In this instance it is the pieces of a mosaic of cards and, in particular, the sequence of the cards that create the context and the story of the mysterious travelers.[37] The author explains the method of constructing his stories with the cards this way:

> I began by trying to line up tarots at random, to see if I could read a story in them. "The Waverer's Tale" emerged; I started writing it down; I looked for other combinations of the same cards; I realized the tarots were a machine for constructing stories; I thought of a book and I imagined its frame: the mute narrators, the forest, the inn; I was tempted by the diabolical idea of conjuring up all the stories that could be contained in a tarot deck. (126)[38]

Once again we find an analogy with Borges, namely with his "Pierre Menard, Author of *Don Quixote,*" where the text undergoes infinite changes because each reader gives it a different meaning. Therefore, every time we read a book we have to rewrite it, which is precisely what the Borgesian protagonist does. The same holds true in Calvino's case: each card is read differently by the various narrators, including the author himself.

By printing the cards in the margin of the pages as they are laid down, Calvino allows the reader to follow the pictorial narrative and simultaneously the written narrative that is commenting on it. Clearly both *The Castle* and *The Tavern* are experimental in construction and, as noted by Updike, "the act of narration is double and cunningly merges, in the voiced uncertainties and multiple possibilities of interpretation, with the act of listening, of understanding."[39] In Constance Markey's characterization, the book is "a gigantic card game in which both the readers and the characters participate, puzzling together in bewilderment over the card signs and deciphering life's events as best they can for themselves."[40] Potentially, the full tarot deck represents Derrida's notion that there is nothing outside textuality, that perhaps all the world is a text.

The muteness of the participants allows Calvino to play the games learned so well from Jarry's "science of imaginary solutions" and Queneau's combinatorial potentials of language and text. Additionally, it could also represent, according to Baroni, "a renunciation of ordinary communication in the thick and inextricable forest of other people's signs, as well as a choice for a correlated communication in a unitary design."[41]

In *The Castle* the tarots of each story are arranged in a double file, horizontal or vertical, and are crossed by three further double files of cards (horizontal and vertical) which constitute other tales. This way we can read three stories horizontally and three vertically. Furthermore, each of these sequences can also be read backward, giving us a total of twelve stories. The central part of this scheme offers episodes based on Ariosto's *Orlando Furioso* and other Carolingian themes: tales of love and death, horrors, follies, betrayed monarchs and doomed brides, all intersecting in a perfect geometric pattern.[42] In *The Tavern* we encounter Hamlet, Macbeth, Lear, Faust, Parsifal, Oedipus, Helen of Troy, and even a reference to T. S. Eliot's *The Waste Land.* Marilyn Schneider comments that the volume is "a tapestry of European literature, from Homer to Calvino, that its author has craftily snipped and pieced together again with all the seams dazzlingly displayed."[43] While the scheme of *The Castle* is coherent, logical, and has horizontal and vertical patterns, the cards of *The Tavern* follow no set rules or any special order, and therefore the narrators' tales do not "proceed in a straight line nor according to a regular path."[44] Some cards appear in all the narratives and at times more than once, so that "they form blocks with more irregular outlines, superimposed in the central area of the general pattern, where cards that appear in almost all the tales are concentrated'' (126).

"The Waverer's Tale," the first story Calvino managed to complete and told with thirty-one cards, deals with the same problems found in Borges's "Garden of the Forking Paths": our difficulty in understanding the complex machinery of the world, as well as the "metaphoric image of bifurcating time" and space which have many threads that determine the destiny of the individual caught up in an absurd chain of events destined to recur.[45] Both stories seem to be designed to mock the reader who searches for rationality in the absurd tales and therefore becomes victim to them, just as Calvino became victim to his own different, all-consuming literary undertaking.

Calvino's story deals with a sad young man (indicated by *The Knight of Cups*) who has deserted his wedding feast on the very day of his marriage. Apparently there are two women in his life, and he can't choose between them. Every time he is about to decide, he vacillates between one and the other, "for every choice has an obverse, that is to say a renunciation, and so there is no difference between the act of choosing and the act of renouncing" (56). He sets out on a journey through the forest, allowing his horses (*The Chariot*) to choose the way. But when they reach a crossroads (*Two of Clubs*), they start pulling each in a different direction, immobilizing the vehicle, as happens to many people when they are "free to go everywhere, and everywhere is always the same" (56–57). The young man allows chance to decide for him by tossing a coin which falls on edge in a bush, right in the middle of the roads. Unable to decide which way to go, he climbs a tree, "among the branches which, with their succession of repeated forks, continue to inflict the torment of choice on him" (57). He cannot see where the roads lead because his vision is obstructed by the thick foliage and the burning sun. Then suddenly he notices twin urchins in the tree who point out to him the walls of a city, apparently "suspended on the highest branches like a bird's nest" (58). At this point the guests in the tavern watch carefully as the young man lays down the cards slowly and hesitantly, following him with their own conjectures: "What city is this? Is this the City of All? Is this the city where all parts are joined, all choices balanced, where the void between what we expect of life and what we draw is filled?" (58). After getting lost in the city, the young man encounters the two women "of his eluded choice" who seem to prevent him from leaving.

After many perplexing and surrealistic occurrences, including a great surging tide that engulfs the tree he has climbed and into which he plunges, the young man eventually resumes his own human form lost during his ordeal.

"But is this really he," he wonders, "or is it rather a double whom he saw coming through the forest, the moment he was restored to himself?" (63).[46] When asked who he is, he responds: "I am the man who was to marry the girl you did not choose, who was to take the other road at the crossing, quench his thirst at the other well. By not choosing, you have prevented my choice" (63).

An explanation for the two women's roles may be gleaned from their graphic description. Both are holding unsheathed swords, one of which, we are told, could also be a goose-quill pen, compasses, a flute, or a knife, signifying that "two different ways are open to him who still has to find himself" (59). This is precisely the dilemma of Calvino, who is floundering, does not yet know exactly what he is doing with this questionable narrative tour de force, and who faces the dreaded plight of the author who must decide on form and style, choose one idea over another, one word over others: "the existential anxiety, the energy of the adventure spent in a slaughter of erasures and crumpled paper" (104). Likewise, each time one of the book's characters picks up a card, he too faces the problem of choosing and renouncing, reading, interpreting, and finding both a sequential order and a logical conclusion. In this parody of himself and of reading, writing, and the creative process, Calvino suggests that he may also end up like the young man in the story, hanging from a gallows different from the one where the reader will have hanged himself (63). A. H. Carter points out that in *The Castle* and *The Tavern* famous characters such as Oedipus, Faust, and Hamlet become parodies of the originals and that the first part of the book is a parody of the second. We can also add that the projected third part, "The Motel of Crossed Destinies," would have been a parody of the other two.[47]

When asked by Constance Markey why all the stories in *The Castle* and *The Tavern* have an unhappy ending, why they are pervaded with gloom, and if he meant to convey a negative message, Calvino replied that a happy ending is not always part of a hero's tale, particularly in modern literature; that despite the chivalric theme, the book is really written for modern times and there is no room in it for self-confidence. He also added that if he ever "deliberately set out to include a moral" in his books, "it's surely in this one," and that to find his message one has to look at the chapter entitled "I Also Try to Tell My Tale." Yet when the interviewer pointed out that this tale has no definable message and that the very last lines—"Thus I have set everything to rights. On the page, at least. Inside me, all remains as before"—are ambiguous, uneasy, and disconcerting, Calvino replied: "Well, let's just say that it's the best I can offer in the way of a moral. It serves me. I can't say whether it will be useful to others. Today we live with just such an uneasy moral testament. This is where we are today."[48]

In "I Also Try to Tell My Tale," the "I" of the story's title refers to the unidentified narrator who has been reporting and commenting on his companions' individual stories. Now he tries to tell his own tale, which, unlike the others, consists only of reflections. De Lauretis notes that appearing as the author himself, Calvino is "unmediated by the persona, and metanarratively" he reflects on the nature of writing. "Here language, imagery, and metalinguistic references are all dictated by the particular narrative code (the tarot) that the author imposes, as a strictly constraining grill, on his material."[49] The author/narrator finds it difficult to start his tale because the deck has already been used up by the others. He recognizes that the cards previously laid down to portray Parsifal and Faust and other combinations of events can also be used to describe his own experiences, which consist of "a series of nasty encounters that is perhaps only a series of missed encounters" (99).[50] He selects the *King of Clubs* because he is holding a pointed implement that resembles "a pen or a quill or a well-sharpened pencil or a ballpoint" whose large size signifies the importance of writing. Next he chooses the *Two of Coins*—the coins are joined together by a decorative serpentine letter *S*—because just as writing implements and their products serve for communication and the passing of information, it too is a sign of exchange,

> of that exchange that is in every sign, . . . the sign of writing wed to exchanges of other things . . . involved in the currents of currency as in the circulation of gold coins, the letter that must not be taken literally, the letter that transfers values that without a letter are valueless, the letter always ready to grow upon itself and deck itself with blossoms of the sublime, . . . the letter as prime element of Belles-Lettres, though always enfolding in its significant coils the currency of significance, the letter Ess that twists to signify it is ready and waiting to signify significations, the signifying sign that has the form of an Ess so that its significations can also assume the form of Ess. (100)

Like the deconstructionists, in this bravura display of rhetorical figures[51] Calvino paradoxically both "valorizes and at the same time disqualifies" and subverts language, including the accepted norm that a text establishes meaning.[52] In these rarefied experiments, full of fragmentation and dislocation, he plays with semiotic ideas, with structural linguistics—in particular with *signified* and *signifier*—and with connotative ideas, attitudes, or emotions associated with a word or sign in the mind of the writer or reader vis-à-vis denotative language. For Calvino, the author—the "combinatorial

machine''—is but a ''juggler, or conjurer, who arranges on a stand at a fair
a certain number of objects and, shifting them, connecting them, interchang-
ing them, achieves a certain number of effects'' (105). Indeed, according to
JoAnn Cannon, Calvino bases this work on the theoretical hypothesis that
''fiction is produced through the combination of a limited number of prefab-
ricated elements subject to fixed rules of association.''[53] Furthermore, when
Calvino worked on his *Fiabe italiane*[54] he became familiar with the work of
Vladimir Propp, who, in his analysis of one hundred Russian folk tales
(1928), found that they all consisted of thirty-one ''functions.'' Although the
names may change from one tale to the next, the ''functions'' performed by
the characters, remain limited and always the same.[55] It is not difficult to see
that these functions are present also in Calvino's tarot cards: the cards (structure) remain the same, but their reading constantly changes according to relations between elements rather than because of the elements themselves.
Therefore, not only are the cards a machine for constructing stories, but also
''a labyrinth where all the world's stories can be found.''[56]

Unlike all the other stories, the last seven pages of ''I Also Try to Tell My
Tale'' are told without cards on the margin of the page; only the written narrative appears. Quite possibly this indicates that Calvino is reverting back to
a more traditional narrative mode, where the pictorial icon no longer vies
with the written one. Ironically, in the pages in question, Calvino combines
elements of the lives of Saint George and Saint Jerome as they are depicted
in well-known paintings; but this is done exclusively by means of written language. ''The trick of arranging some tarots in a line and making stories
emerge from them,'' the narrator tells us, ''is something I could perform also
with paintings in museums'' (105). If the colorful and suggestive tarot cards
are indeed paintings that are about reading, it is only logical that Calvino
should also include in his gallery canvases depicting well-known images
and incidents. What catches his interest is the ever-present lion next to Saint
Jerome, ''curled up, domestic, serene,'' as well as the proverbial dragon associated with Saint George.[57] The import of the analogy between the paintings and narrative writing becomes clear when Calvino discusses the taming
and symbolically redemptive qualities of the lion and literature. ''Why the
lion?'' he asks, ''Does the written word tame passions? Or subdue the forces
of nature? Or does it find a harmony with the inhumanity of the universe? Or
incubate a violence, held back but always ready to spring, to claw?'' (105).

Evidently the author identifies with Saint Jerome because of his scholarly
attributes as the translator of the Vulgate, the humanizing or taming function
of literature, and also because ''the job of writing makes individual lives

uniform'' (106), he informs us. Yet he is far more intrigued with Saint George, always depicted with an ''impersonal face,'' and with his battle against the dragon as ''a scene on a coat of arms, fixed outside of time'' (108). Whenever we see the saint performing his famous feat with the dragon, he is ''always closed in his breastplate, revealing nothing of himself'' because ''psychology is no use to the man of action.'' It is in the beast that Calvino finds psychology, because ''he is the psyche, he is the dark background of himself that Saint George confronts . . . an internal enemy who becomes an object of loathsome alien-ness. Is it the story of an energy projected into the world, or is it the diary of an introversion?'' (109).

The common element to both saints is their relationship to dangerous animals: ''the dragon-enemy or the lion-friend'' (110). The former is a threat to a city, the latter to solitude. Yet, as in the case of a creative writer, both are part of one animal, since we encounter the fierce beast

> both outside and inside ourselves, in public and in private. There is a guilty way of inhabiting the city: accepting the conditions of the fierce beast, giving him our children to eat. There is a guilty way of inhabiting solitude: believing we are serene because the fierce beast has been made harmless by a thorn in his paw. The hero of the story is he who in the city aims the point of his lance at the dragon's throat, and in solitude keeps the lion with him in all its strength, accepting it as guard and domestic genie, but without hiding from himself its animal nature. (110–11)

For the first time in his literary career, Calvino expresses his fear of failure. Dissatisfied with his craft, and in particular with the text under discussion, as he tells us in his *nota* to *The Castle of Crossed Destinies,* he shows the frustrations of an author at a crossroad who, although filled with inspiring new ideas, suddenly feels incapable of expressing himself on paper to his satisfaction. In fact, the third card chosen by the tale's narrator, the *Page of Cups,* ''depicts me as I bend to peer into the envelope of myself; and I do not look content; it is futile to shake and squeeze, the soil is a dry inkwell'' (100). Regardless of Calvino's combinatorial games and tricks, as a writer he ''can only try to follow an unattainable model'' (101), because writing ''warns like the oracle and purifies like the tragedy'' (103), and what it ''speaks is what is repressed'' (102). This is why ''I Also Try to Tell My Tale'' ends with a claim to have set things straight, at least on paper, although inside the author ''all remains as before.'' The writer, like Saint George and Saint Jerome, must be both warrior and sage; either he succeeds in all his narrative undertakings or he will be neither one nor the other.

Does Calvino succeed with *The Castle of Crossed Destinies?* As a theorist, unequivocally yes; as an artist, alas no. Kathryn Hume admits that Calvino's last works, although original, beautiful, and well-crafted, are "perhaps a bit brittle? artificial? self-absorbed? tedious? overly complex? lacking in human warmth." She suggests that one needs to acquire a taste for these sophisticated narratives, the way we do for new music, painting, and food.[58] Perhaps she is right, though in all frankness Calvino reaches a point of exhaustion with his belabored combinatorial game which borders on self-parody with such an intense virtuoso performance. He overdoes his own card tricks and thereby loses the reader, the ostensible master of this game,[59] whose deciphering codes have been disrupted by a short circuit caused by an excessive surge of energy. In short, a reader may find it a bit overbearing to confront this prodigious text, consisting of "subtle and ingenious Rorschachs";[60] Indeed it is a text that is more interested in allegorizing the making of fiction than in presenting fiction. No wonder that Calvino himself intimates in his *nota* that writing these stories was agony for him. He is very much like the alchemist in "Two Tales of Seeking and Losing," who has spent his life "investigating the combinations of the elements and their metamorphoses," and now tries to arrange the cards in a manner in which all the stories can be read, his included. "But when he seems to have succeeded in deploying the stories of the others, he realizes his own story has been lost" (90).

Invisible Cities

In *Invisible Cities,* published in 1972, Calvino once again put into practice the structuralist/semiotic concepts presented at the beginning of this chapter.[61] In the novel (actually an antinovel), Marco Polo (1254–1324), the famous Venetian traveler who opened for Europe the Asian continent, relates to the great emperor Kublai Khan his findings concerning the cities within the vast Tartar empire. It is significant that Calvino chose to set his novel in China, which in 1972 was under the political and cultural hegemony of Mao Tse-Tung, who, despite his tyranny and destructive policies, was regarded by some progressive elements in Western society as the great creator of an ideal society.

The novel is based on Marco Polo's famous book *Il Milione* (*The Travels of Marco Polo*). The son of a Venetian banker, Polo spent about twenty-five years traveling and exploring the Asian continent and seventeen years as ambassador to Kublai Khan, whose empire reached from the Yellow River in China to the shores of the Danube in Eastern Europe and from Siberia to the Persian Gulf. Soon after his return to Venice in 1298, Polo was captured during a naval battle by the Genoese. While held captive, he dictated his adventures to a fellow prisoner who wrote them down. The book, whose title suggests unbelievable, exciting, and countless adventures, provided the medieval reader with a detailed description of Asian countries, cities, landscape, laws, religions, customs, trade routes, commerce, and leaders; above all, it gave a fascinating account of conditions in the Far East, especially in China and at the emperor's court. The content was so remarkable that Marco Polo's contemporaries found it difficult to believe. Indeed, the first sentence in Calvino's *Invisible Cities* indicates that the fictionalized Marco Polo protagonist/narrator is utterly unreliable:

> *Kublai Khan does not necessarily believe everything Marco Polo says when he describes the cities visited on his expeditions, but the emperor of the Tartars does continue listening to the young Venetian with greater attention and curiosity than he shows any other messenger or explorer of his.*[62]

Calvino's novel—one critic's reading is that it "poses as a rewriting" of Polo's "cosmography of the East"[63]—consists of Polo's descriptions of the empire's "invisible cities" to the khan, who, because of old age, has given up trying to control directly his large, crumbling, and unmanageable domain; these reports are accompanied by dialogues written in italic which take place each time the Venetian returns to court from his travels as ambassador. Structurally, the book is divided into nine chapters, each containing two dialogues and descriptions of the cities. In the first and last chapters there are ten cities each, and each of the seven intervening chapters present five cities. Every city's narrative is preceded by a caption. Each caption is repeated five times but not in sequential order—almost like a countdown (1; 2-1; 3-2-1; 4-3-2-1; 5-4-3-2-1, etc.)—and all together there are fifty-five cities under eleven categories.[64] Giovanni Falaschi explains Calvino's countdown by regarding *Invisible Cities* as "a series of mental designs continuously subjected to frustration that lead to zero degree." The book is therefore "set as an adventure of the mind, as a mathematical construction that at the end leads to nothing."[65] In John Updike's view, the cities "are cunningly grouped, with a mathematical complexity and subtlety of modulation worthy of Marco Polo's contemporary, Dante."[66] There are eighteen dialogues, one preceding and one following each chapter, which serve as extended cornices or frames that give insight and unity to the fifty-five descriptive narratives, and also stand for Barthes's concept of the world as text. In the frame tales the khan functions as the reader of a text as he asks questions, discusses, contradicts, and tries to find a pattern that would allow him to make sense out of Polo's (the writer's) imaginative descriptions concerning his own empire. Calvino's intent as a writer is to open up his text for the reader the way Marco Polo the explorer opened up the continent of Asia for European society, and for the khan as well.

Each city bears a beautiful and arcane feminine name with Arcadian, Classical, and Oriental echoes: Sophronia, Eudoxia, Thekla, Olinda, Diomira, Zaira, Isaura, Zenobia, Euphemia, Chloe, Fedora, etc.[67] However, the imaginary cities do not appear on any of the khan's maps, nor is it clear if they exist in the past, present, or future because their temporal and spatial locus is always in Marco Polo's fluid consciousness.[68] His travels span ancient China and modern megalopolises, which are increasingly taking up more and more of the earth's surface, with no intervening space between sprawling urban settlements. In fact, for the khan, who feels a prisoner of his situation, past and future rise out of an *"unlivable present, where all forms of human society have reached an extreme of their cycle and there is no imagining what new forms they may assume"* (135–36). Since there are no characters, no plots, no events, but only timeless patterns in these metafictional narratives, the world external to Kublai Khan's court cannot live or become visible except through the conversations or meditations that constitute the text itself. According to De Lauretis, both Kublai Khan and Marco Polo, who have no naturalistic attributes in the novel, "are reduced to their mythical names and to the extracontextual resonance that their names evoke." What emerges is not true narration in either the frames or in the framed sections, but rather the "narrating consciousness" of Polo in "the process of creating images of infinite cities of the mind, a purely functional persona, the subject of the writing." This narrating persona is "metamorphosed into the pure voice of a discourse totally rarefied, lyrical, oneiric, beyond the threshold of antinarrative."[69]

The historical Marco Polo describes his travels ranging from the Polar Sea to Java, from Cathay to Zanzibar and to Japan, and in so doing he reveals (makes visible) a world hitherto relatively unknown (invisible) to western Christendom. Calvino's cities, however, are invisible in a different sense inasmuch as they are imaginary both to Polo and the emperor, who readily acknowledges that the Venetian is presenting him *"truly a journey through memory"*; that although his accounts are *"most precise and detailed"* (22), his *"words and actions are only imagined,"* and he is just *"smuggling moods, states of grace, elegies!"* (98). Actually, as Polo discloses in his description of Olivia, one of the "Cities and Signs," the city should never be "confused with the words that describe it," even though there might be a connection between the two (61). This may explain in part why the two men communicate by means of mental images and not traditional language, although at times they also make use of mime, grimaces, glances, props, and the game of chess with its inexhaustible potential for different moves on the board. *"If each city is like a game of chess,"* muses the emperor, *"the day when I have learned the rules, I shall finally possess my empire, even if I shall never succeed in knowing all the cities it contains"* (121). The game, which represents *"the invisible order that sustains cities,"* reflects also the emperor's melancholy at not knowing all of the vast possessions he has created but which are now irrevocably disintegrating and, similar to the pieces on the chessboard, are falling in ruins. Worse still is that the game's purpose is eluding the khan, who, by *"disembodying his conquests to reduce them to the essential,"* understands that his empire like the game of chess is reduced *"to a square of planed wood: nothingness"* (123). But then the ingenious Polo points out to the khan that the chessboard is inlaid with two different woods, that the square on which his

> enlightened gaze is fixed was cut from the ring of a trunk that grew in a year of drought: you see how its fibers are arranged? Here a barely hinted knot can be made out: a bud tried to burgeon on a premature spring day, but the night's frost forced it to desist. (131)

Calvino was to comment years later that when he wrote these words it became clear to him that his "search for exactitude was branching out in two directions," that he was searching for "the reduction of secondary events to abstract patterns" coupled by a wish to express with words "the tangible aspect of things as precisely as possible."[70]

Throughout the dialogues the younger man strives to help his master understand the *"invisible order"* that regulates human existence (122), and to teach him to give a new sense to his life "by challenging the evil forces in his domain and by insuring the safety of whatever is just."[71] Polo shows him that a basic design exists, but that it is so complicated that it cannot be understood by logic alone. Accordingly, the invisible order that rules our existence, as well as that of cities, is like the logic (or illogic) that gives order to dreams:

> With cities, it is as with dreams: everything imaginable can be dreamed, but even the most unexpected dream is a rebus that conceals a desire or, its reverse, a fear. Cities, like dreams, are made of desires and fears, even if the thread of their discourse is secret, their rules are absurd, their perspective deceitful, and everything conceals something else. (44)

All the cities are different and very distinct from one another.[72] Whatever continuity they have does not reside in their composition but rather in being mere images, shadows, of one unmentioned city: Venice. There is a clear parallel between Calvino's *Invisible Cities* and Borges's "Tlön, Uqbar, Orbis Tertius," inasmuch as "the central scheme" of the latter "is an extraordinary mirror-game of successive levels of the unreal." Therefore, it could be argued that as Borges's story is only "nominally about an imaginary book," so Calvino's novel is only nominally about one city, Venice, and the invisible cities represent various levels of the unreal in a similar mirror-game.[73] When the khan wonders why Polo never speaks to him about the city of Venice, the ambassador replies:

> —*What else do you believe I have been talking to you about?* . . . *Every time I describe a city I am saying something about Venice.*
> —*When I ask you about other cities, I want to hear about them. And about Venice, when I ask you about Venice.*
> —*To distinguish the other cities' qualities, I must speak of a [preexisting]*[74] *city that remains implicit. For me it is Venice.* (86)[75]

Upon being told to begin each tale with a full description of Venice, Polo replies that he is afraid of losing it all at once if he speaks of it, and that perhaps by speaking of other cities he "*has already lost it, little by little*" (87). Calvino seems to be indicating that thought and reason destroy reality at the very moment of thinking.[76] One is reminded of Calvino's observation, regarding Cervantes' great novel, that "literary inventions are impressed on our memories by their verbal implications rather than by their actual words."[77] In fact, when Don Quixote is asked at different times to describe Dulcinea, he only manages to tell what she is not like. At one point he says that he paints her in his mind as he desires her, and obviously were he to present a full description of her, he would destroy the ideal Dulcinea. Likewise, the fear of losing the ideal city (or woman) by speaking of it takes us once again to Borges's "Tlön, Uqbar, Orbis Tertius," where when things duplicate themselves they "tend to efface themselves, to lose their detail when people forget them."[78] Raman Selden points out that "the postmodern experience is widely held to stem from a profound sense of ontological uncertainty" and that if the poststructuralist theorists have "a summarizing idea, it is the theme of the absent center," which, in Calvino's case, I think, is represented by the uncertainty of his "ontological ideal."[79]

Furthermore, it could be argued that the uniqueness of the ideal Venice, the only existing city for Marco Polo, also finds precedent in the statement by the narrator in Borges's *ficción* that in literary matters "the dominant notion is that everything is the work of one single author." Since plagiarism does not exist, "all books are the work of one single writer, who is timeless and anonymous." For Borges, it is criticism that invents authors. Similarly, like Polo's invisible cities, all books of fiction "are based on a single plot, which runs through every imaginable permutation."[80] Accordingly, this confirms Marco Polo's hypothesis—actually the underlying rationale for *Invisible Cities*—that "each man bears in his mind a city made only of differences, a city without figures and without form, and the individual cities fill it up" (34). As has been pointed out by Paul Bailey, Venice, "that decaying heap of incomparable splendour, . . . a place where the dead can seem to outnumber the living," still stands as strong evidence "of man's ability to create something perfect out of chaos."[81] San Remo, the unspoiled *locus amoenus* of Calvino's youth, has played a similar role as a literary touchstone. In fact, in his interview with Maria Corti, Calvino explained that San Remo is particularly present in many of the invisible cities; that it continued to persistently "pop out" in his books in "the most varied facets and perspectives, especially as seen from above"; that for him, San Remo was the "nucleus from which one's imagination, psychology and language are derived."[82]

The title *Invisible Cities* may have been partially inspired by the prologue to *The Travels of Marco Polo,* in which Polo states that his account is "a written record made of all the things he had *seen* and had heard by true report, so that others who have not *seen* and do not know them may learn them from this book" (my italics). Then why are the fictionalized Marco Polo's cities invisible, and why are they not included in any of the khan's extensive and exhaustive atlases? The answer may possibly lie in Plato's notion of the ideal. Unlike Aristotelian philosophy, which concerns itself mainly with the visible universe, Platonism is interested primarily in the unseen world. In his idealistic philosophy Plato distinguishes between the ontological real and the actual existent. According to the philosopher, the world of experience—the phenomenal world—is an imperfect shadow of the real and permanent ideal world: the ontological. Plato assumed that ontological reality was superior to the phenomenal world because the latter consists of matter and is restricted to limitations of time and space. The former, however, transcends space and time and is free of all restrictions. The ontological goes beyond the phenomenal world composed of sensory experiences, and it reveals reality that consists of an ideal world of which the world of phenomenal experience is but an imitation. Unlike the phenomenal world which is perceived by the senses and is tangible, the ideal is intangible and created by the mind; it is also enduring, perfect, and unchangeable.

Thus, the distinction between the Platonic ideal and the phenomenal explains why Calvino chose to make the cities conceived in the minds of Polo and the khan sensorially invisible—that is, ontological. Venice, the preexisting city, is the ontologically ideal city. Indeed, whenever Polo speaks about all the other cities he merely presents shadows, images, or replicas of his city. For the Venetian, *"the model city"* from which he deduces all the others is *"a city made only of exceptions, exclusions, incongruities, contradictions."* And if such a city is very unlikely, he continues,

> by reducing the number of abnormal elements, we increase the probability that the city really exists. So I have only to subtract exceptions from my model, and in whatever direction I proceed, I will arrive at one of the cities which, always as an exception, exist. But I cannot force my operation beyond a certain limit: I would achieve cities too probable to be real. (69)

Unlike the amateur philosophers who love concrete beautiful things but have only relative knowledge, the Venetian and the Tartar are true philosophers in the Platonic sense because they love wisdom, have an unquenchable curiosity to know all truth, exalt mind over matter, and do not confuse the Idea with the Particular. Both are able to distinguish between the copy and the real, between the material world of the senses and a supersensory world conceived by reason and emotion. For them, as for Saint Augustine, material cities are impermanent and apt to fall, whereas the concept of an ideal city is an eternal and immutable model according to which all other cities are created and arranged.

Calvino's Platonic discourse also finds resonance in Barthes's essay "From Work to Text," in which the critic distinguishes between a literary "work" and "text." The former is concrete, fixed, and has exact meaning, while the latter has "an irreducible plurality of meaning." Thus, like a literary text, Calvino's invisible cities remain in a state of production, have no fixed signifieds, and exist "in the movement of discourse"; and analogous to a text, they are seen in "the very activity of reading and interpretation."[83] Consequently, the meaning of the invisible cities is to be found not merely in Polo's words, but between words; not in things, but between things. Meaning, therefore, results from differential relations, from signifying relations. The cities are meaningful only in relation to each other because, as in language, there are only differences.

Although each of the nine thematic captions has five variations, every individual city has its own characteristics. At first the cities are described in a positive vein, but gradually they become places of vice, decay, and of man's wanton self-destruction. Isidora, the place of "perfect telescopes and violins," is the city of Polo's dreams with one difference: "the dreamed-of city contained him as a young man," but he arrives there in his old age so that for him "desires are already memories" (8). Zora, on the other hand, is a city that once seen cannot be forgotten in all its particular details. Its secret "lies in the way your gaze runs over patterns following one another as in a musical score where not a note can be altered or displaced." This unforgettable city is like an "armature, a honeycomb in whose cells each of us can place the things he wants to remember" (15). But Polo is unable to visit Zora because, forced to remain always the same in order to be more easily remembered, it "has languished, disintegrated, disappeared. The earth has forgotten her" (16). When one visits Maurilia, one has to examine old postcards which depict the city as it used to be before it changed: "a bandstand in the place of the overpass, two young ladies with white parasols in the place of the munitions factory" (30). One is compelled to show preference for Maurilia's postcard images or else the inhabitants are disappointed; but in fact the modern metropolis no longer has any resemblance at all to the original city; nor do the new inhabitants, composed of outsiders, have any connection with the former ones. In Eudoxia, with its winding alleys, hills, and deadend streets, the inhabitants preserve a carpet that reflects the city's true form. At first glance the city appears different from the carpet

> laid out in symmetrical motifs whose patterns are repeated along straight and circular lines, interwoven with brilliantly colored spires, in a repetition that can be followed throughout the whole woof. But if you pause to examine it carefully, you become convinced that each place in the carpet corresponds to a place in the city and all the things contained in the city are included in the design, arranged according to their true relationship, which escapes your eye distracted by the bustle, the throngs, the shoving. All of Eudoxia's confusion . . . is evident in the incomplete perspective you grasp; but the carpet proves there is a point from which the city shows its true proportions, the geometrical scheme implicit in its very, tiniest detail. (96)

It is easy to get lost in Eudoxia, but the inhabitants find their way by comparing the "carpet's immobile order" with their own image of the city. Moreover, one can also find concealed among the carpet's "arabesques, an answer, the story of his life, the twists of fate" (97). According to F. B. Napoletano, there is a metaphoric identification between the invisible cities and the texture of Eudoxia's carpet; similarly, the inhabitants' relationship between city/carpet is parallel to the one between reader and text.[84] In essence, what Calvino is trying to show is that like the carpet, a literary text (or language) functions like a woven material. By analyzing the similar and dissimilar threads interwoven into different patterns, one gains better insight into its composition and structure. Analogously, not only are the novel's two well-defined tracts perfectly interwoven, but so are the only two protagonists. Polo's imaginary cities themselves are interwoven to form the various patterns which always allude to an ideal city. Reading, therefore, is a structuring activity, and each text, "which is its own model," is "ceaselessly traversed by codes which are the source of its meaning," according to Jonathan Culler. A text, like each city, has plural meanings because "it involves the reader in the process of producing meaning."[85] In "Pierre Menard, Author of the *Quixote*," Borges, too, views reading as a form of writing or rewriting. For him the reader is a participant who by reading changes the text. Juxtaposing two narrative planes whose alternation produces a text, Calvino is able to successfully spin his bivalent story: an apprehension for the plight of the city and an interest in combinatory potentials of narrative text.

Although Marco Polo has to cope constantly with changes of language as he travels from city to city, in Hypatia the change is unique because it "regards not words but things" (47). He discovers young women bathing, "but at the bottom of the water crabs were biting the eyes of the suicides, stones tied around their necks, their hair green with seaweed." Upon questioning the city's sage, Polo is told: "Signs form a language, but not the one you think you know" (48). He realizes that in order to understand Hypatia's language he has to rid himself of the images that in the past had announced to him the things he sought. Finally, he admits that "there is no language without deceit" (48). In Thekla, Polo learns that the construction of the city never stops, "so that its destruction cannot begin" (127); whereas in three-tiered Beersheba the people believe that suspended in the heavens there is another Beersheba "where the city's most elevated virtues and sentiments are poised" (111). If the terrestrial city will take the celestial as its model, the two will become one. They also believe that there is yet a third Beersheba underground, "the receptacle of everything base and unworthy." The hypocritical inhabitants constantly strive to erase from the visible city every tie to the lower one where they imagine in the place of roofs there are "overturned rubbish bins, with cheese rinds, greasy paper, fish scales, dishwater, uneaten spaghetti, old bandages spilling from them" (112). Intent on reaching perfection, Beersheba takes "for virtue what is now a grim mania to fill the empty vessel of itself" (112). It fails to recognize, however, that its only "free and happy action" occurs when "it shits; [then it] is not miserly, calculating, greedy" (113).

Procopia is so densely populated that the inhabitants hide the place and even the sky from newcomers. While Laudomia has at its side the city of the dead who bare the same names as the living, its special endowment is that it includes also a third city, that of the unborn. The living go there to interrogate them in silence, and "it is always about themselves that the living ask, not about those who are to come" (141). The city of the unborn conveys only alarm because the future generations will be so numerous that they "will then go no further." Consequently, the Laudomia of the dead and that of the unborn will be like the two parts of an hourglass that is not turned over; "each passage between birth and death is a grain of sand that passes the neck, and there will be a last inhabitant of Laudomia born, a last grain to fall, which is now at the top of the pile, waiting" (143).

Berenice, the last of Calvino's *Invisible Cities,* is the center of Marco Polo's sphere.[86] It consists of two cities, that of the unjust and that of the just. However, even in the just city a hidden "malignant seed" is fermenting in bitterness. It consists of "the certainty and pride of being in the right," of being more just than others who call "themselves more just than the just" (162). Calvino may be alluding to the "just" reformers or revolutionaries (Lenin, Stalin, Mao, Castro), who at first may indeed have stood for the right ideas, but as soon as they came to power were quickly corrupted by their own sense of what is good for the people, and inevitably replaced the old evil with a new one. Thus, in Berenice, a different, unjust city is germinating secretly inside the just city. Clearly the city also stands for the modern sprawling metropolis, "a temporal succession of different cities, alternately just and unjust." But what Polo wants to warn the emperor about is that "all the future Berenices are already present in this instant, wrapped one within the other, confined, crammed, inextricable" (163), all interwoven like a carpet.

In addition to Polo's imaginary cities, the Great Khan's atlas contains maps of "*promised lands visited in thought but not yet discovered or founded: New Atlantis, Utopia,*[87] *the City of the Sun, Oceana, Tamoé, New Harmony, New Lanark, Icaria*" (164). The khan, who observes in his atlas ominous cities such as Enoch, Babylon, Yahooland, Butua, Brave New Worlds, remarks that it is all useless because the ocean's currents are drawing us to the infernal city.[88] Polo replies that "*the inferno of the living*" is already here, "*the inferno where we live every day, that we form by being together*" (165). Nonetheless, there are two ways out: accept the inferno and become so much a part of it that we can no longer recognize it; or "*seek and learn to recognize who and what, in the midst of the inferno, are not inferno, then make them endure, give them space"* (165). The message is that we must be constantly vigilant and apprehensive in order to overcome the evil of the modern cities; we must preserve what is good in us in order to assure our survival.

What is perhaps most singularly remarkable about Polo's cities is that their inhabitants remain almost "invisible"—children are virtually omitted— throughout the entire book, thus creating an ever greater sense of anguish, foreboding, and desolation; the people are usually referred to indirectly as mere scenic props, demographic data, and the total effect is similar to that of modern cities which after five o'clock become ghost towns, empty shells where one only comes to work and not to live.[89] This is very evident in Chloe, where all are strangers:

> At each encounter, they imagine a thousand things about one another; meetings which could take place between them, conversations, surprises, caresses, bites. But no one greets anyone; eyes lock for a second, then dart away, seeking other eyes, never stopping. . . . When some people happen to find themselves together . . . meetings, seductions, copulations, orgies are consummated among them without a word being exchanged, without a finger touching anything, almost without an eye raised. (51)

This ominous sense of alienation and distancing has been characterized by Cesare Cases as the author's Nietzschean *"pathos* of distance." In his often-quoted 1958 essay, Cases singled out the vital nucleus of Calvino's oeuvre which "lives in the tension between solitude of distance and the essential community, which is disgustedly near and unreliable. In either extreme situation man is mutilated, and one has to put him back together, something that can only happen in fables."[90] *Invisible Cities* is replete with examples of distancing, such as the inhabitants of Baucis, who rarely show themselves, preferring to view the city with spyglasses and telescopes, "contemplating with fascination their own absence" (77). Irene can only be "discerned spread out in the distance below. . . . Irene is a name for a city in the distance, and if you approach, it changes" (124–25).

The *"pathos* of distance" between human beings, which is so prevalent in Marco Polo's cities, is very similar to that found in Calvino's stories "The Adventure of a Soldier" (1949) and "The Adventure of a Reader" (1958). In the first narrative Private Tomagra has sex with a widow seated next to him in a train compartment without exchanging any words with the woman. In the second story, Amedeo, an avid reader, is absorbed by a thick novel he is reading at the beach. He notices a woman sunning herself not far away from him.

They get acquainted, but their conversations are interrupted by long periods of time during which Amedeo, spurred by a strong curiosity to find out what happens next in the novel, resumes reading. When the woman takes off her bathing suit, he is uncertain "whether to look at her, pretending to read, or to read, pretending to look at her." Even during the ecstasy of lovemaking, Amedeo tries "to free one hand to put the bookmark at the right page,"[91] torn between the allure of reading about sex and having sex with a real woman. Ironically, for Freud the act of writing had significant sexual connotations, but for Calvino the act of reading seems to be even stronger.

Likewise, the *"pathos* of distance" that distinguishes the interaction of Calvino's characters parallels that of the author himself. Indeed, as has been noted, Calvino finds it necessary to distance himself from his characters in order to observe them better; but the moment he reaches the proper distance, he "senses a remorse, a nostalgia, an ancestral disability" that prevent him from fully identifying with his protagonists and sharing in their "existential adventures."[92] It is precisely this defamiliarization and distancing that determine how Marco Polo looks at his cities as they gradually become barren like Despina, "a border city between two deserts" (18).

Clearly there are certain similarities between Calvino's *Invisible Cities* and T. S. Eliot's *The Waste Land* (1922) insofar as both authors express the disillusionment of their respective generations. The poem likewise reflects the decay, emptiness, gloom, sterility of modern life, and particularly the tedium of living in modern cities. For Calvino cities are composed only of buildings, structures, canals, and cement, albeit often imbued with sensuality. Yet in spite of this wasteland, Calvino never loses sight of man's irrepressible humanity represented by *"the design of a filigree so subtle it could escape the termite's gnawing"* (6). The cities and their inhabitants are invisible only to those incapable or unwilling to see beyond the surface of things. As Flavia Ravazzoli points out, they are "un-narratable" only for those who are "so deprived of fantasy that they never venture beyond accounts solidly founded on verisimilitude"; they are infernal only for those who are frozen in the "triple compartmentalization of literature–rhetoric–poetry, a thing that still can cause daily astonishment and doubt in the conception of the impossible."[93] In essence, once again, Calvino exhorts the reader to keep challenging the labyrinth without ever submitting to it.

Calvino regards the city as a "complex symbol" which allows him to express "the tension between geometric rationality and the entanglements of human lives."[94] In fact, in order to understand fully his interest in cities and their evolution and decline, one must see them as representative symbols of human behavior. Going back to the beginning of civilization, since their designs and disposition are never arbitrary, cities reflect the doctrine and practices of the society which creates and maintains them. Hence, cities have never been regarded simply as places of human settlement. They have always had religious and cosmic symbolism as an extraterrestrial reality, some being copies of a mythical or divine model, some having descended from heaven, some even having a relationship to the underworld. Even in Plato's *Republic,* the ideal city has its celestial prototype. And according to tradition, not only does Jerusalem stem from a celestial model, but it was also created by God before it was constructed by humans. In Saint Augustine's *The City of God,* which considers the city only as a community of people, there is a clear antithetical contradiction between "terrestrial" and "celestial" cities. Likewise in Marco Polo's time, the earthly city was seen as disconnected from its celestial model. Indeed, during the Middle Ages the city was seen as a place of temptation, debasement, debauchery, avarice, even as inhabited by infernal creatures. During the Renaissance, however, the ideal city came to be identified, at least in part, with the material one. Venice and Florence were invested with many utopian virtues. Thus, Leonardo Bruni (1369–1444) refers to Florence as a model city of justice, harmonious beauty, with functional and rational institutions; and its architecture conforms with the city's social and political structure. The people of the Renaissance saw the city as an earthly rational human structure no longer having any connection to a celestial prototype; they were concerned primarily with problems of civil life: how to make justice and wisdom work effectively.[95]

In modern times, despite well-intentioned urban planning, the drastic increase in city population, combined with environmental abuses and the ensuing social, economic, and demographic problems, have caused the city to be seen once again as a place of vice, crime, and greed. The vision of an ideal city no longer holds true for some, particularly for those compelled to endure the decay, the danger, the pollution, the congestion, the traffic jams, the noise, the constant changes, and the endemic tension that has become so pervasive in all cities to the extent that, as in Eusapia, "there is no longer any way of knowing who is alive and who is dead" (110).[96] It is precisely this sense of despair and loss for the mythical and virtuous city, previously dramatized by Calvino in *Smog* and *A Plunge into Real Estate,* that torments both Kublai Khan and Marco Polo.

In discussing the role of the city in the American experience—urban worthlessness versus the belief that true virtue resides in nature—Jay Martin argues that in addition to the metropolitan evil, which he characterizes as being part of the material "visible" city, there are other essential elements; these manifest themselves in the "invisible" city, seen as "a rich and various metaphor of urban experience." The "value" of the "invisible" city is to help the individual, rendered "invisible by the mass collective life of the modern city," to be "visible again by reviewing himself."[97]

Joseph Hudnut's *Architecture and the Spirit of Man* (1949) makes it clear that in contemporary life people do not live in cities purely for economic reasons and that the positive experiences far outweigh the negative ones. However, in Calvino's novel nothing is categorical; everything is opaque and contradictory. When Polo describes a bridge, stone by stone, and the emperor asks which stone it is that supports the bridge, he explains: *"The bridge is not supported by one stone or another, but by the line of the arch that they form."* When the khan replies: *"Why do you speak to me of the stones? It is only the arch that matters to me,"* Polo answers: *"Without stones there is no arch"* (82). Clearly, in spite of the subtle contradiction, the stones mentioned by Polo stand for the various cities and the line of the arch for the unity of the book. Pier Vincenzo Mengaldo, for whom "stone" and "arch" relate to the reading of the narrative, points out that *Invisible Cities* is a narrative of a narrative; that "the ambiguous relationship between the narrator and his narrating character [Marco Polo], further complicated by the contradictory level constantly imposed by the interlocutor [Kublai Khan], calls primarily into question the very function of narrating."[98] Thus the emperor and the reader get no clear answer from Marco Polo/Calvino. According to Robert Breiner, however, the stones are Venice and the "arch has to do with methods of reading, with techniques of structure both generative and retrospective, and, more generally, with fictions about literary production."[99]

Calvino poses many questions and seldom provides any answers; in fact, he summarized *Invisible Cities* as a book that offers far more questions than solutions,

> that proceeds by discussing and questioning itself, that allows itself to be traversed in different directions and on superimposed layers, that molds itself in an elaborate and accomplished form, but which every reader can take apart and put back together, by following the drift of his motivations and whims.[100]

Calvino offers no answers because in today's world the solutions have become the problems. Motor vehicles, which were supposed to have been the solution to poor communication and transportation, have become serious hindrances that affect our environment, deplete our natural resources, and kill thousands of people daily. The world changes too rapidly, to the extent that the past no longer seems to offer us sufficient guidance or any useful lesson, except, perhaps, that there is no lesson to be learned.

Is Calvino trying to indicate that change is out of control, that our practices and institutions, the defenses of our social and moral existence, are snapping under the strain of modern life? We live today with a feeling of constant crisis, without truly being able to identify its causes or effects clearly. In *The Watcher*, Amerigo arrives at the conclusion that Cottolengo—symbolic of cities and their institutions—should be regarded primarily for its human qualities and for the ingenuity that created it. He laments, however, that the modern individual, unaware, is letting die out the "secret fire without which cities are not founded and machinery's wheels aren't set in motion."[101] This, too, is the apocalyptic revelation and forewarning of Calvino's *Invisible Cities*. We have to learn to live without solutions, without necessarily finding our way out of the labyrinth, by cherishing that which is not *inferno*, by guarding our few remaining positive values. We can hardly even identify what is "positive" and what is not; we aren't sure what to guard or protect.

In a 1985 New York interview with Alexander Stille, when asked if he had a favorite among all his books, Calvino pointed out that *Cosmicomics* and *t zero* are among his best books because they "will be more and more recognized," but that "probably the book that is most finished and perfect is *Invisible Cities*."[102] Elsewhere, Calvino explained that it remains the book

in which I think I managed to say most . . . because I was able to concentrate all my reflections, experiments, and conjectures on a single symbol [the city]; and also because I built up a many-faceted structure in which each brief text is close to the others in a series that does not imply logical sequence or a hierarchy, but a network in which one can follow multiple routes and draw multiple, ramified conclusions.[103]

Indeed, many critics agree with him, especially Gore Vidal, who not only recognizes the narrative's "theme of multiplicity and wholeness," but also admires the "grace and tenderness" of Calvino's "novel (or work or meditation or poem)," which he considers to be "perhaps his most beautiful work."[104] In Falaschi's view, the lyrical foundation of *Invisible Cities* is indicative of the "search for something that does not exist nor could it exist, or has been and can no longer be."[105] The book adheres to Calvino's own precepts concerning "lightness" both in literature and in life; namely, that the gravity of existence can only be borne lightly; that were he to choose a promising image for the new millennium, it would be the agile leap of the poet-philosopher who raises himself above the weight of the world, showing that with all its gravity he has the secret of lightness, and that what many consider to be the vitality of the times—noisy, aggressive, revving and roaring—belongs to the realm of death, like a cemetery for rusty old cars.[106]

Salman Rushdie considers *Invisible Cities* to be not "really a novel at all, but a sort of fugue on the nature of the City" because Polo and the khan are the "only attempts at characters." Although he laments that despite "all those jewelled sentences and glittering notions" there is "no story-telling worth a damn," he finally admits that the book's "true star" is indeed Calvino's descriptive prose.[107] This is particularly so in the dialogues between Marco Polo and Kublai Khan, which, according to Updike, are "a metaphor for the artistic experience" and at the same time "a riddle for communication."[108]

NOTES

1. "Cybernetics and Ghosts," *The Uses of Literature* (New York: Harcourt, Brace, 1986) 15.

2. "Cybernetics" 7.

3. Terence Hawkes, *Structuralism and Semiotics* (Berkeley: University of California Press, 1977) 112.

4. Roland Barthes, "To Write: An Intransitive Verb?" in *The Structuralist Controversy,* ed. Richard Macksey and Eugenio Donato (Baltimore: Johns Hopkins University, 1972) 144.

5. Hawkes 113.

6. "Cybernetics" 13.

7. Jerry Varsava, "Calvino's Borgesian Odysseys," in *Borges and His Successors,* ed. Edna Eizenberg (Columbia: University of Missouri Press, 1990) 184.

8. "Cybernetics" 15–16.

9. "Cybernetics" 10.

10. Hawkes 114.

11. Roland Barthes, *The Pleasure of the Text* (London: Cape, 1976) 9–10.

12. See Malcolm Bradbury, "The Scholar Who Misread History," *The New York Times Book Review* (24 Feb. 1991): 9 (review of David Lehman, *Sign of the Times: Deconstruction and the Fall of Paul de Man*).

13. "Cybernetics" 16.

14. Roland Barthes, "The Effect of Reality," in *French Literary Criticism Today,* ed. T. Todorov (Cambridge: Cambridge University Press, 1968) 147–48.

15. "Cybernetics" 26.

16. Quoted, Gérard Genette, "La utopia literaria," in *Jorge Luis Borges,* ed. Jaime Alazraki (Madrid: Tauros, 1976) 210.

17. "Cybernetics" 7. Unfortunately the English version omits the subtitle of Calvino's lecture: "Appunti sulla narrativa come processo combinatorio" (comments concerning narrative as a combinatory process).

18. "Quickness," *Six Memos for the Next Millennium* (Cambridge: Harvard University Press, 1988) 50.

19. "Cybernetics" 25.

20. George R. McMurray, *Jorge Luis Borges* (New York: Frederick Ungar, 1980) 160–61.

21. Raman Selden, *A Reader's Guide to Contemporary Literary Theory* (Lexington: University Press of Kentucky, 1989) 72.

22. Quoted from Alexander Argyros, "Deconstruction, Quantum Uncertainty, and the Place of Literature," *Modern Language Studies* 20 (Fall 1990): 35. *Aporia* means an impasse, not knowing where to begin or what to say; for Derrida it signifies the impasse of interpretation "between incompatible or contradictory meanings which are 'undecidable,' in that we lack any solid ground for choosing among them." See M. H. Abrams, *A Glossary of Literary Terms*, 5th ed. (Fort Worth: Holt, Rinehart and Winston, 1990) 205.

23. *The Castle of Crossed Destinies* (New York: Harcourt Brace, 1979) 123. The volume also includes *The Tavern of Crossed Destinies*. Page numbers referring to this edition are shown in parentheses.

24. Juan Luis Vives, *Obras Completas* (Madrid: Aguilar, 1948) 2: 957.

25. Louis C. Pérez, "Con relación a los naipes en el teatro del XVII," *Bulletin of the Comediantes* 33.2 (Fall 1981): 139, 140.

26. Wolfgang Iser, *The Act of Reading: A Theory of Aesthetic Response* (Baltimore: Johns Hopkins University Press, 1978).

27. Umberto Eco, *The Role of the Reader: Explorations in the Semiotics of Texts* (Bloomington: Indiana University Press, 1979); see also *The Open Work* (Cambridge: Harvard University Press, 1989).

28. Quoted, Selden 121.

29. *Nota, Il castello dei destini incrociati,* (Turin: Einaudi, 1973) 125. I am quoting from the Italian version because the English one is incomplete; certain paragraphs are either missing or condensed.

30. Tarot cards, often used for fortune-telling, consist of fifty-six numbered cards divided into four suits plus twenty-two trump cards or picture cards. The suit cards are broken down into Minor Arcana and Court Arcana. The trump cards, known as the Major Arcana, are numbered 0–XXI, with the fool being unnumbered.

31. *Nota* 125. Calvino's interest in Ariosto is not surprising given that he saw him as one of his literary forbears. The fantastic world and the parodistic devices found in *Orlando Furioso* often reappear in Calvino's work.

32. It was published in Parma, 1969, by Franco Maria Ricci Editore. In 1976 an English edition was published in New York by the same publisher.

33. *Nota* 126–28.

34. The English version reads: "I always feel the need to alternate one type of writing with another, completely different, to begin writing again as if I had never written anything before" (*The Castle* 129).

35. The beginnings of both novellas make clear allusions to the first six tercets of Dante's *Inferno*.

36. Teresa De Lauretis, "Narrative Discourse in Calvino: Praxis or Poiesis?" *PMLA* 90 (1975): 422.

37. In "Scienza e letteratura," Calvino already indicated his particular interest in the mosaic in which man finds himself encased, the game of relationships, and the image to be discovered amidst the arabesques of the carpet (*Una pietra sopra*, [Turin: Einaudi, 1980] 188). See also ch. 6 of the present study.

38. In his essay "Multiplicity," Calvino writes that to "sample the potential multiplicity of what may be narrated" forms the basis of *The Castle*, "which is intended to be a kind of machine for multiplying narratives that start from visual elements with many possible meanings, such as a tarot pack" (*Six Memos* 120). We have already seen in ch. 6 that in *Exercises in Style*, Queneau related the same episode in ninety-nine different ways.

39. John Updike, "Italo Calvino," *Hugging the Shore: Essays and Criticism* (New York: Knopf, 1983) 464.

40. Constance Markey, "Italo Calvino: The Contemporary Fabulist," *Italian Quarterly* 23 (Spring 1982): 80.

41. Giorgio Baroni, *Italo Calvino* (Florence: Le Monnier, 1988) 90.

42. Calvino's Orlando, strung up by his feet (indicated by the tarot *The Hanged Man*), refuses to regain his senses. He says: "Leave me like this. I have come full circle and I understand. The world must be read backward. All is clear" (34). Orlando refuses to accept the reason that underpins the cards, according to Benussi, knowing that it is pointless to seek a fixed point and think in terms of continuity with the past. See Cristina Benussi, *Introduzione a Calvino* (Rome: Laterza, 1989) 123.

43. Marilyn Schneider, "Calvino at a Crossroad: *Il castello dei destini incrociati*," *PMLA* 95 (1980): 73–74.

44. *Nota* 127–28.

45. McMurray 105.

46. There is an obvious analogy here with *The Nonexistent Knight*.

47. A. H. Carter III, *Italo Calvino* (Ann Arbor: UMI Research Press, 1987) 105.

48. Markey 79–81.

49. De Lauretis 422.

50. Calvino is echoing the theme of "The Waverer's Tale": that there is no difference between choosing and renouncing.

51. The rhetorical figures are alliteration, epanaphora, transplacement, and epanalepsis.

52. Jacques Derrida, *Of Grammatology* (Baltimore: Johns Hopkins University Press, 1976) 141. The poststructuralist term "deconstruction," coined in the 60s by Derrida, is often applied to a method of reading whose aim is to "subvert" and "undermine" the accepted norm that a text establishes meaning through its verbal elements. Therefore no text can express the "truth" of any particular subject. At the same time, however, it also opens up the traditional literary canon to diverse linguistic and interpretative problems. It makes use of phenomenology by adding to it the notion of linguistic semiotic difference, insisting that the written text is the primal signifying activity and not speech. As noted in ch. 7, Derrida coined the word *différance* to express the ambiguity and the divided nature of the sign. Language is based on differences and the text is treated as something expressing signifying relations, something that is *de rigueur* intertextual since it is seen in the context of difference between other signs and other texts. Thus, the meaning of a text, which always depends on intertextuality, is continually open to various and contradictory readings; it can be read in different contexts regardless of the writer's intention. Not only does the author lose prominence vis-à-vis the text, but so does the text with respect to the reader and the act of interpretation. Finally, Derrida's deconstruction questions "the self-identity of signifier and signified and the self-presence of the speaking subject and voiced sign. Namely, the spoken word is given greater value than the written because the speaker and the listener are present. There is an abandonment of all reference to a centre, to a fixed subject, to a privileged reference, to an origin, to an absolute founding and controlling first principle" (Madan Sarup, *An Introductory Guide to Poststructuralism and Postmodernism* [Athens: University of Georgia Press, 1989] 58–59).

53. JoAnn Cannon, "Literature as Combinatory Game: Italo Calvino's *The Castle of Crossed Destinies*," *Critique* 21 (1979): 85.

54. *Fiabe Italiane* (Turin: Einaudi, 1956). There are two English versions: *Italian Fables*, trans. Louis Brigante (New York: Collier, 1961) and *Italian Folktales*, trans. George Martin (New York: Harcourt Brace, 1980).

55. Vladimir Propp, *Morphology of the Folktale*, 2nd ed., trans. Laurence Scott (Austin: University of Texas Press, 1968).

56. Michael Wood, "Fortune Hunting," *New York Review of Books*, 12 May 1977: 36 (review of *The Castle of Crossed Destinies*).

57. St. George (third century, patron saint of Venice and England) is one of the favorite subjects of Renaissance artists, and paintings of him abound all over Italy. He is usually represented

as a mounted warrior holding a book in one hand and in the other a lance poised ready to thrust into the head of a huge dragon or serpent. The saint represents the struggle against evil forces, as well as the triumph of justice and the spirit over oppression and wickedness. The dragon symbolizes the devil and the serpent, the cunning tempter who entices man to sin. St. Jerome (fourth century), translator of the Vulgate Bible, whose life was devoted to scholarship and ascetic practices, is usually depicted as a hermit or as a scholar consulting treatises outdoors. He is seated at the entrance of a cave and near him is a tame lion. According to legend, the saint removed a painful thorn from the paw of the lion, who then became his close and faithful friend. The lion, one of the mystic beings in Christian tradition, represents resurrection.

58. Kathryn Hume, "Calvino's Framed Narrations: Writers, Readers, and Reality," *Review of Contemporary Fiction* 6 (Summer 1986): 71.

59. Reflecting contemporary literary trends, Calvino clearly emphasizes the activity of reading by stressing its "active productive nature." Culler writes that interpretation, or reading, is "an attempt to participate in and observe the play of possible meanings to which the text gives access" (Jonathan Culler, *Structuralist Poetics* [Ithaca: Cornell Univeristy Press, 1975] 247).

60. Carter 107.

61. For Gatt-Rutter, *Invisible Cities* and *The Castle of Crossed Destinies* are "semiological fantasies elaborated" through Polo's description of the cities and the tarot cards respectively (John Gatt-Rutter, "Calvino's Macrocosm: The Politics of Play," in *Writers and Politics in Modern Italy* [New York: Holmes & Meier, 1978] 48).

62. Italo Calvino, *Invisible Cities* (New York: Harcourt Brace, 1978) 5. Page numbers referring to this edition are shown in parentheses.

63. JoAnn Cannon, "The Map of the Universe," in *Italo Calvino: Writer and Critic* (Ravenna: Longo, 1981) 83.

64. In 1971 Calvino wrote the introduction to the Italian edition of Julio Cortazar's *Cronopios and Famas*. Therefore, when he wrote *Invisible Cities*, he was no doubt familiar with Cortazar's radically experimental novel, *Rayuela* (*Hopscotch*, 1963). This novel can be read linearly through ch. 56, ignoring the remaining 99 "expendable" chapters, or by skipping back and forth throughout the 155 chapters, or according to the indications provided by the author (73-1-2-116-3-84).

65. Giovanni Falaschi, "Italo Calvino, *Le città invisibili*," review, *Belfagor* 29 (Sept. 1974): 602.

66. John Updike, "Metropolises of the Mind," *Hugging the Shore* 459.

67. The Old Testament refers to cities as women. Carl Jung sees the city as a mother who shelters the inhabitants as if they were her children. To the best of my knowledge, the mystifying code of the cities' names—if there is one—has not yet been broken.

68. Calvino's cities, as the title clearly denotes, do not exist nor can they be located. For example, one reaches Diomira by "leaving there and proceeding for three days toward the east" (7); and one finally comes to Isidora by riding "a long time through wild regions" (8). Cannon observes that the cities "do not even pretend to exist in any real or identifiable dimension" and that the indications given "could be applied to any point in space" (Cannon, "Map of the Universe" 83). Calvino's process brings to mind the experiments of James Joyce and Italo Svevo in representing consciousness, particularly in the way in which their characters first grasp unrelated observations and experiences, and then bring them together as a whole. Trieste is for Svevo what Dublin is for Joyce, and San Remo is for Calvino what Venice is for Marco Polo.

69. De Lauretis 416–17. In Breiner's reading of the book, the frame is "not quite a frame, just as the accounts of the cities are not quite stories," and the italic sections are more of an addition than a complement because "they pursue their own course" (Laurence A. Breiner, "Italic Calvino: the Place of the Emperor in *Invisible Cities*," *Modern Fiction Studies* 34 [Winter 1988]: 562).

70. "Exactitude," *Six Memos* 74. It should be pointed out that the game of chess symbolizes many binary oppositions: black vs. white, male vs. female, direct moves vs. diagonal, Polo vs. Khan, visible vs. invisible, Orient vs. Occident, author vs. text, text vs. reader, italic type vs. roman, etc.

71. Sara Maria Adler, *Calvino: The Writer as Fablemaker* (Potomac, MD.: José Porrúa Turanzas, 1979) 131. According to Updike, all of Calvino's "investigations spiral in upon the central question of *How shall we live?*" ("Metropolises of the mind" 457).

72. Updike remarks that "Italy's towns, many of them once city-states, are vividly individual, and do seem each to embody a different principle, or to crystallize the differing moods of a volative individual" ("Metropolises of the Mind" 461). Cannon comments that the cities are "composed of identical elements" but are "still unique" ("Map of the Universe" 91).

73. Donald Heiney, "Calvino and Borges: Some Implications of Fantasy," *Mundus Artium* 2 (1968): 68.

74. Weaver translates it as "first city."

75. A parallel can be drawn between the absence of a complete holograph manuscript of *Il Milione* and the impossibility of attaining the ideal city. Although there are numerous manuscripts of Polo's work in various languages, they are all incomplete. Indeed, in Latham's view, "even by fitting them all together like the pieces of a jig-saw puzzle we cannot hope to reconstitute the original text as it left the practised hand of Messer Rustichello." Ronald Latham, introduction, *The Travels of Marco Polo* (New York: Penguin, 1982) 24.

76. Falaschi sees this as proof of the "insufficiency of human instruments, of the separation of intellectual work from manual work, of theory from experience" (Falaschi 602).

77. "Lightness," *Six Memos* 17. Calvino was a great admirer of Cervantes. In an interview (August 1981), having been asked about the absence of great heroes in modern literature, he remarked: "After all, we live in a time of very little faith. Anyway, I believe that even in the time of the Renaissance, the idea of the hero had already come to be treated a bit tongue in cheek. Ariosto is, in many respects, already a modern writer. But, of course, it's with Cervantes that modern literature actually begins" (Markey 79).

78. Jorge Luis Borges, "Tlön, Uqbar, Orbis Tertius," in *Ficciones*, ed. Anthony Kerrigan (New York: Grove Widenfeld, 1963) 30.

79. Selden 72. Peter Ackroyd, in his review of the novel, finds it spurious because there "is a hole right through the middle" of it which "lies within the narrator himself who has his circumference everywhere and his centre nowhere" (*The Spectator* 22 Feb. 1975: 214).

80. Borges 28. As in the case of Polo's invisible cities, Borges's city and planet are likewise not found in any encyclopedia or atlas.

81. Paul Bailey, "Italo Calvino: *Invisible Cities,*" *Times Literary Supplement* 21 Feb. 1975: 185.

82. Maria Corti, "Intervista: Italo Calvino," *Autografo* 2 (Oct. 1985): 51.

83. Quoted from *Literary Criticism and Theory*, ed. Robert Con Davies and Laurie Finke (New York: Longman, 1989) 712–18.

84. Francesca Bernardini Napoletano, *I segni nuovi di Italo Calvino* (Rome: Bulzoni, 1977) 186.

85. Culler 243.

86. "Berenice's Hair" is Mr. Palomar's favorite constellation.

87. Various critics have commented on Calvino's understanding of Utopia in *Invisible Cities*. Mengaldo sees "the delicate equilibrium between reality and Utopia moving gradually toward the latter" (Pier Vincenzo Mengaldo, "L'arco e le pietre (Calvino, *Le città invisibili*)," in *La tradizione del Novecento: Da D'Annunzio a Montale* [Milan: Feltrinelli, 1975] 414); Pautasso compares Calvino's utopian invisible city with the Augustinian *City of God* (Sergio Pautasso, "Favola, allegoria, utopia nell'opera di Italo Calvino," *Nuovi Argomenti* 33–34 [1973]: 67–94); Napoletano relates Polo's idea of Utopia to the aspirations of the Enlightenment (Napoletano

169–201); Olken considers Calvino's Utopia as a "loose but convenient metaphor" representative of every city, "real and imagined, no longer a locus of only dreams for an ideal future, nor only of vain nostalgia for the past" (I. T. Olken, *With Pleated Eye and Garnet Wing: Symmetries of Italo Calvino* [Ann Arbor: University of Michigan Press, 1984] 84); and finally, Christensen concludes that Calvino is "interested in his readers' Utopian projects, not with the historical backdrop of his text" (Peter G. Christensen, "Utopia in Calvino's *Invisible Cities,*" *Forum Italicum* 20 [Spring 1986]: 19).

88. In the Old Testament and in Christian literature, from Dante's *Inferno* to John Bunyan's *Vanity Fair,* hell has been traditionally symbolized as a crowded and evil city. Calvino seems to be echoing Josiah Strong's prophecy and concern, at the end of the last century, regarding metropolitanism: "The new civilization is certain to be urban; and the problem of the twentieth century will be the city" (Strong, *The Twentieth Century* [New York: Baker & Taylor., 1898] 53).

89. Carter sees Calvino's book as "very nearly . . . without characters: the cities are full of nameless 'inhabitants,' and the Khan and Polo are like disembodied oracles" (Carter 121).

90. Cesare Cases, "Calvino el il 'pathos della distanza,' " *Città aperta* 7–8 (1958): 33–35.

91. *Difficult Loves* (New York: Harcourt Brace, 1984) 270. The English version appropriately groups these two stories under the caption "Stories of Love and Loneliness."

92. Giuseppe Bonura, *Invito alla lettura di Italo Calvino* (Milan: Mursia, 1987) 143. According to Calligaris, at the center of *Difficult Loves* one finds "the mimesis of alienated existence" (Contardo Calligaris, *Italo Calvino* [Milan: Mursia, 1985] 63). Gatt-Rutter, on the other hand, notes that in these stories "Calvino's play comes most closely to grips with the world we live in and its everyday tension between Eros and Alienation" (Gatt-Rutter 50). Elsewhere, Gatt-Rutter observes that the taboo against Eros is political and that these stories show how "this repressed Eros seeks fulfillment (a meeting of human beings as *persons*) but never meets with more than a fraction of success" ("Calvino Ludens: Literary Play and Its Political Implications," *Journal of European Studies* 5 [1975]: 324).

93. Flavia Ravazzoli, "*Le città invisibili* di Italo Calvino: utopia linguistica e letteratura," *Strumenti Critici* 54 (May 1987): 201.

94. "Exactitude," *Six Memos* 71.

95. For my discussion regarding medieval and renaissance cities, I have availed myself to a great extent of Moshe Barasch's essay "The City," in *Dictionary of the History of Ideas,* ed. Philip P. Wilner (New York: Scribner's, 1973) 1: 427–34.

96. The city of Argia has earth instead of air, and ugly Zobeide is a trap; Leonia is being buried by its own garbage, and eventually the whole world will be covered by mounds of rubbish.

97. Jay Martin, "The Visible and Invisible Cities," in *Harvest of Change: American Literature 1865–1914* (Englewood Cliffs, New Jersey: Prentice-Hall, 1967) 277–78.

98. Mengaldo 415.

99. Robert Breiner, "Italic [sic] Calvino: the Place of the Emperor in *Invisible Cities,*" *Modern Fiction Studies* 34 (Winter 1988) 565.

100. Back cover, *Le città invisibili.*

101. *The Watcher and Other Stories* (New York: Harcourt Brace, 1975) 72.

102. Alexander Stille, "An Interview with Italo Calvino," *Saturday Review* (Mar–Apr. 1985): 39.

103. "Exactitude" 71.

104. Gore Vidal, "Fabulous Calvino," *The New York Review of Books* (20 May 1974): 20. In 1985 Calvino referred to *Invisible Cities* as "something between a fable and a *petit poème en prose*" ("Quickness" 49).

105. Falaschi 602.

106. "Lightness" 12. According to Bailey, the "lightness of the style works as a counterpart to the sombre view of human life it is expressing" (Bailey 185).

107. Salman Rushdie, "Calvino," *London Review of Books* 17–30 Sept. 1981: 16–17.

108. Updike, "Metropolises of the Mind" 462. Apropos Calvino's language, Angela Jeannet argues that he is "an author who truly lives in a world from which no one voice of the past is absent, and to which no human experience—but despair—is denied access" (Jeannet, "Italo Calvino's Invisible City," *Perspectives on Contemporary Literature* 3 [May 1977]: 47).

CHAPTER NINE

Calvino's Ultimate Hypernovel: *If on a winter's night a traveler*

I love his [Borges's] work because every one of his pieces contains a model of the universe or of an attribute of the universe (infinity, the innumerable, time eternal or present or cyclic).[1]

"The idea of infinite contemporary universes in which all possibilities are realized in all possible combinations" is one of the bases of what Calvino calls the "hypernovel" and which he put into practice when he wrote *If on a winter's night a traveler* in 1979.[2] His aim, writes the author, "was to give the essence of what a novel is by providing it in concentrated form, in ten beginnings; each beginning develops in very different ways from a common nucleus, and each acts within a framework that both determines and is determined."[3] Indeed, this successful combinatorial narrative experiment is composed of twelve numbered chapters interpolated with ten novels—or fragments of novels—all written by different authors. The numbered chapters function as frame tales for the fragments, while the action takes place on two distinct planes, one external and the other internal. On the first one, constituted by the the frames, the principal agents are an unnamed male reader, a female reader named Ludmilla, a mysterious swindler, and an Irish novelist; while on the second one, consisting of the narrative segments, the actions of both planes are intermingled.[4]

In this highly self-reflexive novel—or better, a novel about novels— Calvino questions once again, but with a keen sense of humor, his own narrative voice by satirizing modern fiction, particularly the poststructuralist discourse concerning the supremacy of reading over writing. Essentially, the author both restates and subverts, in perhaps his most complicated work, what he expressed in 1967: that once "the process of literary composition has been taken to pieces and reassembled, the decisive moment in literary life is bound to be the act of reading."[5] Calvino consecrates the process of narrative writing and at the same time demonstrates its failings. Geoffrey Green confirms this by indicating that for Calvino, "Any written text must submit to reading, an act that distorts as well as integrates, creates as well as reflects; in the process of reading the author's text, the reader becomes the author of a new and different text.''[6] This is corroborated in a sense by Calvino himself, who, upon the publication of the English edition of his novel in 1981, stated that his original intention was to write ''a book in which the reader would not be reading the text of a novel but a description of the act of reading *per se.*''[7] Thus Calvino becomes what Roland Barthes calls an *écrivain,* not a *scripteur,* who writes in an intransitive mode and whose concern is nothing but the activity of writing itself.

Now, if I may be permitted to adopt Calvino's narrative device, let us suppose that *you,* an avid admirer of Calvino's works (and the reader of *this* modest book, *Understanding Italo Calvino* by B. Weiss), have just found out that after several years of novelistic inactivity his latest novel, *If on a winter's night a traveler,* is available at your favorite bookstore.[8] You rush there and eagerly make your ways through the narrow passageways restricted by barricades of books, ''Books You Haven't Read, Books You Needn't Read, Books Made For Purposes Other Than Reading, Books Read Even Before You Open Them Since They Belong To The Category Of Books Read Before Being Written,'' and so forth. Finally, after many additional encounters with all sorts of book categories, you arrive at the location of ''New Books Whose Author Or Subjects Appeal To You, New Books By Authors Or On Subjects Not New, and New Books By Authors Or On Subjects Completely Unknown,'' and there, at last, you find a stack of *If on a winter's night a traveler* fresh off the press. Being impatient to see what the novel is about, you read the comments on the back of the jacket, ''reading around it before reading inside it,'' savoring the physical pleasure of a new book and anxiously waiting for the more ''substantial pleasure of the consummation of the act, namely the reading of the book'' (9). You suspect that you are in for a surprise because Calvino is known to change his way of writing from one book to the next, and it is this constant changing that allows ''you to recognize him as himself'' (9). This time, however, you will find that the change is far more pronounced because the novel shows absolutely no connection with what he has written before.

When you get home, you start reading the first page. But instead of a narrative text, you find the author's instructions, similar to those found in how-to manuals, on how to make yourself comfortable in preparation for reading:

You are about to begin reading Italo Calvino's new novel. . . . Relax. Concentrate. Dispel every other thought. Let the world around you fade. Best to close the door; the TV is always on in the next room. Tell the others right away, ''No, I don't want to watch TV!'' Raise your voice—they won't hear you otherwise—''I'm reading!

I don't want to be disturbed!'' Maybe they haven't heard you, with all that racket; speak louder, yell: "I'm beginning to read Italo Calvino's new novel!" Or if you prefer, don't say anything; just hope they'll leave you alone. (3)

By the time you have been told how to find an ideal reading position—stretch your legs on cushions, take your shoes off, adjust the light, cigarettes at hand, etc., you have reached the end of chapter 1.

The next chapter, entitled "If on a winter's night a traveler," begins in an almost traditional manner, except that we have to confront both internal and external actions. The first lines of the narrative text make this clear: "The novel begins in a railway station, a locomotive huffs, steam from a piston covers the opening of the chapter, a cloud of smoke hides part of the first paragraph" (10). The smoke, part of the internal action of the novel, affects also the reader's reading of the text by actually enveloping the physical body of the book and then by obscuring his view of the printed page. Then, the unnamed first person narrator tells "you" (*tu*, the familiar form of address), the internal fictive reader, of his mysterious encounter with a police chief named Gorin, to whom he is to hand over a suitcase. Yet when he tries to do so, he is told to clear out with the suitcase because "they have killed Jan''— apparently another secret agent—or he will meet with a similar fate. The narrator barely manages his escape on an outbound train. So ends the first narrative chapter.

What is striking is that Calvino addresses his novel to us, the traditional readers, and at the same time he creates an entirely new category of readership—the reader who is also a protagonist of the novel he is reading. One wonders who is or are the narratees, to use the critic Gerald Prince's term. How does one distinguish between reader and narratee? At times the actual reader may coincide or may not coincide with the person addressed by the narrator; at times they are distinct, synonymous, or overlapping. The other thing that catches our attention is that the first chapter, containing the author's instructions, is numbered while the second unit, containing the interrupted spy narrative, is not. You suspect that Calvino may be repeating the structure of *Invisible Cities,* insofar as there are both frame and narrative chapters in this novel as well. The other curiosity is that of narrative perspective, given that it is not the authorial voice which addresses the reader, but rather the narrator called "I." The latter is distinct from the author because he frequently refers to him and makes comments on his writing, such as: "For a couple of pages now you have been reading on. . . . Perhaps the auhor still has not made up his mind, just as you, reader, for that matter, are not sure what you would most like to read'' (12). This becomes even more pronounced when the narrator/protagonist enters the bar at the station and notices a woman patron:

> Your attention, as reader, is now completely concentrated on the woman, already for several pages you have been circling around her, I have—no, the author has—been circling around the feminine presence, for several pages you have been expecting this female shadow to take shape the way female shadows take shape on the written page, and it is your expectation, reader, that drives the author toward her; and I, too. (20)

Calvino's device of integrating the internal action of the text with the external action of the reader—one reality with another—recalls the dramatic techniques of Pirandello, especially his *Six Characters in Search of an Author*. In that play a distinction is made between the actors who play the role of actors engaged in rehearsing a play, and those actors who play the role of characters and lead the spectators, including the director and the other actors, into believing that they are living characters and not actors. Whereas Pirandello deals with the mystery of dramatic creation and the inability of the characters to materialize on the stage and present a drama never written for them, Calvino plays with the process of writing and reading. Like Pirandello, he too presents us with the passage from person (reader) to character, from having form to being form. In the dramatic instance we have the characters' desperate search for an author who would be willing to grant them their wish, while in the second case we have the readers' yearning for the complete story which keeps eluding them. In *The Purple Rose of Cairo*, Woody Allen's 1985 film, we encounter a similar integration of two distinct realities when players and audience participate in what happens in the film, which in turn is influenced by the goings-on in the theater where it is being shown. In fact, the hero of the movie notices from the screen one of his ardent admirers, speaks to her, comes out of the screen, joins her in the auditorium, and finally runs off with her, leaving the film and all its characters in complete disorder. We have here another example of the narrow line between external and internal realities, between art and life, as the character virtually enters the life of the admiring woman, and she enters into the make-believe world of the screen.[9]

Now back to Calvino's novel. When the fictive or internal reader turns to the next unit, or numbered chapter 2, there is no narrative text; there are only comments by the narrator/author to the reader/protagonist. We read:

> You have now read about thirty pages and you're becoming caught up in the story. . . . Just when you were beginning to grow truly interested, at this very

point the author feels called upon to display one of those virtuoso tricks so customary in modern writing. (25)

You wonder what is happening, and why all these interruptions. Upon turning the page, you become aware that from page 32 you have gone back to page 17. You would like to know what has happened to the man with the suitcase and anxiously look for page 33, but can't find it. The rest of the book keeps going from page 31 to 32 and then back to 17. It must be a printer's mistake which occurred during the binding of the volume, you are eventually told by the narrator.

The next day, when you take Calvino's novel back to the bookstore, you can't wait to get hold of a nondefective copy. The bookseller informs you that a part of the edition of the volume is defective and is being withdrawn from circulation. Apparently because of an error in the bindery, the printed signatures of Calvino's book got mixed up with those of the Polish novel *Outside the Town of Malbork* by Tazio Bazakbal. There are available, however, sound copies of Calvino's novel, and the clerk offers to exchange your copy. But since you have gotten so involved with the beginning of Bazakbal's narrative, you no longer are interested in Calvino's book and you request the Polish one instead. At this moment the clerk points to a young woman in the store who has come in with the same problem and also has exchanged her book for the Polish one. Consequently, the narrator tells you:

> The Other Reader makes her happy entrance into your field of vision, Reader, or, rather, into the field of your attention; or, rather, you have entered a magnetic field from whose attraction you cannot escape. (29)

You meet the woman, her name is Ludmilla, and start talking about books and particularly about Bazakbal's novel. You are impressed by her feminine beauty, her knowledge of literature, and her insights. She tells you: "I prefer novels that bring me immediately into a world where everything is precise, concrete, specific" (30). You want to impress her so you say that it would be funny if you thought you were reading the Polish novel and it turned out to be Calvino's instead. Before parting, you exchange telephone numbers so that you can call each other in the event the new volume should turn out to be defective too. "If there are two of us," you tell her, "we have a better chance of putting together a complete copy" (31). You go home with two different expectations: the pleasure of continuing your reading and the thought of seeing her again.

As you start reading, you realize that this activity is no longer solitary because the Other Reader is doing the same thing, and "the novel to be read is superimposed by a possible novel to be lived, the continuation of your story with her, or better still, the beginning of a possible story'' (32). From this moment on, the narrative will progress at various levels, and the Reader will pursue Ludmilla with the same excitement and curiosity with which one follows an interesting and titillating novel. Thus, the male and female readers enter into a relationship based solely on their passion for reading, which for them becomes a total experience as they pursue it together and experience it both literally and figuratively.

After you have cut open the pages of *Outside the Town of Malbork*—for you, too, reading becomes a *total* experience—from the very first lines you realize that this narrative has nothing to do with the previous one. The novel is a rather boring account of how the narrator, a young man, is forced by his family to leave home and spend some time on another farm in an exchange with Ponko, the son of the owner of another estate. When Ponko opens up his trunk and the narrator shows great interest in the picture of Zwida, Ponko's girl, the two come to blows. As the narrator leaves for Ponko's village, he savors the moment he will meet Zwida and take the other man's place. But suddenly, just when your attention as reader, ''is gripped by the suspense, in the middle of a decisive sentence, you turn the page and find yourself facing two blank sheets'' (42). You keep turning the pages and find that the next two are printed properly, but they too are followed by blanks. This is repeated until the end of the book. Worse still, the various parts of the narrative text are not connected: the names are not Polish, the characters are different, and so are the settings. You finally conclude that this is not the Polish novel you thought you were reading. You look up the places in an encyclopedia and learn that the action is taking place in Cimmeria.[10]

As you continue with your reading, the same interruptions and frustrations will occur with the remaining novels, always left unfinished at the most interesting point.[11] You note that each of the ten narratives has its own style and takes place in a different country, ranging from Italy, to Eastern Europe, the Soviet Union, and South America; there are even some imaginary countries. All in all, the narratives represent a parody of contemporary fiction— the magic realism characteristic of Latin American novels, Eastern European political fiction, Japanese erotic prose, and detective stories. Eventually even the frame tales are interrupted by dreams, diary entries, political plots, repressive censors, secret agents, and other fortuitous events over which the Reader has no control.

In the Italian version the terms *Lettore* (Reader) and *Lettrice* (Other Reader) are used; the first denotes a generic or male reader and the second strictly a female reader. This is significant because of the pronounced sexual connotations regarding the act of reading in which Calvino's text abounds.[12] In fact, by stating that reading results in a "substantial pleasure of the consummation of the act" (9), and that a book must be "properly bound, so we won't be interrupted right at the climax" (31), the author echoes the connection between reading and lovemaking (for Freud the act of writing was wrought with sexual symbolism) found in Roland Barthes's *The Pleasure of the Text*. Indeed, Calvino stated quite categorically that literature is for him the "only aphrodisiac" and that "reading is a possession, a march toward a possession. It has many degrees of eroticism. It can be a caress or a complete intercourse."[13] Nonetheless, the entire reading experience of both male and female readers will turn out to be a classical example of coitus interruptus because every time they think that they have gotten hold of a complete novel, at the very moment of excitement their reading suddenly is interrupted, at first, ostensibly, because of a printer's error and then by the machinations of a shady character by the name of Ermes Marana.

Perhaps the best example of the sexual metaphor of the act of reading, as well as an example of identification between the reader who is reading and the reader who is being read, occurs in chapter 7, when the unnamed *Lettore* and Ludmilla, the *Lettrice,* are in bed together, and the narrator for the first time addresses them in the second person plural because he considers them a "single subject." As their bodies are "trying to find, skin to skin, the adhesion most generous in sensations, to transmit and receive vibrations and waves" (154), they both carefully and passionately read each others anatomies. As Ludmilla is being read, her "body is being subjected to a systematic reading, through channels of tactile information, visual, olfactory, and not without some intervention of the taste buds. Hearing also has its role, alert to your gasps and your trills" (155). And when the woman reads her partner's physique, she reviews his body "as if skimming the index, and at some moments she consults it as if gripped by sudden and specific curiosities, then she lingers, questioning it and waiting till a silent answer reaches her, as if every partial inspection interested her only in the light of a wider spatial reconnaissance." She carefully covers his body as one covers a book, "pages and pages from top to bottom without skipping a comma" (155–56). The only difference from the reading of written pages is that reading each other's bodies is not linear. In either case, however, the experience is unique and unrepeatable, observes the novel's narrator. The scene is a perfect example of the novel's self-referentiality or self-reflexive reading: one internal reader reads the other the way we external readers read about them reading each other. For

Calvino the pleasurable act of reading is not only tantamount to the act of sex and the excitement leading to it, but, as has been pointed out by Wiley Feinstein, the author also "uses the sexual metaphor in order to focus on reading's most disturbing aspect. Calvino's doubt is that reading, like sex, does not allow escape from separateness for either reader or author. . . . Reader-author relationships are therefore just as doomed to failure as sexual relationships."[14]

So far, we have seen how *If on a winter's night a traveler* is not just one novel, but a composite of ten unfinished narratives (plus twelve frames), each reflecting a different author, story, style, place, and theme. But why are the narratives unfinished, and who is the culprit that interrupts them at the reader's highest moment of suspense? Who is this mysterious archenemy of reading who takes pleasure in frustrating both internal and external readers and bears the name of the Greek divinity Hermes, which means "interpreter" or "mediator"? Although the god's task was to conduct the souls of the dead to Hades, for the ancients he also epitomized the power of the spoken word and was regarded a most sinister thief. Having stolen the bow and quiver of Apollo, the girdle of Venus, the trident of Neptune, the tools of Vulcan, and the sword of Mars, he was appropriately called the god of thieves. Indeed, as we continue reading the hypernovel, at every turn we get the impression of confronting someone comparable to Professor Moriarty, the malevolent mastermind of crimes and inveterate enemy of Sherlock Holmes. Calvino's swindler and plotter of literary intrigues, who creates chaos among writers, readers, and in the publishing world, is truly a modern version of Ser Cepelletto, Boccaccio's notorious notary who felt great shame and disappointment when any legal document he had drawn up was discovered to be "anything but fraudulent" (*Decameron* 1.1). Calvino's "I" narrator characterizes Marana as "a serpent who injects his malice into the paradise of reading" (125), while Ludmilla, the Other Reader, laments that "whatever he touches, if it isn't false already, becomes false" (152). It is he who has created havoc in the publishing world by mixing up the signatures of the ten novels "that begin and don't continue" (97), and by translating a trashy novel and then passing it off to the publishers as Cimmerian, Cimbrian, and then Polish without knowing a single word of these languages. He claims to be the founder of OAP (Organization of Apocryphal Power), a sect of pirates "consecrated to the worship and the unearthing of secret books" (119), and a representative of OEPHLW of New York (Organization for the Electronic Production of Homogenized Literary Works), which offers technical assistance to writers incapable of finishing their novels. And finally, true to his name, among his many shady deals he also passes himself off as an agent of the Mercury and Muses Agency, "specializing in the advertising and exploitation of literary and philosophical works" (120).

It is quite possible that Calvino may be using the name Ermes (Hermes) in order to parody hermeneutics as a theory of interpretation. Richard Palmer notes Martin Heidegger's insistence that the term be understood as related to the Greek god; that *hermeneuein* not only signifies to "interpret," but also it has come to mean "to say," "to explain," "to translate." Palmer adds that "*hermeneuein* is that laying-open of something which brings a message, insofar as what is being exposed can become a message."[15] Calvino's intent may very well have been to show that hermeneutics, once used strictly for the interpretation of sacred texts, now is applied to all kinds of texts; and that on the basis of the hermeneutic circle a paradox emerges from "the fact that the reader cannot understand any part of the text until the whole is understood, while the whole cannot be understood until the parts are understood."[16] Clearly the paradoxical hermeneutic circle is present in *If on a winter's night a traveler* because both the parts and the whole are either missing or incomplete, thereby making understanding or interpretation impossible. For Calvino the text has become profane, it is no longer sacred, and therefore all interpretation (or reading) is misinterpretation. In spite of Marana's feverish activities, he is never present; we never see him or meet him directly in the text. Figuratively he is representative of translators, who, regardless of their significant contributions to literature as a whole, are never seen or regarded in high esteem by critics and readers, who take them for granted. Like Hermes/Mercury, Ermes Marana is a mediator between the original source of text and the final book, whose task as translator requires him to falsify, to change, and to deceive. Because of this, Marana is condemned by Calvino to fulfill the aphorism that every translator is a traitor (*traduttore traditore*). William Weaver, who has translated into English most of Calvino's fiction, notes that the author did not "cherish his translators" and was extremely suspicious of them; that he found him difficult to translate and hard to please: "With Calvino, every word had to be weighed. . . . Every word had to be sounded. . . . Every repetition had to be judged; every rhythm had to be tested." Weaver adds that "Calvino would have preferred to translate his books for himself, if that had been possible."[17]

But in a literal sense, why is Marana bent on bringing devastation to literary circles throughout the world? As we eventually find out in chapter 7, his machinations were not set in motion because of his criminal tendency, but rather by a jealousy brought about by Ludmilla's extreme love for reading books. He is resentful of

> the invisible rival who came constantly between him and Ludmilla, the silent voice that speaks to her through books, this ghost with a thousand faces and faceless, all the more elusive since for Ludmilla authors are never incarnated in individuals of flesh and blood, they exist for her only in published pages, the living and the dead both are there always ready to communicate with her, to amaze her, and Ludmilla is always ready to follow them, in the fickle, carefree relations one can have with incorporeal persons. (159)

Marana is no doubt a Calvino incarnation of deconstruction. He dreams of a "literature made entirely of apocrypha, of false attributions, of imitations and counterfeits and pastiches" (159), and rather than sever the last thread that ties him to her, he goes on "sowing confusion among titles, authors' names, pseudonyms, languages, translations, editions, jackets, title pages, chapters, beginnings, ends," so that Ludmilla will be compelled to acknowledge "those signs of his presence, his greeting without hope of an answer" (239). By creating a literature made entirely of apocrypha, false attributions, imitations and counterfeits, Marana hopes that he will no longer feel abandoned by Ludmilla, now totally absorbed in her reading, and that between "the book and her there would always be insinuated the shadow of mystification, and he, identifying himself with every mystification, would have affirmed his presence" (159).

To this end, Marana targets the Irish novelist Silas Flannery,[18] Calvino's obvious alter ego, who is trying to cope with a dry period of artistic creativity: he can no longer complete the numerous novels he has begun to write and for which he has received advances from various publishers. Thus, Calvino injects a different impasse into the text; the narratives are now interrupted by both external and internal causes, when they are being constructed as well as when they are being read or consummated. The same happens to Marana's letters, which are also all incomplete. Moreover, because of Marana the Irishman's manuscripts first disappear and then, when they are mysteriously returned, they are no longer the same. Although a team of ghost writers, "experts in imitating the master's style in all its nuances and mannerisms," is standing by to step in and complete the unfinished narratives so that "no reader could distinguish the parts written by one hand from those of another" (121), Flannery refuses to be helped. Instead, he starts writing a diary, a record of reflections, in which nothing really happens. This diary—the only true book he can write—is revealing because it allows us to penetrate Calvino's most intimate ideas pertaining to the relationship between writer, reader, and text. In these self-conscious reflections on the telling and reading of stories, Calvino lays bare his artistic spirit, his satisfactions and frustrations.[19] According to Teresa De Lauretis, these are meditations, "but in the form of fiction, in the style of a consummate narrative art that is conscious of being at once fantasy and reality."[20]

Like Calvino, who worked extensively as both editor and writer, Flannery too has gone astray and lost the capacity for "disinterested reading." Whenever he reads something written by someone else, he cannot help but compare it to his own work to the extent that he has become "a slave laborer of writing" and "the pleasure of reading has finished for me" (169). He is similarly dissatisfied with his inability to express himself fully as he would like: the distance between his writings and his readers seems "unbridgeable" and whatever he writes "bears the stamp of artifice and incongruity" (170). A similar distance exists between the author and his writings because he considers himself less important than they are. For Flannery, reading is clearly paramount to writing because it is quite personal and a far more individual act: "If we assume that writing manages to go beyond the limitations of the author," notes the novelist, "it will continue to have a meaning only when it is read by a single person and passes through his mental circuits" (176).

But who is this powerful reader who controls the outcome of narrative texts? Is it the *Lettore,* or the beautiful *Lettrice?* The former could at least be satisfied if he were provided with the continuation of the stories he has begun to read, including the object of his desire, the *Lettrice.* Ludmilla, however, can never be satisfied with the books she is reading. In fact, she is constantly rejecting Marana's and Flannery's works, including, by implication, those of Calvino. The reason, notes Feinstein, is that the author is "incapable of pleasing this typical reader" who "also represents the author himself as his own (always unsatisfied) reader." Thus, Calvino is not only identified with Marana and Flannery, but he also "peers at us from behind the mask of yet another character in the novel," the independent female reader.[21]

Ludmilla is a curious and insatiable reader who uncovers truths hidden in fakery and falsity. For her, reading "is going toward something that is about to be, and no one yet knows what it will be. . . ." (72); and the novel should have "as its driving force only the desire to narrate, to pile stories upon stories" (92) and "make you feel uneasy from the very first page" (126). In keeping with the structure of *If on a winter's night a traveler,* she reads several books at once in order "to avoid being caught by the disappointment that any story might cause her'' (147); and the novels that attract her the most are ''those that create an illusion of transparency around a knot of human relationships as obscure, cruel, and perverse as possible'' (192). But what makes her an impossible reader more than anything else is that

> reading means stripping herself of every purpose, every foregone conclusion, to be ready to catch a voice that makes itself heard when you least expect it, a voice that comes from an unknown source, from somewhere beyond the book, beyond the author, beyond the conventions of writing: from the unsaid, from what the world has not yet said of itself and does not yet have the words to say. (239)

Hoping to satisfy such a reader, Flannery perseveres in effacing the presence of the author vis-à-vis the text and reader by musing about the true book he would like to write. Its subject matter consists of ''something that already exists: thoughts already thoughts, dialogue already spoken, stories already happened, places and settings seen'' (171). The book ''should be simply the equivalent of the unwritten world translated into writing'' or it should be ''the written counterpart of the unwritten world; its subject should be what does not exist and cannot exist except when written'' (172). Inevitably, Calvino leads to the conclusion that the entire literary process is one of mystification, as exemplified by Marana. That it is all a hoax, and instead of a book one could write ''lists of words, in alphabetical order, an avalanche of isolated words which expresses that truth I still do not know, and from which the computer, reversing its program, could construct the book, my book'' (189). This being the case, it is not surprising that Calvino's texts are unfinished and are marked by so many interruptions that create voids and blanks which ask to be filled. But this should not matter because, according to Borges's notion of the Book as the Universe, all books are written by the same author, whose stories are only variations of a single plot which runs through every conceivable permutation.[22] And Salman Rushdie points out that all ten of the unfinished novels are ''transformations of the eternally-beginning story.''[23] In fact, for Flannery (read Calvino) ''the author of every book is a fictitious character whom the existent author invents to make him the author of his fictions'' (180). In essence, Calvino remakes the image of self and reader, very much in accordance with Wayne Booth's findings that ''the author creates, in short, an image of himself and another image of his reader; he makes his reader, as he makes his second self, and the most successful reading is one in which the created selves, author and reader, can find complete agreement.''[24] But Calvino deliberately fails to follow the latter part of

Booth's statement; not only does he diminish the significance of the author vis-à-vis the text and the reader, but he also sabotages the identity and integrity of the author, "who is dissolved in the cloud of fictions that covers the world with its thick sheath" (180). This accounts for Calvino's narrator's apologia for producing too many stories at once: "What I want is for you to feel, around the story, a saturation of other stories that I could tell and maybe will tell or who knows may already have told on some other occasion" (109). Similarly, Silas Flannery conceives of writing a fragmentary book consisting only of an "*incipit,* that maintains for its whole duration the potentiality of the beginning, the expectation still not focused on an object. But how could such a book be constructed? Would it break off after the first paragraph? Would the preliminaries be prolonged indefinitely?" (177). Iban Hassan notes that "fragmentation—literature as bits and pieces rather than as an integrated totality"—is a basic property of postmodernism. Yet these fragments, adds the critic, give us the impression that they are part of a "hidden matrix, or synthesis."[25]

Feinstein argues convincingly that Flannery "represents Calvino the Writer," that Marana "is a stand-in for Calvino the Critic," and that the unity of *If on a winter's night a traveler* is to be found in "the simultaneity of narrating and theorizing."[26] In fact, the entire book is devoted to questions pertaining to the creation of a story, its writing, narrating, reading, as well as the fundamental reality of a text. Therefore, Calvino's novel does not tell a full story, but rather the novel offers instead itself. Nuccia Bencivegna argues this point when she explains that the novel's stories are unrelated and always interrupted because for the author they do not really matter:

> The only thing that matters here is the process of writing and reading stories. . . . The book wants to have no story. The book wants to put all possible stories in parentheses, and does so by having different stories cancel each other. The book wants to talk about the text and its vicissitudes, about its being written and immediately transformed by its readers.[27]

Similarly, Linda Hutcheon notes that postmodernist fiction is self-referring or autorepresentational; that it is narcissistic because it "provides, within itself, a commentary on its own status as fiction and as language, and also on its own processes of production and reception."[28]

One is never sure where Calvino stands because he never firmly commits himself. Perhaps this is due to the new expectations a contemporary writer has to face and fulfill—what Said refers to as "an intensified confusion of production with product, of career with text, of textuality with sexuality, of image with career."[29] In fact, after meandering from semiotics through post-structuralism to total textual self-referentiality, what Calvino seems to refute is Barthes's contention that the novel is a lie[30] and that fiction's only reference can be found in itself. But even though he questions the predominance of reader over author, he does not deny the centrality of the text. Eventually, by taking contemporary literary trends and discourse and stretching them to their logical and chilling conclusions, he humorously satirizes the notion that only the interaction between reader and text counts; that the author is no longer vital, that he is dead. And finally, in undermining his own novel through an intense deconstructive reading by treating it as a self-referential play devoid of any certainty, Calvino tries to show the absurdity reached by the practitioners of modern literary theories who with their zeal are killing invention and fantasy in literature. These fads, which have passed their limit, have resulted in chaos rather than in reason and order; and like the apocryphal Marana, they are destroying our ability to write and to read. In this vein, Giorgio Bárberi Squarotti correctly characterizes *If on a winter's night a traveler* as

> a discourse, conducted with a margin of irony and playfulness, concerning the dissolution of the forms of literature. The work which is sought in the book is always different from the one which keeps presenting and revealing itself. Similarly, the author changes into another name, in another face, another time, another country of origin, another program of writing, another style, another way of being. He exists in too many different ways for us to say that he really exists, just as the work starts in too many different forms for us to identify its comprehensiveness.[31]

Literature, continues Bárberi Squarotti, although it still has beginnings of stories, no longer offers any unraveling or conclusions. "The modern encyclopedia of literature can therefore be only the collection of all the beginnings," and its conclusion can be found in life because, after all, the male reader marries Ludmilla. Another possibility is that the true conclusion exists in literature itself, in the new book which encompasses all styles, various contents and forms, and is offered to the protagonist "as the beginning of the unfindable book." What remains in the end, even after both readers' literary and carnal consummation, is a "new book on the impossibility of finding books, reading novels after the first few pages, identifying authors, knowing their nationality, intentions, poetics, language, age."[32] In spite of the fact that literature is irremediably unfinished and lost, concludes Bárberi Squarotti, it is also all that remains.

Ironically, the contention of the primacy of reading over writing is paradoxically self-defeating because Calvino uses text to underscore this primacy in the first instance, and writing is used to undermine itself in the second instance. A similar paradox is noted by Linda Hutcheon, who points out that the readers of postmodernist fiction are "the distanced, yet involved, co-producers of the novel," and that "it is fiction itself that is attempting to bring to readers' attention their central and enabling role."[33] Ultimately we may all end up using a computer for the creation of stories and an electronic scanner for reading them.[34] In fact, this is what Ludmilla's sister, Lotaria, puts into practice by using a computer that reads an entire novel in a few minutes and records the frequency of all the words contained in the text. The list of word frequencies allows her to "form an idea of the problems the book suggests," and directs her "straight for the words richest in meaning," which give her "a fairly precise notion of the book" (186). Thus, reading loses the ability to be *utile et dulce* (useful and pleasurable) as it is reduced to the mechanical recording of word frequencies and thematic recurrences.

The dénouement of the puzzling interruptions comes in chapter 11, when it is time for the forlorn reader's "tempest-tossed vessel to come to port"(253). The Reader decides to go to the library in the hope of finding the "ten novels that evaporated" in his hands. But even though the authors and the titles he is looking for appear in the catalog, they are all unavailable: on loan, at the bindery, inaccessible, wrongly cataloged, etc. While the library staff is searching for the vanished novels, the Reader (*Lettore*) meets seven other readers, each of whom expresses an opinion on the act of reading and also expounds on reader-oriented theories—what Calvino has referred to as "a kind of encyclopedia on the art of reading."[35] The first one states that if a book truly interests him, he can only follow it for a few lines because his mind becomes so stimulated that he wanders from thought to thought, image to image. It is the stimulus of reading that is important to him, and therefore he manages to read only a few pages which, nonetheless, already enclose for him "whole universes" that he "can never exhaust" (254). For the second reader, reading is a discontinuous, fragmentary operation and it has no end. This is why he keeps rereading everything, "each time seeking the confirmation of a new discovery" (255). The third reader agrees with the previous one, although at each rereading he confronts a new book and experiences "different and unexpected impressions" (255). He wonders if it is he who is changing or if it is the activity of reading, "a construction that assumes form," and something "that cannot be repeated twice according to the same pattern" (255). He concludes that "reading is an operation without object; or that its true object is itself. The book is an accessory aid, or even a pretext" (255). For the fourth, every new book he reads becomes a part of all the books, the sum of all his readings. Therefore, following the Borgesian paradigm, he has done nothing "but continue the reading of a single book" (256). The same is true for the next speaker, for whom all books lead to a single book containing a story of which all the stories he reads carry its echo. For the sixth reader what counts most is the moment that precedes reading. At times, a title, the *incipit*,[36] or the first sentences of a book, sets his imagination going. It is the expectation of pleasure that excites him. And finally, the last reader explains that for him it is the end that counts; that his "gaze digs between the words to try to discern what is outlined in the distance, in the spaces that extend beyond the words 'the end' " (256).

When it is the turn of the novel's "absolute protagonist" (219)—that is, the Reader (*Lettore*)—to speak, not surprisingly he turns out to be rather traditional in his expectations: he likes to read only what is written; he wants to be able to connect the details with the whole and to consider what he reads as something definitive; he separates one book from another and prefers to read books from beginning to end without any interruption or sudden suspension. At this point the fifth reader explains that the story he was referring to, but of which he only remembers the beginning, comes from the *Arabian Nights*;[37] and that although he is collating various editions of the text, he has not been able to find that story. Hoping to find the answer to his quest, he starts to narrate the story whose ending he cannot remember. One night, the Caliph Harun-al-Rashid leaves his palace disguised as a merchant. In a palace court he meets a beautiful maiden seated on a silver chair and surrounded by seven men—identical to the number of readers. She takes a pearl necklace consisting of seven white pearls and one black pearl, breaks the string, and drops the pearls into a cup. She tells the men that he who draws by lot the black pearl must kill the caliph and bring her his head. As a reward she will give herself to him. But if he refuses to kill the caliph, then the other seven men will kill him, also repeating the drawing of lots for the black pearl. When the disguised caliph draws the ominous pearl, he is ready to obey " 'on condition that you tell me what offense of the Caliph has provoked your hatred,' he asks, anxious to hear the story" (258). As one might expect, we never find out the answer because at this point Calvino's narrator, who cannot remember the title of the story, tells the Reader to give it a title. And so the Reader adds "*He asks, anxious to hear the story*" to the list of titles he has asked for unsuccessfully in the library. This way he discovers that the list containing all the titles of the ten unfinished narratives, plus the one based on the last line of the *Arabian Nights* unfinished story, form a complete grammatical sentence:

> *If on a winter's night a traveler, outside the town of Malbork, leaning from the steep slope without fear of wind or vertigo, looks down in the gathering shadow in a network of lines that enlace, in a network of lines that intersect, on the carpet of leaves illuminated by the moon around an empty grave—What story down there awaits its end?—he asks, anxious to hear the story.* (258)

The text's circularity and reliance on repetition is paradigmatic of postmodernism, and Calvino uses the same device at various points of *If on a winter's night a traveler.* A good example of this as well as of the novel's self-referentiality can be found in chapter 8, in Flannery's diary:

> I have had the idea of writing a novel composed only of beginnings of novels. The protagonist could be a Reader who is continually interrupted. The Reader buys the new novel A by the author Z. But it is a defective copy, he can't go beyond the beginning. . . . He returns to the bookshop to have the volume exchanged. . . .
> I could write it all in the second person: you Reader. . . . I could also introduce a young lady, the Other Reader, and a counterfeiter-translator, and an old writer who keeps a diary like this diary. . . . (197–98)

As Szegedy-Maszák has pointed out in his discussion of postmodernism and in reference to the writings of authors such as Borges, Barth, and other postmodernists—which could also be applied to Calvino's hypernovel—"there is no progress, only repetition. Accordingly narration is not teleological but circular."[38] The other readers of *If on a winter's night a traveler,* who think that the titles are actually the start of yet another novel, continue to quibble over whether every story ought to have a beginning and an end. When they lament that in ancient times, after having passed all tests, "the hero and the heroine married, or else they died" (259), the Reader reflects on these words and suddenly he decides to marry Ludmilla. Thus he follows in the footsteps of Italo Svevo's Zeno, who declares himself cured of his neuroses when he realizes that the only cure for life, or disease, is death.

Silas Flannery notes in his diary that on the wall facing his desk there is a poster of the dog Snoopy seated at a typewriter, with the caption: "It was a dark and stormy night . . ." (176). Every time the frustrated author sits down to write, he reads the poster's *incipit* (heading or beginning), which allows him to leave this reality for "the time and space of the written word" and lets him "feel the thrill of a beginning that can be followed by multiple developments, inexhaustibly" (177). The poster captures the essence of Edward W. Said's book *Beginnings*. Said considers "a beginning" a creative and critical activity, as well as a frame of mind. And for all writers the choice of a beginning is crucial because it determines much of what follows, given that it is "the main entrance to what it offers." A beginning, which also implies return and repetition, becomes "*making* or *producing difference* . . .—difference which is the result of combining the already-familiar with the fertile novelty of human work in language," rather than a linear attainment or completion.[39] Calvino begins his novel with the knowledge that he does not really know where to start, as well as with a full awareness of the difficulty of creating a beginning when all traditional forms of discourse are undermined by the practitioners of contemporary literary theories. But he is not interested in just one beginning, but in ten beginnings—a virtual periphrastic sequence of beginnings—all without endings, because the *topos* of his narratives, their idée fixe and internal coherence, consists precisely of their Pirandellian incompleteness. In fact, in this multidirectional novel the point of departure is really the conclusion, and the discontinuity of the stories is actually continuity. As Said points out in his study, every writer's desired goal is a true whole, one in which "individual segments are subordinated to the totality of collective integration and collective affirmation."[40] This is why Calvino's novel culminates in the Readers' conjugal bed with a blissful merging of both external and internal actions, that is, with the final and conclusive reading of *If on a winter's night a traveler* by its two major protagonists. Indeed, the ultimate consummation of the novel, both in terms of reading and sex, occurs in the matrimonial bed of both Readers, when Ludmilla says to her new husband: "Turn off your light, too. Aren't you tired of reading?" And he replies: "Just a moment, I've almost finished *If on a winter's night a traveler* by Italo Calvino" (260). By giving the frametale a traditional happy ending yet refusing to do so to the novels, Calvino underlines the primacy of the former over the latter.[41] With this conclusion Calvino shows that there is after all meaning in fiction, and that not every literary text collapses or destroys itself when subjected to literary analysis or when reduced to nothing but codes, patterns, or language.

At the beginning of *If on a winter's night a traveler*, Ludmilla notes that for her "reading is going toward something that is about to be, and no one yet knows what it will be" (72). Perhaps Calvino had in mind the sultan's curiosity about the outcome of Sheherezade's tales, as well as the ability of the reader "to enter the text from any direction" and, at the same time, "to open and close the text's signifying process without respect for the signified."[42] Although Calvino shows that the novel, far from being a dead form, is still breathing and capable of manifesting itself in many forms, he nonetheless yearns nostalgically for a return to good old-fashioned natural reading, when a sense of marvel, of innocent curiosity and suspense, drove unspoiled readers to discover new worlds, new ideas, new experiences, and new situations. This, I think, is the lesson we can learn from Calvino's ironic, self-conscious, and metafictional tour de force, as well as from the two Readers' search for a readable and pleasurable text.

NOTES

1. "Multiplicity," *Six Memos for the Next Millennium* (Cambridge: Harvard University Press, 1988) 119.
2. *If on a winter's night a traveler* (New York: Harcourt Brace, 1981) 8–9. Page numbers referring to this edition are shown in parentheses.
3. "Multiplicity" 120.
4. Instead of *Lettore* and *Lettrice*, William Weaver's terms "Reader" and "Other Reader" will be used throughout this chapter.
5. "Cybernetics and Ghosts," *The Uses of Literature* 15.
6. Geoffrey Green, "Ghosts and Shadows: Reading and Writing in Italo Calvino's *If on a winter's night a traveler*," *Review of Contemporary Fiction* 6 (Spring 1986): 101.
7. Francine du Plessix Gray, "Visiting Italo Calvino," *The New York Times Book Review* (21 June 1981): 22.
8. *If on a winter's night a traveler* was Calvino's last major work to appear in print (1979) prior to his move from Paris to Rome, and almost seven years after the publication of *Invisible Cities*.
9. Maurizio Nichetti's film *Il ladro di saponette* [1990] (*The Icicle Thief*), a comic satire of De Sica's *Il ladro di biciclette* (*The Bicycle Thief*), follows in the same Pirandellian artistic tradition. However, this time the text is framed within a TV movie broadcast which is constantly interrupted by commercials and mindlessly viewed by a family. At a certain point, the various levels of reality interact with each other: a blonde from the glamorous commercial enters the bleak world of the black and white feature film; the neorealistic characters of the film enter the colorful and rich milieu of the commercial world, and, finally, the director enters his own film in a desperate attempt to bring order back to his artwork.
10. This is remindful of Borges' story "Tlön, Uqbar, Orbis Tertius," where the narrator searches atlases and encyclopedias, but can't find the slightest mention of Uqbar.
11. Salman Rushdie points out that each of the ten novels is a "transmogrified avatar of the previous one" (Rushdie, "Calvino," *London Review of Books* 17–30 Sept. 1981): 16.
12. Regarding the role of the reader, in his novel *Hopscotch*, Cortázar distinguishes among various types of readers: the *lector-hembra* (easily satisfied passive reader), the *lector-alondra* (a derogatory synonym for passive reader), and the *lector cómplice* (active, demanding reader). It is the last one who truly interests him. *Hembra* means female, *alondra* lark, and *cómplice* accomplice.
13. Francine du Plessix Gray, "Visiting Italo Calvino," in *The New York Times Book Review* (21 June 1981): 23.

185

14. Wiley Feinstein, "The Doctrinal Core of *If on a winter's night a traveler,*" *Calvino Revisited,* ed. Franco Ricci (Toronto: Dove Editions, 1989) 152.

15. Quoted from Chris Schreiner, "Modern Critical Terms, Schools, and Movements," *Dictionary of Literary Biography: Modern American Critics Since 1955,* ed. Gregory S. Joy (Detroit: Gale Research Co., 1988) 67: 292.

16. Quoted from Greig E. Henderson, Glossary, *Critical Survey of Literary Theory,* ed. Frank N. Magill (Pasadena: Salem Press, 1987) 4: 1809.

17. William Weaver, "Calvino: An Interview and Its Story," *Calvino Revisited* 19.

18. Calvino may have chosen the name Silas Flannery because of its association with that of Flannery O'Connor or George Eliot's *Silas Marner;* or perhaps that of movie actor, Sean Connery. In O'Connor's "A Good Man Is Hard to Find," a psychopathic murderer kills in an attempt to force God to reveal himself.

19. The diary is actually a "paratext," according to Said's definition of the term, because Calvino explores in it his "working problems in making a text." According to the critic, "One of the critical distinctions of modern literature is the importance given by the writer to his own paratexts." Said goes on to cite James's *Notebooks,* Gide's *Journals,* Rilke's *Letters,* Valéry's *Cahiers,* and Kafka's journals as examples of paratexts (Edward W. Said, *Beginnings: Intention and Method* [New York: Basic Books, 1975] 251).

20. Teresa De Lauretis, "Italo Calvino: In Memoriam," *Science-Fiction Studies* 13 (Mar. 1986): 98. Rushdie characterizes the novel as "the most outrageous fiction about fiction ever conceived." (Rushdie 17).

21. Feinstein 153.

22. See epigraph at the beginning of this chapter. In Borgesian terms, if all men are one man, it follows that all books have been written by the same author, who is timeless, anonymous, and whose stories are variations of a single plot ("Tlön, Uqbar, Orbis Tertius" 27).

23. Rushdie 17.

24. Wayne Booth, *The Rhetoric of Fiction* (Chicago: University of Chicago Press, 1971) 138. In his 1967 essay "Whom Do We Write For? or The Hypothetical Bookshelf," Calvino states that literature must anticipate a public that is "*more cultured than the writer himself,* and invent a 'himself' who knows more than he does," in order "to speak to someone who knows more still" (*The Uses of Literature* [New York: Harcourt Brace, 1986] 85).

25. Ihab Hassan, "Pluralism in Postmodern Perspective," in *Exploring Postmodernism,* ed. Douwe W. Fokkema (Philadelphia: J. Benjamins, 1987) 19.

26. Feinstein 151.

27. Nuccia Bencivegna,"Caliphs, Travelers, and Other Stories," *Forum Italicum* 20 (Spring 1986): 4.

28. Linda Hutcheon, *Narcissistic Narrative: The Metafictional Paradox* (New York: Rutledge, 1991) xii. In addition to the terms self-referring, autorepresentational, and self-conscious used to describe narrative narcissism, she also includes the following not quite synonymous adjectives: self-reflective, self-informing, self-reflexive, and auto-referential (p. 1–2).

29. Said 263.

30. Roland Barthes, *Writing Degree Zero* (New York: Hill and Wang, 1968) 33.

31. Giorgio Bárberi Squarotti, "Dal *Castello* a *Palomar:* Il destino della letteratura," in *Italo Calvino. Atti del Convegno internazionale* ed. Giovanni Falaschi (Milan: Garzanti, 1988) 340.

32. Bárberi Squarotti 341.

33. Hutcheon xii.

34. It is ironic that Calvino, who was so well versed in the latest scientific advances and wrote repeatedly about the use of the computer in our civilization, never owned one. During an interview in 1984 he stated: "I don't have one yet, but I'm beginning to feel the need for one. I think it might free my mind from many menial duties and open up my memory space to higher tasks. . . . Yet the presence of a new gadget in the home would only increase my irritabilities"

(Giulio Nascimbeni, "A colloquio con lo scrittore in occasione dell'uscita di *Cosmicomiche vecchie e nuove*," *Corriere della Sera* (5 Dec. 1984): 3.

35. Gregory L. Lucente, "An Interview with Italo Calvino," *Contemporary Literature* 26 (1985): 248.

36. Apparently, Calvino contemplated using *Incipit* as a title for his novel. (Guido Almansi, "The Gnac Factor," *London Magazine* 20 (Oct. 1980): 62.

37. In *The Arabian Nights' Entertainment* or *A Thousand and One Nights*, the sultan takes a new wife each night and puts her to death the next morning. The ingenious wife Scheherezade, however, avoids being killed by keeping him amused from one night to the next by telling him stories which she breaks off before they are finished, and then completes the following evening. The sultan cannot bear to kill her because he wants to know how each story ends. After 1001 nights he revokes his decree. Very much like Calvino's interrupted stories, Scheherezade's tales cover a wide spectrum of places, people, and events which are unconnected and different in plot but unified by an ingenious narrative framework.

38. Mihály Szegedy-Maszák, "Teleology in Postmodern Fiction," *Exploring Postmodernism*, 224.

39. Said 3, xiii.

40. Said 226.

41. Olga Ragusa indicates that traditionally stories within a frame have always been favored and that Calvino's real contribution to the genre is that "the self-reflexive part of the novel engages author and reader to the point that the stories told are only incidental" (Ragusa, review of *Se una notte d'inverno un viaggiatore, World Literature Today* 55 [Winter 1981]: 81).

42. Selden 79.

CHAPTER TEN

Posthumously: *Under the Jaguar Sun;*
La strada di San Giovanni

I consider that my books which are made up of brief texts are never concluded. Each one represents a direction of work in which I continue to probe deeply.[1]

Since Calvino's death in 1985 two volumes of short stories have appeared, edited by Esther Calvino, the author's wife: *Sotto il sole giaguaro* (*Under the Jaguar Sun,* 1986) and *La strada di San Giovanni* (The San Giovanni Road, 1990). Both collections are reprints and rewrites of previously published materials.

Under the Jaguar Sun

Under the Jaguar Sun consists of three short stories: "The Name, the Nose," "Under the Jaguar Sun," and "A King Listens."[2] In 1972 Calvino started writing a book about the five senses, but only completed the stories dealing with smell, taste, and hearing; he also failed to provide the narratives with a frame, which he deemed fundamental insofar as "it allows the picture to exist, isolating it from the rest; but at the same time, it recalls—and somehow stands for—everything that remains out of the picture."[3] We do not know the planned sequence of the stories, which in the Italian edition—but not in the English—follow a chronological order. Speaking in 1984 of the projected volume, Calvino stated that unlike our primitive ancestors, contemporary man has lost the full use of the five senses:

> Modern man perceives certain things but fails to intercept others: olfaction is atrophied, taste is limited to a restricted range of sensations. And as far as our sight is concerned, given our habit of reading and interpreting fabricated images, it no longer has the ability to distinguish details, traces, signs, the way tribal man no doubt was able to do.[4]

Of course, this doesn't appear entirely so in the spectacular display of visual and mental experiences in *Mr. Palomar*. Certainly the sense of sight is dominant throughout that novel, and Calvino exploits to the fullest the visual acumen of the protagonist. But in *Under the Jaguar Sun,* Calvino is reacting against a society which he felt was oversaturated with theories and abstract discourses; consequently he tries to rely only on things he "could see, on objects, on pictures."[5] In other words, although mankind has become sophisticated and enlightened with new knowledge, the primordial senses, of which we are still prisoners, remain the most direct, unadulterated, and sincere way to perceive reality.

"The Name, the Nose," the first story in *Under the Jaguar Sun,* consists of three sequences in which three males, living in different historic periods, use the sense of smell to search for the woman of their desires, but are unsuccessful because in each case the search ends with her death. In the narrative, evocative of Mr. Palomar's quasi-carnal experience produced by the seductive aromas of a Parisian cheese shop, Calvino shows his familiarity with the latest scientific information concerning the scent lure both in man and in the animal kingdom. The sense of smell used for communication, for finding food or a mate, and as a warning of impending danger is far older than the sense of sight and hearing in the evolution of life. Dogs, for example, have an exceptional ability to smell their masters, which is surpassed only when a male dog smells a female dog in heat. Indeed, olfaction plays a prominent role in the mating instinct of countless species.

In the first sequence of the story, which takes place in *belle époque* Paris, a well-to-do gentleman visits a great *parfumerie* on the Champs-Elysée. He hopes to trace by means of her scent a lady with whom, the night before, he had been intimate at a masked ball but who had refused to reveal her identity. After smelling a variety of delicate perfumes in his venture to "give a name to an olfactory sensation," he becomes lost in "Madame Odile's liquid labyrinth" (77), unable to distinguish one scent from another but confident that "there lurked that perfume" which, for him, was "a complete woman" (71). Finally, he leaves the *parfumerie* with an address wrested from Madame Odile. When he arrives at the indicated house, he sees in a coffin the body of a woman whose face is hidden by a veil. He recognizes "the echo of that perfume that resembles no other, merged with the odor of death now as if they had always been inseparable" (81). When he mentions to a mourner that the night before at midnight she was alive and dancing with him at a ball, he is told that at midnight she was already dead.

In the second sequence the protagonist thinks of primitive man—whose olfaction was far more acute than his eyesight—when a network of smells governed his behavior either for food, danger, or sex. Each female had an odor that identified her with the herd, but she also had a distinct odor that distinguished her from the other females and with which she summoned him "in the midst of all those other odors" (72). He recalls how at that moment of human evolution the sense of smell was crucial for "recognizing the hostile male who has recognized on me his female's odor . . . and I recognize her smell on him and I am filled with fury" (79). Although he wins the contest with a rival male, he cannot smell clearly the female's scent because of the blood in his nostrils sustained during the clash. So, for the first time, he stands erect in order to keep his nose suspended in the air and at the same time be able to see better. He now senses "the stink of clawed cadavers, the breath of jackals," which announce the death of the woman.

In the third sequence the narrative shifts to modern times, a drug scene in a squalid London flat where a wild party, actually an orgy, is going on— Milanini describes it as "the kingdom of a loud incapacity to communicate."[6] The protagonist, a rock drummer, wakes up smelling "grass." As he gropes his way on all fours in the darkness, recognizing people, especially the women, by the smell of their sweat, he is stricken by the scent of a girl, "breathing and smelling nothing but her" (75). After he has had sex with the female,[7] he temporarily leaves her in order to put some shillings in the gas stove to heat the freezing room. But when he tries to find her scent again in the darkness, he loses his direction and can't locate her. Upon returning to the flat, after having gone outdoors to clear his head, the drummer finds all the rooms empty except one, which is locked and from which a smell of gas is escaping. He breaks down the door and inside he finds the stiffened body of a woman. He smells "her odor within the asphyxiating odor, her odor" which he follows in the ambulance, then in the hospital, "among the odors of disinfectant and slime that drips from the marble slabs in the morgue, and the air is impregnated with it, especially when outside the weather is damp" (83). It is interesting to note that even though olfaction is the leitmotif of "The Name, the Nose," Calvino's males make use of their other senses in the pursuit of the opposite sex because the five senses are closely related and often interdependent. For example, at the end of the first sequence we note the use of hearing when the male recognizes the "echo" of the woman's scent; in the second section sight complements scent when primitive man stands erect in order to see better; in the last segment sight is also used in the macabre depiction of the morgue ("slime that drips from the marble slabs") and touch in the description of the damp weather.

All three sequences—each denoting a different aspect of smelling, each told in the first person and written in a different style—end in an apocalyptic vision in which the aroma of females inexplicably and disturbingly blends with the stench of death. The bodies' putrefying odors and those of gas and disinfectants recall the Nazi extermination camps with their crematoria, spewing from their stacks the stench of death which impregnated the surrounding air with its unmistakable smell. Calvino is not only trying to show that man is an instinctive being whose moral life and behavior are determined and manifested by smell, but to warn us about the putrefaction of our existence and our environment, doomed to decay and die. He also alerts us about the progressive weakening of our senses, which are being destroyed by all kinds of environmental pollution. Like primitive man, we too must heed the presence of danger detected in our nostrils.

In spite of Calvino's protestation that he never felt compelled to explore man's inner psychological nature, that he lacked any interest in introspective probing, and that he felt that our society was oversaturated with the analysis of the psyche,[8] one cannot avoid certain psychological conclusions when confronting the irrational and compulsive behavior pattern of the protagonists in the title story, "Under the Jaguar Sun." The narrative's idée fixe is a cannibalistic obsession which affects the narrator and his wife, Olivia; both feel compelled to satisfy their gluttony by metaphorically replicating in their gastronomic habits certain anthropophagous rituals practiced by the ancient inhabitants of Mexico. The story is full of psychoanalytic implications such as oral eroticism, oral primacy, and even oral sadism. Psychologists have long documented the oral dynamism pertaining to the derivation of erotic pleasure from activities such as sucking, smoking, talking, biting, and chewing. The tendency of a young baby during the oral stage to put things into the mouth is usually interpreted to reflect not only a desire to satisfy hunger but also to incorporate the mother or other objects of attachment into the self. Later on, such behavior may be indicative of oral sadism; that is, when sexual satisfaction is associated with the infliction of pain or desire to hurt someone by biting or chewing.

"Under the Jaguar Sun," devoted to the sense of taste, focuses on the gustatory adventures of two tourists in Mexico who are bent on finding new and intriguingly palatable aphrodisiac experiences. The protagonists, already familiar with the fiery Mexican cuisine, are staying at a former convent, now a hotel, where they are savoring the exotic dishes "of conventual gastronomy" (5), which are always accented with native varieties of hot peppers that "opened vistas of a flaming ecstasy" (7). In the hotel they are intrigued with a large painting of a young nun and an old priest standing side by side; "their hands, slightly apart from their sides, almost touched" (3). An inscription identifies them as the abbess of the convent and the chaplain, painted together because of the extraordinary love that had bound them for thirty years;

when the priest died, the abbess immediately fell ill "and literally expired of love" to join him in "Heaven" (4). It is via the former convent and the painting that Calvino introduces the void in the tourists' marriage, the gustatory theme, and the notion of unselfish sacrifice.

Although the husband—Olivia calls him "insipid"—and the more imaginative, intense, and inquisitive wife are no longer sexually intimate and are unable to communicate verbally with one another, they nonetheless do so erotically by eating the spicy Mexican dishes. When at dinner Olivia seems self-absorbed, the narrator realizes that with her passion for food she is actually expressing a strong desire to involve him in her emotions, "communicating with me through flavors, or communicating with flavors through a double set of taste buds, hers and mine" (9). During a visit to the temples on Monte Albán, they are fascinated by the Olmec ritual of human sacrifice and try to envision "the hot blood spurting from the breast split by the stone axe of the priest" (13). What draws them even more to these practices is the knowledge that the victims participated willingly in such rites, that their flesh was eaten by the priests as a ritual meal, and, in particular, that in many instances the sacrificers would eventually be sacrificed as well. The husband and wife are sexually aroused as they return to the hotel. He is especially overcome by the realization that his "gaze was resting not on her eyes but on her teeth," which for the first time he sees "not as the radiant glow of a smile but as the instruments most suited to their purpose: to be dug into flesh, to sever it, tear it" (16). As they pursue their fascination with Aztec and Olmec sacrificial rites and "sacred cuisine" (19), they learn that the spiciness of Mexican food derives from the seasoning used by the ancient people to hide the taste of human flesh, or "perhaps the other flavors served to enhance that flavor, to give it a worthy background, to honor it" (22). Later, while dining in a restaurant on spicy exotic dishes "that melted in the mouth," the narrator fantasizes that he is being devoured by his wife:

> I could feel her tongue lift me against the roof of her mouth, enfold me in saliva, then thrust me under the tips of the canines. . . . It was as if a part of me, or all of me, were contained in her mouth. . . . The situation was not entirely passive, since while I was being chewed by her I felt also that I was acting on her, transmitting sensations that spread from the taste buds through her whole body. . . . It was a reciprocal and complete relationship, which involved us and overwhelmed us. (23)

Eventually the husband comprehends that his problems with Olivia stem from not understanding that each individual is potentially both sacrificer and victim; that his mistake was to have taken a passive role in their relationship and given his wife the responsibility of making the marriage work. He is surprised to have considered himself "eaten by her, whereas I should be myself the one to eat her. . . . It was only by feeding ravenously on Olivia that I would cease being tasteless to her palate" (26). That evening, while consuming a dish called *gorditas pellizcadas con manteca* (plump girls pinched with butter), the husband concentrates on devouring, with "every meatball, the whole fragrance of Olivia—through voluptuous mastication, a vampire extraction of vital juices" (27). Later, for the first time during their Mexican sojourn, they join again in sexual union. Although the story ends happily for the couple, who keep ecstatically eating with the intensity of the serpents carved on the stones of the ruins; it nonetheless strikes a somber note on marriage in general because we are all ingested and digested "in the universal cannibalism that leaves its imprint on every amorous relationship and erases the lines between our bodies and *sopa de frijoles, huachinango a la vera cruzana,* and *enchiladas.*" (29)[9]

Silvana Borutti's reading of the story is that Calvino's intent was to suggest that taste is the sense with which we discover "the nexus between pleasure and knowledge, between orality and intellectuality." She also points out that Olivia's obsessive curiosity about the ancient Indian cannibalistic and ritual practice is the key to the narrative because it suggests "that comprised in a way of eating there is a way of thinking."[10] Indeed, this may very well have been Calvino's rationale for originally publishing the story under the title "Sapore Sapere" (Taste Means Knowledge) before settling on "Under the Jaguar Sun"—the jaguar sun being a relief carved in the Mayan Temple of the Sun.

Cynthia Ozick, who rightly identifies the couple's "comic immersion in the psychology of that 'universal cannibalism,' " sees the three narratives of *Under the Jaguar Sun,* and in particular the title story, as indications of Calvino's qualification as an authentic postmodernist, one who does not experiment because "the self-conscious post-modernist is also a devil-may-care post-experimenter." Aside from her tongue-in-cheek characterization, Calvino's postmodernism is for Ozick "a literalism so absolute that it transports myth to its organic source, confining story to limits of the mouth, the ear, the nose."[11] In her *Postmodern Italian Fiction,* JoAnn Cannon discerns in Calvino's works a "*fabulist* quality, an apotheosis of storytelling that seems to be one of the distinguishing characteristics of a great deal of postmodernist fictions." Cannon also sees postmodernist tendencies in Calvino's "self-conscious text," his "firm understanding of science," and his proposition that literature, philosophy, and science "should continuously call each other into question"; and finally, he is a postmodernist for writing, like Robbe-Grillet, Cortázar, and Gass, "not as if the world existed for literature to mirror it, but rather as if literature, as a language game, could offer various grammars for ordering the world of words."[12]

"A King Listens," the last story in the collection, deals allegorically rather than literally with the sense of hearing, the important sense that makes it possible for us to communicate through speech. Calvino indicates that hearing, like the sense of smell, can both alert us to danger and provide pleasures such as listening to music, to the sound of the sea, and to the wind. At the same time, when not linked to our other senses, "hearing can create a paranoid relationship to reality."[13] And finally, Calvino allegorizes the concept that our ears help us keep our sense of orientation and balance because of certain fluids which respond to the movement and position of the head, and messages from the brain are sent to various muscles that keep our body steady as we move or sit or stand.

A king, figuratively tied to his throne for fear of losing it and insulated from society, finds it critical for his survival to know all the secrets of his palace whose corridors and chambers are "the ear of the king." The dynamics of the story recall those of "The Count of Monte Cristo" in which Edmond Dantès, while plotting his escape, listens to the sounds made by his jailers' movements which allow him to reconstruct mentally a detailed picture of the fortress. In "A King Listens" the brain, its nerve cells, and its fibers are all paradigmatic of the king and the palace; and it is only through eavesdropping on his people and the sounds and silences that reach him as he is "crouched at the bottom, in the innermost zone of the palace-ear" (38), that he keeps himself guarded and informed. He has no other way of keeping his reign balanced because the news given him by his officials is slanted and totally unreliable:

> Voluminous bundles of secret reports are turned out daily by electronic machines. . . . It is pointless for you to read them: your spies can only confirm the existence of conspiracies, justifying the necessity of your espionage; and at the same time they must deny any immediate danger, to prove that their spying is effective. . . . The assumption is that a king need not read anything, the king already knows what he has to know. (39)

The king knows that he must never let down his guard lest he be toppled from power, the way he himself had brutally eliminated his predecessor. He knows that it is only a matter of time before it will be his turn; there is no escape from it. To be able to hear and not see poses a problem for the immobilized ruler, who is obsessed with fears of impending dangers, all magnified by his fantasy and paranoia. "The ear is all petrified anxiety," writes Ozick; "to listen acutely is to be powerless, even if you sit on a throne. . . . The ear turns out to be the most imagining organ, because it is the most accomplished at deciphering."[14] The king's plight is similar to that in a fable narrated by Italo Svevo in his *Confessions of Zeno*. A little bird one day discovers that the door of his cage is unlocked. On one hand the animal is eager to fly out and enjoy the newly found liberty, but on the other hand it is afraid that during its absence someone might close the cage and prevent it from reentering. Thus Calvino's message in this Kafkaesque story is that power does not merely liberate, but that inevitably it also imprisons, isolates, and destroys us.

Calvino's tale is told by a narrative voice that is not well defined. At times it appears to be the king's inner voice, and at other times an external voice speaking to and even berating the monarch; the interior voice reflects upon and illuminates the exterior one and vice versa. In the end the king is no longer able to define what surrounds him aurally, nor his own identity, until he can combine the sense of hearing with that of sight. This occurs at the conclusion of the story, when the expected doom finally materializes. The city erupts "in flames and shouts. The night has exploded, turned inside out. . . . There is no night darker than a night of fires. There is no man more alone than one running in the midst of a howling mob" (59). However, as he wanders outside the palace, we never learn whether the king holds on to his scepter or has been overthrown: "The dogs are barking, the birds wake, the colors return on the world's surface, things reoccupy space, living beings again give signs of life. And surely you are also here, in the midst of it all, in the teeming noises that rise on all sides" (64). Robert A. Morace rightly points out that "The King Listens" comes to an end elliptically, "with the voice silent, the ruler overruled, or at least overwhelmed, first by the city's sounds and then by the narrative silence."[15]

Besides the questions of power that inevitably make one think of those set forth in Niccolò Machiavelli's *The Prince*—how principalities are acquired, how they are maintained, why they are lost—and the dramatization of the sense of hearing, the most fascinating aspect of "The King Listens" is its extremely subtle and lyrical language. Indeed, as in a musical drama, Calvino's evocative lyricism blends harmoniously with the anonymous narrative voice which keeps alternating between inner monologue and dialogue, and which is stimulated by the protagonist's imagination that "imposes raving words on those formless reverberations" (47). Moreover, when all is silent in the palace, it is a summoning, feminine voice coming from the city which brings the king the first comforting sound and makes him take an interest in something not connected to rule or power. Now "it is no longer fear that makes you prick up your ears," but rather "the dream of a woman's voice singing in the nightmare of your long insomnia" (52). When the king is unable to sing back because he can't find his "true voice," the narrative voice comments, like the chorus in a Greek tragedy:

> If you had known how to sing, perhaps your life would have been different, happier; or sad with a different sadness, a harmonious melancholy. Perhaps you would not have felt the need to become king. Now you would not find yourself here, on this creaking throne, peering at shadows. (54)

The singing voice echoes Mr. Palomar's thoughts, stirred by listening to the birds' melody, which makes him see that his life has been a series of missed opportunities. Likewise, in the pursuit of progress, selfish power, and control, we too have mislaid our "true voice" and, as with the king, it is unclear whether we are the rulers or the ruled, whether we have become indeed masters or prisoners of our life-styles. In this connection, Alix Kates Shulman remarks that the king's "inside and outside worlds are indistinguishable, you and your nemesis are one."[16] Calvino's lesson is that we are no longer able to sing the melody which defines identity, and every attempt to escape from our "cage is destined to fail: it is futile to seek yourself in a world that does not belong to you, that perhaps does not exist" (58–59).[17]

The entire story is full of varied sounds and noises that alternate with a melancholic melody like an operatic ensemble. In fact, the melodramatic elements of "A King Listens" stem from the fact that in 1977 Calvino wrote the narrative for an opera based on Roland Barthes's entry *ascolto* (listening) in the *Enciclopedia Einaudi*. In this essay Barthes distinguishes between hearing, a physiological phenomenon, and listening, a psychological activity; unlike the former, which can be described by means of acoustics or by the physiology of hearing, the latter, which is far more complex for humans, functions at various levels, necessitating the ability to decipher the *signs* captured by the ear according to certain codes analogous to the act of reading. What must have been of great interest to Calvino was the French critic's observation that like sight, hearing is connected to the ability to judge our spatial-temporal situation, and that "the appropriation of space is in part based on sound." However, the ability to discriminate between sounds has become compromised by sound pollution "that is nothing but the intolerable alteration of human space, in which man tries hopelessly to *recognize him-*

self.'' Thus this pollution undermines the senses (sight, smell, hearing) which allow both man and animal to recognize their own territory, their own habitat, and impedes our *listening.*[18] In the view of Claudio Varese, Barthes's essay offered Calvino an opportunity for expressing "plurality in a series and, almost, in a dance of different *listenings* which are differently interpreted and interpretable."[19] Eventually the Calvino libretto was revised by Luciano Berio, the Italian avant-garde composer renowned for using all means of sound communication in his operas, who published it in the magazine *Duo* (1982). Berio later used it for several successful opera performances in Salzburg and Vienna in 1982, and at the Teatro della Scala of Milan in 1986. Calvino had previously collaborated with Berio on other musical ventures, notably the operas *Allez-hop!* which includes material from *The Baron in the Trees,* and *La vera storia,* which represents "the confusing, painful, tangled truth of the contradictory human condition."[20]

What then is the meaning of the three dazzling and perturbing stories (parables?) in *Under the Jaguar Sun?* Is it that, like Svevo's little bird, we no longer can leave our self-made cages? That our freedom is illusory and our reality is shaped by irrevocable choices? That, as in Milan Kundera's *The Unbearable Lightness of Being,* life seems to lose its substance and weight? That we have become prisoners of our power and of our fears, and that all is for nought? Perhaps. But in spite of this ominous possibility, Calvino intimates that all is not lost. In fact, we glimpse a sense of hope, of redemption, in the concluding paragraph of "A King Listens." The king has undergone quite an ordeal, and we are unsure if he is going to survive. Yet, as he walks the streets of his city under the brightening morning sky, he makes full use of his capacity to hear, to smell, and to see. He feels the wind, hears the dogs barking and the birds waking. He notices colors, and "living beings again give signs of life" that erupt in a crescendo of hammering, roaring, and all absorbing noises characteristic of all metropolises (64). Despite the loss of our primeval ability to fully perceive reality through the senses, it is only by means of them, no matter how feeble they may have become, that mankind can improve its lot and safeguard its existence today. Calvino does not present the senses as merely avenues of pleasure, writes Alan Wade; instead the novelist gives us "an epistemology of the senses, or rather, he invents worlds in which a system of knowledge must be elaborated from a single sense alone."[21] Regardless of our advanced place on the evolutionary scale, smelling, tasting, hearing—and of course seeing and touching—when honed are still the best, if not our only, means of perceiving authentic reality in our contradictory human condition and imperfect but nevertheless satisfying life.

Like the phenomenologists, Calvino's aim is to bring essence back to existence, reachieve "a direct and primitive contact with the world," and endow "that contact with a philosophical status."[22]

La strada di San Giovanni

In the prefatory note to *La strada di San Giovanni* (The San Giovanni Road) Esther Calvino informs the reader that in 1985 Italo Calvino had in mind a collection of stories consisting of a series of "memory exercises," bearing the title "Obligatory Passages." Since the project was never completed, the volume contains only previously published material written between 1962 and 1977, but with some deletions and corrections made by the author.[23] *La strada di San Giovanni* is a collage of five stories flimsily held together by the theme of memory. In addition to the author's essentially imaginative nature and delightful aesthetic qualities, these writings tend to be more of an autobiographical sentimental journey than fiction proper. Although they do not add significantly to Calvino's narrative canon, they nonetheless do offer some additional insight into his artistry. They are very much like musical études, designed to develop and strengthen a particular technique.

In the title story, written in 1962, the author goes back in memory to the beginning of the Second World War, when as a teenager he would observe his father leave their San Remo home early every morning and go to the family farm in San Giovanni to carry out his research work. He recalls somewhat painfully how difficult father and son found it to communicate with each other despite their talkative natures. Even then Italo felt lured by the call of the city and by his literary chimera. He already knew that his parents' way of life was not meant for him, as he writes wistfully:

I was already what I am today, a citizen of the city and of history—a consumer—and victim—of the products of industry—a consumer candidate, a barely designated victim—and already destinies, all the destinies were decided, ours and the general ones. (36)

In the second memoir, "Autobiografia d'uno spettatore" (The Autobiography of a Movie Watcher), Calvino recalls his passion for the movies, especially American films. During this critical phase of development as a teenager, he was able to escape into a world different from the one he lived in: "Only what he saw on the screen possessed the characteristics of a world, the fullness, the necessity, the coherence" which did not exist on the outside

(43). He recalls in particular walking into the theater in the middle of a film, seeing the second half, and then, when viewing it from the beginning, the immense pleasure of discovering the genesis of the mysteries and dramas rather than their denouement. Interestingly, Calvino first formed a negative perception of fascism when in 1938 the regime imposed an embargo of certain American films, more for commercial protectionist reasons rather than for ideological-political ones (the latter were finally imposed when Italy went to war in 1941). Having known only a Fascist Italy, young Calvino had not yet become fully aware of the repressions of Mussolini's regime. In the instance pertaining to American films, however, he felt personally deprived:

> It was the first time that a right I was enjoying was being taken away from me personally: more than a right, a dimension, a world, a mental space; and I saw this loss as a cruel oppression, one that contained all the forms of oppression I was aware of by hearing people speak about them or by having seen others suffer from them. (59)

In essence, what the movies meant to him at that time was evasion, distance; above all they conveyed a need to broaden his mind beyond the constraints of actual reality and to open for himself new and immense dimensions. Now that so many years have gone by, instead of distance, they signify for him only "absolute nearness . . . the irreversible sense of all that is close to us, next to us, on top of us" (64).

In "Ricordo della battaglia" (Remembering a Battle) Calvino goes back to his own experiences in the Resistance, previously narrated in *The Path to the Nest of Spiders* and in several other war stories. What intrigues him, as he describes a defeat suffered by his group of partisans, are the tricks memory now plays on him: he can only vaguely recollect his own participation in the battle, but recalls in great detail what he was told about it afterward by his comrades. In "La poubelle agréé" (The Agreeable and "officially" approved Garbage Can), which bears a French title, the scene moves to the Calvino apartment in Paris. This recollection deals with a comic ingenious description of putting out the garbage each day: "Of all the domestic chores, it is the only one he fulfills with a degree of competence and satisfaction" (89). Interesting is the analogy between discarding garbage and the purgative effect of writing: "To write is to dispossess oneself, no less than throwing things away; to write is to get rid of a bunch of crunched-up pieces of paper or a pile of densely written pages, the former and the latter no longer belonging to me, put aside, expelled" (115). Memories, like recycled refuse—"the eternal return of the ephemeral" (114)—cannot be gotten rid of and invariably come back to haunt us.

"Dall'opaco" (From Opaqueness), the last story in the volume and perhaps the most challenging and artistically revealing, is actually a practice exercise in reflection and recollection, and lacks the sentimentality and humor of the other pieces. It consists of various essaylike fragments, devoid of any complete sentences except for the concluding one, in which Calvino describes his difficulty in viewing the world and the resulting opaqueness. The following is typical:

> I shall therefore start by saying that the world is composed of broken and oblique lines, with segments that tend to extend beyond the corners of each step, in the manner of the agaves that often grow at the edge and climb in vertical lines like palms that provide shade to the gardens or terraces overlooking those where the roots of the plants are planted. (120)

In the final part of this meditative investigation of the shape of the world, Calvino "blends earthly and cosmic dimensions with lexical terms."[24] After explaining that *ubagu*, the Ligurian word for opaque, denotes a place where the sun does not shine, and that *abrigu* means the contrary, in a cryptic and morose philosophical conclusion, he claims to be writing from

> *ubagu*, from the depth of opaqueness, reconstructing the map of an *aprico* which is only an unverifiable axiom for memory's calculations, the geometric place of the "I," of a myself needed by the myself in order to know that it is a myself, the "I" whose only function is to make sure that the world receives continually news of the world's existence, a device the world has at its disposal so that it can tell if it exists. (134)

In this memory exercise, rather opaque in its hermetic meaning, Calvino no longer seems to be interested just in memory or in the shape of the world, but rather in the boundary of our unconscious and in the difficulty of determining and regaining our lost identity. Clearly, the cited passage recalls Silas Flannery's musing in *If on a winter's night a traveler,* in which he envisions the death of certainty, of the Cartesian I: "I, too, would like to erase myself and find for each book another I, another voice, another name, to be reborn; but my aim is to capture in the book the illegible world, without center, without ego, without I" (180). For Hans Robert Jauss, Flannery's reverie thematizes "the new change of horizon in a way which no longer sees the dawn of the new looking backwards, in epigonic awareness of the *post*, of 'afterwards', of what has come 'too late.' "[25] Likewise, Lorna Sage's reading of "Dall'opaco" is that in these mediations Calvino seems to be "about to deconstruct external reality, but/and does the same for the self, for good measure.''[26] The antithesis *ubagu/aprico* is illusory because the two are linked and interchangeable; thus Calvino's memory is not one which creates a mosaic composed of pieces from the past, but rather that "memory is future to be explored retrospectively, a source of images having inexhaustible meanings."[27] This is a fitting commentary apropos Calvino—someone avowedly unfriendly toward the disciples of Freud—and the meandering realm of the subconscious. However, in the meditative—or better, stream-of-consciousness—pieces of "From Opaqueness," the postmodernist writer may be finally trying to come to terms with his own existence as he probes deeply into the human mind and explores the recesses of the unconscious.

NOTES

1. Paul Fournel, "Italo Calvino: cahiers d'exercise," *Magazine Littéraire* June 1985: 88.

2. "Sotto il sole giaguaro" first published under the title "Sapore Sapere" (Savor and Sagacity, or better, Taste Means Knowledge) in *FMR*, 1 June 1982, was revised and given a new title in July of the same year; "Un re in ascolto" appeared in *la Repubblica* 13 Aug. 1984; and "Il nome, il naso," written in 1972, in *Antaeus* 20 (Winter 1976).

3. *Under the Jaguar Sun* (New York: Harcourt Brace, 1988) 85–86. Page numbers referring to this edition are shown in parentheses.

4. Giulio Nascimbeni, "A colloquio con lo scrittore in occasione dell'uscita di *Cosmicomiche vecchie e nuove*," *Corriere della Sera* 5 Dec. 1984: 3. Similarly, at a public lecture, Calvino spoke again of the projected volume: "Writing it, I have the problem that my sense of smell is not very sharp, I lack really keen hearing, I am not a gourmet, my sense of touch is unrefined, and I am nearsighted. For each one of the five senses, I have to make an effort in order to master a range of sensations and nuances. I don't know if I shall succeed, but my efforts, in this case as in the others, are not merely aimed at making a book but also at changing myself, the goal of all human endeavor." "The Written and the Unwritten Word," *The New York Review of Books*, 12 May 1983: 39.

5. Nascimbeni 3.

6. Claudio Milanini, *L'utopia discontinua* (Milan: Garzanti, 1990) 185.

7. Hume notes that in this story "odors frame a world of sexual oppression," and that the Parisian's relationships with women are "overtly exploitative" (Kathryn Hume, "Sensuality and the Senses in Calvino's Fiction," *Modern Language Notes* 107 [1992]: 171).

8. Nascimbeni 3.

9. Bean soup, red snapper cooked in spicy citrus juices, and enchiladas.

10. Silvana Borutti, "Metafisica dei sensi e filosofia involontaria nell'ultimo Calvino," *Autografo* 4 (Mar. 1987): 14–15.

11. Cynthia Ozick, "Mouth, Ear, Nose," *The New York Times Book Review* 23 Oct. 1988: 7.

12. JoAnn Cannon, *Postmodern Italian Fiction: The Crisis of Reason in Calvino, Eco, Sciascia, Malerba* (Madison, NJ: Fairleigh Dickinson University Press, 1989), 9, 10, 11. In the last quotation Cannon cites Allen Thiher, *Words in Reflection: Modern Language Theory and Postmodern Fiction* (Chicago: University of Chicago Press, 1984) 112.

13. Hume 169.

14. Ozick 7.

15. Robert A. Morace, "Under the Jaguar Sun," *Magill's Literary Annual 1989* (Englewood Cliffs, NJ: Salem Press), 2: 875.

16. Alix Kates Shulman, "Senses and Sensibility: Italo Calvino Solves the Mind-Body Problem," *Village Voice* 14 Feb. 1989: 53.

17. The king's uncertainties and bewilderment bring to mind the experiences of Sigismundo, the prince in Calderón de la Barca's (1600–1681) play *Life Is a Dream,* who has been kept imprisoned since infancy by his father. When he is finally released, although confused about what is real, he has learned to control his passion and to conquer himself rather than his father, who eventually hands him the crown. Sigismundo restores peace to the kingdom and rules wisely.

18. R. Barthes and R. Havas, "Ascolto," *Enciclopedia Einaudi* (Turin: Einaudi, 1977).

19. Claudio Varese, "Calvino librettista e scrittore in versi," in *Italo Calvino: Atti del Convegno internazionale,* ed. Giovanni Falaschi (Milan: Garzanti, 1988) 360. Excellent source of information about Calvino as a librettist and his other collaborative musical activities.

20. Varese 355.

21. Alan Wade, "An Epistemology of the Senses," review of *Under the Jaguar Sun, The New Leader* (1 Jan. 1989): 20.

22. M. Merleau-Ponty, *Phenomenology of Perception* (New York: Humanities Press, 1974) vii.

23. *La strada di San Giovanni* (Milan: Mondadori, 1990). The volume has not yet been translated into English. Page numbers referring to this edition are shown in parentheses. In addition to the five stories included in the Mondadori volume, Calvino also intended writing among others the following: "Cuba," "Gli oggetti," and "Istruzioni per il sosia." Just before he was stricken by illness, he also planned to rewrite the five Casanova amorous recollections, originally published as "Le memorie di Casanova (Sofia, Fulvia, Tullia, Cate e Ilda, Irma)" in *la Repubblica* (15–16 Aug. 1982): 15–16.

24. *La strada di San Giovanni,* dust jacket.

25. Hans Robert Jauss, "The Theory of Reception: A Retrospective of its Unrecognized Prehistory," in *Literary Theory Today,* ed. Peter Collier and Helga Geyer-Ryan (Ithaca: Cornell University Press, 1990) 68.

26. Lorna Sage, "From the Mind's Balcony," review of *La strada di San Giovanni, Times Literary Supplement,* 5–11 Oct. 1990: 1060.

27. *La strada di San Giovanni,* dust jacket.

CHAPTER ELEVEN

Conclusion: The Unredeeming Author: *Mr. Palomar*

They knew each other. He knew her and so himself, for in truth he had never known himself. And she knew him and so herself, for although she had always known herself she had never been able to recognize it until now.[1]

Italo Calvino was, and continues to be, regarded as the most ingenious, the most innovative, the most unconventional, exciting, and admired writer of contemporary Italy—to the extent that Hans Robert Jauss calls him "Borges' most important successor."[2] Whether he was writing seriously about Italy's war and postwar turbulent periods, or ironically about medieval and recent times, or even tracing the evolution of the cosmos by detailing its various prehuman phases, he always endeavored to make sense of the entire universe, to seek harmony with it, to grasp the meaning of existence, and to constantly insist on his faith in humanity by auguring a world of transcendence, respect, and love for both nature and mankind.

And yet, we the readers are left at times unfulfilled, a bit frustrated, as we confront some of Calvino's narrative texts, particularly those written after the mid-1960s in which he "moves away from emotions and more toward intellectual responses."[3] One identifies with the travelers of *The Castle of Crossed Destinies* who, when confronting the tarot cards, are reluctant to question the future since they are "as if drained of all future, suspended in a journey that had not ended nor was to end" (6). Reading is of course an individual process measured according to different scales; but regardless of whether one chooses to be an "implied," "informed," or "competent" lector, as reader-response criticism has declared the engaged reader to be,[4] Calvino leaves us at times unsatisfied. In a phenomenological sense we do not always perceive the registering of Calvino's intentional acts in the text, and therefore find it difficult to adequately reexperience the work of his consciousness.[5] Indeed, phenomenology—a movement with which Calvino identified[6]—stresses the perceiver's central role in determining meaning. Hence, when readers are no longer fully appreciative of what the artist is offering, when they fail to respond properly to the text, then something has surely gone awry. No doubt this should concern us, though we are somewhat reassured by Calvino's own comments regarding *Mr. Palomar*. He writes that in this "pedagogy of observation and reflection" the reader must "learn to keenly observe and never be satisfied with what he has seen."[7]

When approaching Calvino, what is it that leaves us at times no longer totally involved and our consciousness (phenomena) unfulfilled? First of all, it may the fact that the author does not always strike an emotional chord with the reader—this in spite of the fact that he is very capable indeed in making "cells speak as if they were people," and conceiving "human figures and language in the primeval void" of his cosmicomic tales.[8] Calvino is often more concerned with form, ideas, systems, scientific principles, combinatorial games, mental impulses, than with the human qualities of his characters. As readers, our minds may delight in his abstractions and novel ideas, but it is our emotions that ultimately provide an aesthetic and dramatic response, and they respond to the personal, to the particular, to the concrete, and to the human dimension with all its passions. The later Calvino, with his almost exclusively emblematic characters, is not always successful in bringing his abstractions into the range of our personal sensory experience, especially when his fiction becomes subservient to science, and at times even turns into sheer method. Indeed, starting with some cosmicomic stories in *t zero,* it is scientific logic that inevitably becomes a key that fits and operates all his narrative texts. Because of Calvino's propensity for continuous rationalization and a tendency to depersonalize with a highly artistic prose, always making deductions in logic by means of an endless series of variants and exercises, both his point of origin and interest are neither characterization nor plot, but rather a proposition, an idea, a metaphor. Above all, he seems to be intentionally lacking in pathos, the quality in art which stimulates our emotions: pity, tenderness, sorrow, joy, love, affection. Feelings and emotions are relegated to mental images and to the physical senses of smell, taste, hearing, touch, and vision. In other words, there appears to be too much emotional distancing in several of his writings. Although Calvino is indeed capable of pathos, as we glimpse it in many of his short stories, particularly those involving Marcovaldo, he is at times (e.g., *The Castle of Crossed Destinies*) more interested in breaking everything down into a geometric and algebraic grid that permits him to translate everything not only into words, but even better, into codes, signs, signifiers, signified, etc., so that a potential computer can scan these inputs and decipher them for him and the reader. Consequently one can identify with Mr. Palomar, who, in spite of his detailed phenomenological sense of observation, discovers that seeing is not the same as understanding. And because he no longer considers himself to be in control of his world, any other reality or "thought of time outside our experience is intolerable" for him.[9]

As has already been indicated in chapter 6, there is an almost deliberate absence of psychological elements in Calvino's writings because, as the author has stated, he was "not attracted to psychology, to the analysis of feelings, or to introspection"; what interested him more was the "whole mosaic in which man is set, the interplay of relationships."[10] Let us take Pin, the protagonist of *The Path to the Nest of Spiders*, as an illustration of distancing, decentering, and defamiliarization.[11] According to Michel David, his psychology is reduced to a few elementary reactions, usually limited to: "I like," "I don't like," "it's nice," "it's ugly," "it amuses me," "it angers me." There are hardly any dreams, remarks David, given that Calvino "decidedly refuses a literature of inner testimony, of innermost shock, personal confession, because these inner zones have turned out to be less rich for him" than others. Calvino is too intent on analyzing Pin's "political puberty" rather than the boy as a developing adolescent. The author, David concludes, who no longer participates in "the sea of subjectivity" so characteristic of Proust, Joyce, Kafka, and Svevo, has instead turned to a "different and disquieting sea of objectivity."[12]

Yet Calvino never totally loses sight of man's irrepressible humanity. And although a certain ironic resistance may keep the author from always being closely connected to some of his characters' psychology, when he chooses to do so, he can ably express emotion, sentiment, and thus bring us close to his characters. This certainly is the case with *Marcovaldo or the Seasons in the City*, which is unquestionably a compassionate and lyrical account of a family's struggle for survival in the modern city, marked throughout not only by pathos and humor but also by a delicately rendered psychological subtlety. Indeed, the *paterfamilias* Marcovaldo, perhaps one of Calvino's most human characters, shows remarkable emotion, even though he seems to be totally absorbed in his own world of fantasy. The fact that he finds himself out of step with his surroundings—perplexed, questioning the world and wasteland existence in the city—does not keep him from sharing his plight with his wife and children, who long to come closer to the unspoiled world of his dreams. The same holds true for Cosimo, who, though living a lofty arboreal life, still craves human contact and affection. In most of Calvino's other writings, however, the manifestation of human behavior is of secondary interest for the author because it is merely the starting point of his inquiry into the human predicament on a vaster scale. Indeed, his work may very well be reflective of the spiritual paralysis modern society has brought upon itself.

Calvino, "the squirrel of the pen," always on the move and toying with both text and readers, is difficult to pin down, as he himself admitted with reference to *If on a winter's night a traveler:*

> There is always something sadistic in the relationship between writer and reader. In this new novel I may be a more sadistic lover than ever. I constantly play cat and mouse with the reader, letting the reader briefly enjoy the illusion that he's free for a little while, that he's in control. And then I quickly take the rug out from under him; he realizes with a shock he's *not* in control, that it is always I, Calvino, who is in total control of the situation.[13]

And Claudio Marabini notes that in *Cosmicomics* game and entertainment are dominant and that "the game of ingenious remarks" plus "chaos and causality coincide in the undecipherable game of reality."[14] In fact, Calvino's games are intellectual, fantastic, and pseudo-scientific not only in their treatment of reality but in style, form, content, character, and point of view as well. Admittedly, all are ingenious and extremely reflective, and many are highly entertaining; but sooner or later some invariably grow heavy. As the author proceeds on his "Oulipo" literary direction and strains the self-reflexive and metaliterary thrust of his fantasy-framing devices, he loses traditional narrative supports and with these the human element whose voice and actions are reduced to signs. Deeds and character no longer matter; dialogue and action virtually disappear. Enzo Siciliano comments that in Calvino's later writings, narrative became a type of "recipe-book of itself," as if you invited someone to dinner and "offered the menu as the meal rather than food itself, and instead of wine the wine list, perhaps embellished with the most beautiful imaginable colors."[15] Because of his penchant for such rationalistic games, Calvino exhausts himself in vicious circularity as he tries to go deeper into the vortex of literary cosmic spaces. Everything becomes too schematic, too graphic, to the extent that man is left spineless, and reality assumes a geometric configuration where there is room left only for calculations, computations, and theorems. This explains why Mr. Palomar, whose "activity is mental and perceptual," is no longer a living character, but rather an "aspect of looking, a wide-opened eye taking in the horizon in its totality."[16]

In a recent essay Enzo Siciliano deplores the changes that took place in Calvino's late 1960s writings, and that his "fable-like grace which had accompanied the impeccable flights of his style and had saturated every spiral curve" eventually turned serious and in time grew too thin. Siciliano blames in part Borges's spellbinding effect on Calvino, who was led to believe "that existence contains something unauthentic, if not downright fetid, and that in writing one must guard against it."[17] The same lamentation is made by Calvino's friend the novelist Luigi Malerba, when he states that "Calvino used to assert that he had turned his back on reality, preferring instead a written mediation of it." In this connection, Luigi Malerba is reminded of a tourist he once saw in the Piazza del Duomo of Orvieto, who instead of admiring directly the cathedral's façade, preferred looking instead at a photographic reproduction.[18]

In addition to Calvino's distancing as an author, there is also a degree of incompleteness and disability reflected in many of the titles of his narrative works (*The Cloven Viscount, The Baron in the Trees, The Nonexistent Knight, Invisible Cities, The Watcher, Mr. Palomar*); this also applies to the narratives' respective characters, all vivid icons of alienation and anxiety. In fact, as Renato Barilli pointed out in 1959, Calvino's narrative is one of absence, given that it is impossible to find characters ready to confess their inner selves and allow us to enter their private world. These characters are constantly subverted by a distancing and "distanced narrator who delights in unsettling and thwarting the reader's expectations."[19] It is quite possible that Calvino's personality may have contributed to this attitude. The author was a timid, solitary person, partly because he stuttered and spoke haltingly; even though he was quite open and congenial with his family and intimate friends, he felt ill at ease and awkward in society. Furthermore, he also refrained from revealing his intimate feelings, and often spoke ambiguously about his writings. He rightly expected his readers to know him through his works and nothing else! In fact, after a 1985 interview, Paul Fournel referred to him as "a man of few words" who nonetheless explained himself extremely well through his works.[20]

Let us take the first novel of Calvino's trilogy as an example of, in my view, this alienating syndrome. Its title, particularly in Italian (*dimezzato*), clearly denotes something incomplete, flawed, diminished, whose parts are separated and distanced. The same words apply to Cosimo, the baron who lives distanced in the trees, where from above he acquires an advantageous view of the society he has fled. He reflects the writer's need to distance himself from life, to interpose between himself and his characters a lens, a filter that permits him to be apart from the world he is representing and at the same time try to come to terms with it. Agilulfo, the nonexistent knight, is only an image, an idea, who is nonexistent because he no longer "makes friction" with anything; he merely functions "abstractly" and has no relationship with what surrounds him.[21] The individual thus has lost significance and has no control over his life and destiny. Like the knight's hollow suit of white armor, we too are abstractions and fail to matter in a world in which there are now robots programmed to perform tasks and functions once relegated only to humans. Qfwfq, the mysterious creature whose nature and composition are always changing and eluding us, soars beyond the trees of the *Baron in the Trees* into the infinite heavens, into unfathomable space and time, very far indeed from actual reality. In *Invisible Cities* Calvino again turns to the past in order to see the present and future. The khan has distanced himself from his possessions, which are seen through the eyes of Marco Polo. This is all in keeping with Calvino's remarks in *Six Memos for the Next Millennium*, in which he underscores his greater interest in the visualization and verbalization of thought rather than of sentiment; he also reveals a "fondness for geometrical forms, for symmetries, for numerical series, for all that is combinatory, for numerical proportions" and a "devouring and destructive obsession" to write about "everything that can happen in time and space,"[22] with hardly any regard for the pathos of the human element. Indeed, the manifestations of human behavior are of secondary importance because they are merely the starting point of Calvino's inquiry into the predicament of the individual in contemporary society. These distancing titles and works are manifestations of dissatisfaction, protest, and dissidence from social and political values.[23] Through them Calvino expresses perceptions deeply entrenched in our modern society, above all the individual's isolation from nature and from our technological world. However, alienation is also seen as a positive force for change and as a prerequisite for hope. And his work is always of vivid images, the inexhaustible and continuing source of his art.

As far as this dichotomy (pathos vs. logos) is concerned, Calvino's narratives reflect to some degree the opposition expressed by Friedrich Nietzsche in his *Birth of Tragedy from the Spirit of Music* (1872). In this treatise the German poet and philosopher first drew attention to the antithesis between Apollo and Dionysius as symbols of extreme views of art and life. Ironically, according to Derrida, Western thought has always been shaped in terms of dichotomies or polarities: good vs. evil, being vs. nothingness, presence vs. absence, etc. Apollo, the god of peace, is associated with leisure, repose, and also with aesthetic emotions and intellectual contemplation. He is known as the god of logical order and philosophic calm, and the Apollonian is the basis for all analytical distinctions. Everything that is part of the unique individuality of a man or thing is Apollonian in character. All types of form and structure are Apollonian since form serves to define or individualize that which is formed. Rational thought is also Apollonian since it is structured and makes distinctions. In this sphere of rationality the geometric, the static, and the formal predominate. Thus Calvino clearly demonstrates many Apollonian characteristics, and, as has been noted by Ghidetti, he is constantly "litera-turizing" life, and reducing the "disorder of life to the order of literature, and searching for life's fathomless geometry."[24] On the other hand, Dionysius, the god of revelry and wine, symbolizes the free expression of desire, the lifting of any inhibition or repression. He represents the ascending life, joy in action, ecstatic emotion and inspiration, instinct, adventure, and fearless suffering. He is the god of song, music, dance, and drama. Drunkenness and madness are Dionysian because they break down individual character. In fact, all forms of enthusiasm and ecstasy are Dionysian for, in such states, one gives up individuality and submerges within a greater whole. Music is the most Dionysian of the arts since it appeals directly to man's instinctive frenzied emotions and not, as in Calvino's instance, to a formal, structured, and logical mind.

Mr. Palomar, the last narrative text published during Calvino's lifetime,[25] and in which only reflection and description prevail, expresses best the author's Nieztschean "pathos of distance" as well as a marked phenomenological estrangement. There is hardly any plot or characterization in what A. H. Carter labels "a series of somewhat claustrophobic prose pieces, high in thought, low on emotional content."[26]

Following Dante's scheme for the Divine Comedy, Mr. Palomar is divided into three parts: "Mr. Palomar's Vacation," "Mr. Palomar in the City," and "The Silences of Mr. Palomar." Each part is subdivided into three sections, which in turn are divided into three subsections. Altogether the book consists of twenty-seven short narratives, meditations, independent microtexts—or, as Calvino called them, cahiers d'exercise (exercise notebooks)—all unified by a macrotext constituted by Palomar's quest; according to Nathalie Roelens, "by their orientation toward a well-defined ending: the death of the protagonist."[27] Hence, as in many of Calvino's previous writings, this collection too is arranged in a precise mathematical pattern. Furthermore, the "Index" contains a key that is supposed to facilitate a better understanding of the units: each title is marked by the numbers 1, 2, 3, which, by their position indicate "three thematic areas, three kinds of experience and inquiry that, in varying proportions, are present in every part of the book." The titles marked "1" refer to a visual experience, and the text is descriptive; those marked "2" contain anthropological or cultural elements, and the text, which tells a story, also involves visual data, language, meaning, and symbols; the stories marked "3" are more speculative and progress from the purely descriptive

209

and narrative to the meditative. Although Calvino perhaps wanted to facilitate the reader's understanding of the book, the result is contrary to his intent, and particularly to Palomar's visionary qualities, because, by programming a priori how one should read, the "Index" restricts one's imagination and interpretation of the texts. Ultimately, it gives the book a directory-like quality which creates a disturbing and unnecessary distancing effect. Thus the reader is better off not consulting the index at all.

Mr. Palomar, named after the famous observatory in California, is ironically nearsighted and detached. He is a "nervous man who lives in a frenzied and congested world" and tends to "reduce his relations with the outside world." In order to "defend himself against the general neurasthenia, he tries to keep his sensations under control insofar as possible" (4). To a large degree he follows the example set forth in *De rerum natura* by the poet Lucretius (ca. 98–55 B.C.), whom Calvino very much admired. "I have two bedside books: Lucretius' *De rerum natura* and Ovid's *Metamorphoses*," stated Calvino in 1985. "I would like that everything I write be related to one or the other, or better to both." *Mr. Palomar,* he concluded, "is definitely closer to Lucretius; my aim was to dream of achieving a minute knowledge of the nature of things to the point that their very substance dissolved at the moment of being grasped."[28] To be sure, when Palomar swims in the sea and gazes at the setting sun's reflections in the water, only the sun matters for him and all "the rest is reflection among reflections," himself included (15). Eventually, as he gazes upward while doing a deadman's float, he feels as if his

> swimming ego . . . is immersed in a disembodied world, intersections of force fields, vectorial diagrams, bands of position lines that converge, diverge, break up. But inside him there remains one point in which everything exists in another way, like a lump, like a clot, like a blockage: the sensation that you are here but could not be here, in a world that could not be but is. (17)

Palomar's peculiar voyeurism is not provoked at all by a vicarious impulse to view the naked body—"Eros is a program that unfolds in the electronic clusters of the mind" (21)—but rather by a phenomenological desire to observe life and nature from afar, to quest after knowledge and to "nullify himself as a subject in order to become an instrument through which the world looks at the world."[29] Nonetheless, although his aim is to view the world through the powerful lenses suggested by the famous observatory, the magnifying glasses become instead powerful reflections of Mr. Palomar's inner anguish and introspective reflections. He is a taciturn individual "who has perhaps lived too long in a world polluted by the bad usage of language." He "intercepts signals beyond any code, weaves mute dialogues and tries to form for himself a morality that will permit him to remain silent as long as possible."[30] He is the progeny of another Calvino observer, Amerigo Ormea of *The Watcher*, but a keener one who relies more on ocular and speculative processes, striving to show, as Calvino does in his 1982 essay "La luce negli occhi" (Light in the Eyes), "that the retina is a peripheral part of the cerebral cortex. In other words, the brain starts in the eye."[31] Nonetheless, Mr. Palomar does not fully succeed in capturing the infinite multiplicity of visual and mental experiences, because he dies in the last sentence of the novel, just as Calvino was ironically to do shortly after the book's publication. For the critic Pietro Citati, the novel expresses the aesthetic and moral attitude of Calvino's last writings, and its fundamental sentiment is

> a perplexity so radical and metaphysical that it prevents him from having feelings, from sharing ideas, from noticing the shape of an object, or simply noticing: "this thing exists," "this feeling is mine," "I exist." Every word of the book gives off this corrosive perplexity, this frightening uncertainty.[32]

Palomar represents not only Calvino's doppelgänger,[33] but also at times his opposite, engaged in an internal confrontation best illustrated in the first narrative, "Reading a Wave." As the protagonist tries in vain to isolate a wave and keep it separate from those immediately following it, overtaking it, and sweeping it away, he realizes that "to understand the composition of a wave, you have to consider . . . opposing thrusts" caused by the beach and submerged sandy shoals (5). The task is made even more difficult by Palomar's impatience, keeping him from completing his visual operation which "could perhaps be the key to mastering the world's complexity by reducing it to its simplest mechanism" (6). When he finally concentrates his attention on the backward thrusts caused by the waves' reflux, the narrative voice asks:

> Is this perhaps the real result that Mr. Palomar is about to achieve? To make the waves run in the opposite direction, to overturn time, to perceive the true substance of the world beyond sensory and mental habits? No, he feels a slight dizziness, but it goes no further than that. The stubbornness that drives the waves toward the shore wins the match. (7)

Palomar observes his lawn, the stars, lizards, turtles, a topless bather on the beach, visits a Parisian cheese shop, goes to the zoo. But, similar to the ever-changing waves which seem to come either from the shore or from the sea, like Calvino he too typically continues to provide suggestions without arriving at definitive answers. His gift, according to Michael Wood, is not for presenting two sides of a question, "but for seeing how a question conceals other, endlessly shifting and multiplying questions, and even some unlikely answers; for seeing how a word can drift among a family of meanings."[34] Indeed, when from the vantage point of his Roman terrace Mr. Palomar tries to conceive the world as it is seen by birds, he arrives at the conclusion that "it is only after you have come to know the surface of things, . . . that you can venture to seek what is underneath. But the surface of things is inexhaustible" (55).

Palomar's already pessimistic tone becomes one of pure anguish in "The Model of Models," where implications are made not only concerning the failure of government and its institutions, but also pertaining to the unlikeliness of finding a countermeasure that will not "cause worse ill and abuses" (111). The "model of models" in question is Marxism; it is seen as the last hope of modern society, although its "enlightened reformers" are also "foolish perhaps, perhaps frauds, perhaps frauds and foolish at once" (112). This anguish reaches its climax in the concluding story, "Learning to Be Dead," in which Mr. Palomar "decides that from now on he will act as if he were dead, to see how the world gets along without him." Much to his surprise, he finds out that "being dead is less easy than it might seem" (121). Given that the world no longer bothers with him and he no longer has to wonder what is in store for him as a dead person, he expects to be relieved of his constant state of anxiety and agitation. But instead, "the very expectation of enjoying this calm" makes him even more anxious. Mr. Palomar's reaction clearly parallels the *noia* (ennui) concept of the Italian neo-romantic poet Giacomo Leopardi (1798–1837), who, incidentally, appears again and again in many of Calvino's writings, particularly in *Six Memos for the Next Millennium*. The *noia* results from the fact that Nature, seen as a cruel stepmother, is inexorable toward us and from the awareness that pleasure is nonexistent: that what we call pleasure is nothing but a reduction of suffering, and that our expectation of pleasure is far greater than the illusory pleasure which we imagine we feel. Thinking that "each instant, . . . when described, expands so that its end can no longer be seen," Mr. Palomar proposes to describe every instant of his life, so that, "until he has described them all, he will no longer think of being dead" (126). But at that instant he dies. As Irving Malin points out, there are several ironies: "Palomar 'dies,' but he is never alive—he is made of lifeless words."[35]

Nietzsche believed that both Apollonian and Dionysian qualities were present in Greek tragedy, and that true tragedy—true art—could only be produced by the tension between the two opposite forces in man. No doubt Calvino's propensity for being Apollonian does not mean that he is lacking in opposite attributes. In fact, one can say that his subtle humor and ironic wisdom, the urgency of his playfulness, his keen fantasy, his unsparing zest for combinatorial games, his persistent quest for new forms and ideas, and his sense of wondering and adventure are certainly reflective of his uninhibited unbridling of Dionysian desire and the lifting of restraint. It is perhaps in the tension resulting from pathos and logos, from hope and despair, that we find the true essence of Italo Calvino's art. And despite some perceived weaknesses, "self-indulgence," "gamesmanship," and a loss of the "vital tension between reality and artifice,"[36] Calvino always asserts man's undeniable if vulnerable right to exist in a humane society. As with much self-conscious fiction, Calvino requires that we (the manipulated readers) work up to his texts, demystify them, search for synthesis, and bring them within our reach. The demands of his dazzling works may be great, but so are the rewards.

NOTES

1. *The Baron in the Trees* (New York: Random House, 1959) 159.

2. Hans Robert Jauss, "The Theory of Reception: A Retrospective of Its Unrecognized Prehistory," in *Literary Theory Today,* ed. Peter Collier and Helga Geyer-Ryan (Ithaca: Cornell University Press, 1990) 68.

3. Kathryn Hume, "Calvino's *La memoria del mondo:* The Forgotten Record of Lost Worlds," *Calvino Revisited,* ed. Franco Ricci (Toronto: Dovehouse, 1989) 97–98.

4. I am referring to the writings of Wolfgang Iser, Stanley Fish, and Jonathan Culler.

5. I am using M. H. Abrams's definition of phenomenology, the philosophical perspective established by the German philosopher Edmund Husserl. Husserl has greatly influenced contemporary literary criticism, primarily Roman Ingarden (1893–1970), which sees the work of art as something existing only in the consciousness of the perceiver. Ingarden states that "a literary work of art originates in the intentional acts of consciousness of its author. . . . These intentional acts are recorded in a text, and so make it possible for a reader to reexperience the work in his or her own consciousness." See M. H. Abrams, *A Glossary of Literary Terms,* 5th ed. (Chicago: Holt Rinehart, 1990) 224–27.

6. "An important international trend in the culture of our century, what we may call the phenomenological approach in philosophy, the estrangement effect in literature, urges us to break through the screen of words and concepts and see the world as if it appeared for the first time to our sight" (Calvino, "The Written and the Unwritten Word," *The New York Review of Books* 12 May 1983: 33–38).

7. Paul Fournel, "Italo Calvino: cahiers d'exercice," *Magazine Littéraire* June 1985: 87.

8. Calvino, "Two Interviews on Science and Literature," *The Uses of Literature* (New York: Harcourt Brace, 1986) 33.

9. *Mr. Palomar* (New York: Harcourt, Brace, 1985) 88. Page numbers in parentheses refer to this edition.

10. "Two Interviews" 34.

11. See Lucia Re, *Calvino and the Age of Neorealism: Fables of Estrangement* (Stanford: Stanford University Press, 1990).

12. Michel David, *La psicoanalisi nella cultura italiana* (Turin: Boringhieri, 1966) 548. David plays with the title of the essay "Il mare dell'oggettività" (The Sea of Objectivity) in which Calvino points out that from "a culture based on the relationship and contrast of individual consciousness, will, and judgement on one side and the objective world on the other, we are passing or have already passed to a culture in which the first term is submerged by the sea of objectivity, by the uninterrupted flux of what exists" and our individuality is taken over by it. As a remedy he proposes to reorient literature from one of objectivity to one of conscience ("Il mare dell'oggettività," *Un pietra sopra* [Turin: Einaudi, 1980] 39–45).

13. Francine du Plessix Gray, "Visiting Italo Calvino," *New York Times Book Review* 21 June 1981: 24.

14. Claudio Marabini, "Italo Calvino," *Gli Anni Sessanta: narrativa e storia* (Milan: Rizzoli, 1969) 180.

15. Enzo Siciliano, "Italo Calvino imbalsamato?" *Corriere della sera* 7 June 1990: 3.

16. Claudio Milanini, *L'utopia discontinua* (Milan: Garzanti, 1990) 171. Ironically, Borges too was accused of "lacking in humanity" and "escaping reality for a world of books" (Martin S. Stabb, *Borges Revisited* [Boston: Twayne, 1991] 128).

17. Siciliano 3.

18. Luigi Malerba, "Tavola Rotonda," in *Italo Calvino: Atti del Convegno internazionale,* ed. Giovanni Falaschi (Milan: Garzanti, 1988) 396–97.

19. I do not agree with one critic's conclusion that Calvino "remains an abstract entity, never having reached full artistic maturity" (Renato Barilli, "My Long 'Infidelity' Towards Calvino" in *Calvino Revisited* 14–15). See also Barilli's "I racconti di Calvino," *La barriera del Naturalismo: Studi sulla narrativa italiana contemporanea* (Milan: Mursia, 1964) 210–20.

20. Fournel 84.

21. Calvino, Prefazione, *I nostri antenati* (Turin: Einaudi, 1960).

22. *Six Memos for the Next Millennium* (Cambridge: Harvard University Press, 1988) 68.

23. Calvino's alienation, or distancing, is somewhat similar to the idea of literary fragmentation which, according to Hassan, is a basic characteristic of postmodernism. The critic views literature no longer as an integrated totality, but rather as a composite of different bits and pieces (Ihab Hassan, "Pluralism in Modern Perspective" in *Exploring Postmodernism,* ed. Douwe W. Fokkema [Philadelphia: J. Benjamins, 1987] 91).

24. Enrico Ghidetti, "Il fantistico ben temperato di Italo Calvino," *Italo Calvino: Atti del Convegno internazionale* 180.

25. Prior to the publication of *Palomar* by Einaudi in 1983, most of the stories first appeared in 1975, 1976, 1977 in *Corriere della sera* and in 1983 in *la Repubblica.*

26. A. H. Carter III, *Italo Calvino: Metamorphoses of Fantasy* (Ann Arbor: UMI Research Press, 1987) 139.

27. Roelens refers to the narratives of *Mr. Palomar* as a "collection of short stories, a serialized narrative, suite narratives, art prose, snapshots, days in the life of . . . fragments, *cahiers d'exercice,* comic strips, *école du regard, littérature objective,* chronicles, ship's log, circumstantially prompted pieces, reportage, essays" (Nathalie Roelens, *L'odissea di uno scrittore virtuale: Strategie narrative in 'Palomar' di Italo Calvino* [Florence: Franco Cesati Editore, 1989] 147–48).

28. Fournel 85.

29. Fournel 85.

30. *Palomar* (Turin: Einaudi, 1983), [*Nuovi Coralli*], back cover.

31. *Collezione di sabbia* (Milan: Garzanti, 1984) 125.

32. Pietro Citati, review of *Palomar, Corriere della Sera* 11 Dec. 1983.

33. Calvino repeatedly stated that he *was* Mr. Palomar, and that the settings in which Palomar makes his observations and inquiries are reconstructions of his own milieu. In fact, he even suggested that he be filmed as Mr. Palomar on his private beach at Castiglion della Pescaia, his lawn

at Roccamare, and his apartment in Rome. See Patchy Wheatley, "The World minus Calvino," *The Listener* 26 Sept. 1985: 9.

34. Michael Wood, "On the Edge of Silence," *The New Republic* 17 Oct. 1988: 38.

35. Irving Malin, review of *"Mr. Palomar,"* *Review of Contemporary Fiction* 6 (Fall 1986): 131.

36. Alter uses these terms in discussing metafiction, and Borges's works (Robert Alter, *Partial Magic: The Novel as a Self-Conscious Genre*, [Berkeley: University of California Press, 1975] 227–28).

BIBLIOGRAPHY

Calvino's Major Works

Fiction

Il sentiero dei nidi di ragno. Turin: Einaudi, 1947. [*The Path to the Nest of Spiders,* trans. Archibald Colquhoun. Boston: Beacon, 1957. Also published by Ecco Press: New York, 1976; this edition includes Calvino's 1964 preface, translated by William Weaver.]

Ultimo viene il corvo (The Crow Comes Last). Turin: Einaudi, 1949. A selection of these short stories is found in *Adam, One Afternoon, and Other Stories,* trans. Archibald Colquhoun and Peggy Wright. London: Collins, 1957.

Il visconte dimezzato. Turin: Einaudi, 1952. [*The Nonexistent Knight and the Cloven Viscount,* trans. Archibald Colquhoun. New York: Random House, 1962. Also Appleton-Century-Crofts, 1968; Harcourt Brace, 1977.]

La formica argentina. Turin: Einaudi, 1965. First published in *Botteghe oscure* 10 (1952): 406–411; subsequently in *La nuvola di smog e La formica argentina.* ["The Argentine Ant" and "Smog" in *The Watcher and Other Stories,* trans. William Weaver. New York: Harcourt Brace, 1971.]

L'entrata in guerra (Entrance into War). Turin: Einaudi, 1954. The volume contains 3 stories ("L'entrata in guerra," "Gli avanguardisti a Mentone," and "Le notti dell'UNPA"); republished in *I racconti.*

Il barone rampante. Turin: Einaudi, 1957. [*The Baron in the Trees,* trans. Archibald Colquhoun. New York: Random House, 1959. Also Harcourt Brace, 1977.]

La speculazione edilizia. Turin: Einaudi, 1957. First published in *Botteghe oscure* 20 (1957); also in *I racconti.* ["A Plunge into Real Estate," trans. D. S. Carne-Ross, in *Difficult Loves.* Toronto: Lester and Orpen Dennys, 1984.]

I giovani del Po (The Young of the Po River). In *Officina* 8–11 (1957) and 12 (1958): 331–552.

I racconti (The Stories). Turin: Einaudi, 1958. Many of these short stories appear in the following English collections: *Adam, One Afternoon, and Other Stories; The Watcher and Other Stories; Difficult Loves.*

Il cavaliere inesistente. Turin: Einaudi, 1959. [*The Nonexistent Knight and the Cloven Viscount*, trans. Archibald Colquhoun. New York: Random House, 1962; also Harcourt Brace, 1977.]

I nostri antenati. Turin: Einaudi, 1960. The volume, consisting of *Il visconte dimezzato, Il barone rampante*, and *Il cavaliere inesistente*, includes a preface by the author. [*The Cloven Viscount, The Baron in the Trees*, and *The Nonexistent Knight*.]

La giornata d' uno scrutatore. Turin: Einaudi, 1963. [*The Watcher and Other Stories*, trans. William Weaver. New York: Harcourt Brace, 1971.]

Marcovaldo, ovvero le stagioni in città. Turin: Einaudi, 1963. [*Marcovaldo or the Seasons in the City*, trans. William Weaver. New York: Harcourt Brace, 1983.]

La nuvola di smog e La formica argentina. Turin: Einaudi, 1965. ["Smog" and "The Argentine Ant" in *The Watcher and Other Stories*, trans. William Weaver. New York: Harcourt Brace, 1975.]

Le cosmicomiche. Turin: Einaudi, 1965. [*Cosmicomics*, trans. William Weaver. New York: Harcourt Brace, 1968.]

Ti con zero. Turin: Einaudi, 1967. [*t zero*, trans. William Weaver. New York: Harcourt Brace, 1969.]

La memoria del mondo e altre storie cosmicomiche. Milan: Club degli Editori, 1968. [The Memory of the World and More Cosmicomic Stories.]

"Il castello dei destini incrociati" in *Tarocchi: Il mazzo visconteo di Bergamo e di New York*. Parma: Franco Maria Ricci Editore, 1969. [*The Castle of Crossed Destinies*, trans. William Weaver. New York: Harcourt Brace, 1979.] The deluxe Italian edition includes illustrations of the Bergamo and Morgan Library Visconti tarot cards as well as a note by the author. In 1976 an English edition, *Tarots: The Visconti Pack in Bergamo and New York* was published in New York by the same publisher and translated by William Weaver. In 1973 Einaudi published a volume containing both *Il castello dei destini incrociati* and *La taverna dei destini incrociati*.

Gli amori difficili. Turin: Einaudi, 1970. Several of these stories appear in "Stories of Love and Loneliness," in *Difficult Loves*, trans. William Weaver, Archibald Colquhoun, and Peggy Wright. New York: Harcourt Brace, 1984.

Le città invisibili. Turin: Einaudi, 1972. [*Invisible Cities*, trans. William Weaver. New York: Harcourt Brace, 1974.]

Se una notte d'inverno un viaggiatore. Turin: Einaudi, 1979. [*If on a winter's night a traveler*, trans. William Weaver. New York: Harcourt Brace, 1981.]

Palomar. Turin: Einaudi, 1983. [*Mr. Palomar*, trans. William Weaver. New York: Harcourt Brace, 1985.]

Cosmicomiche vecchie e nuove. Milan: Garzanti, 1984. [Old and New Cosmicomics.]

Essays and Other Writings

Fiabe italiane. Turin: Einaudi, 1956. [*Italian Fables*, trans. Louis Brigante. New York: Collier, 1961. *Italian Folktales*, trans. George Martin. New York: Harcourt Brace, 1980; also Pantheon, 1980.]

Orlando Furioso di Ludovico Ariosto raccontato da Italo Calvino, con una scelta del poema. Turin: Einaudi, 1970. Calvino's reading of the epic poem and selections.

La panchina. Opera in un atto di Italo Calvino; Musica Sergio Liberovici. Turin: Tipografia Toso, 1956; also in *Strumenti critici* 36–37 (Oct. 1978): 192–210. Introduction by Maria Corti. [The Bench: One-Act Opera by I. Calvino with Music by S. Liberovici.]

Una pietra sopra: Discorsi di letteratura e società. Turin: Einaudi, 1980. Many of these essays appear in *The Uses of Literature: Essays,* trans. Patrick Creagh. New York: Harcourt Brace, 1986. The same English edition is available in *The Literature Machine: Essays.* London: Secker and Warburg, 1987.

Collezione di sabbia (Collection of Sand). Milan: Garzanti, 1984. Essays (1974–84) previously published in *Corriere della sera* and *la Repubblica.*

Posthumous Publications

Sotto il sole giaguaro. Milan: Garzanti, 1986. [*Under the Jaguar Sun,* trans. William Weaver. New York: Harcourt Brace, 1988.] Three short stories.

Lezioni Americane: Sei proposte per il prossimo millennio. Milan: Garzanti, 1988. [*Six Memos for the Next Millennium.* The Charles Eliot Norton Lectures: 1985–86. Cambridge: Harvard University Press, 1988.]

Sulla fiaba. Turin: Einaudi, 1988. Essays on fables.

La strada di San Giovanni (The San Giovanni Road). Milan: Mondadori, 1990. Collection of short stories.

I libri degli altri: Lettere 1947–1981, ed. Giovanni Tesio with a note by Carlo Fruttero. Turin: Einaudi, 1991. A collection of letters written by Calvino to various authors while working for Einaudi.

Perché leggere i classici (Why Read the Classics). Milan: Mondadori, 1991. Essays.

Selected Critical Works

Bibliographies

Benussi, Christina. "Bibliografia," *Introduzione a Calvino.* Rome-Bari: Laterza, 1989.

Bertone, Giorgio. "Appunti per una bibliografia di Italo Calvino" *Italo Calvino: la letteratura, la scienza, la città. Atti del Convegno nazionale di studi di Sanremo,* ed. Giorgio Bertone. Genoa: Marietti, 1988.

Ferretti, Gian Carlo. "Bibliografia" *Le capre di Bikini. Calvino giornalista e saggista 1945–1985.* Rome: Editori Riuniti, 1989.

Frasson-Marin, Aurore. "Bibliographie" *Italo Calvino et l'imaginaire.* Paris: Editions Slatkine, 1986.

Books

Adler, Sara Maria. *Calvino: The Writer as Fablemaker.* Studia Humanitatis. Potomac, MD: Ediciones José Porrúa Turanzas, 1979. A good introduction to Calvino's pre-1977 writings. Emphasis on his narrative skills as fable maker and as a "literary adventurer" shaped by the cultural and political trends of his time.

Baroni, Giorgio. *Italo Calvino: Introduzione e guida allo studio dell'opera calviniana.* Florence: Le Monnier, 1988. Multipurpose introduction to the author's life and works. It includes a brief bibliography and an extremely useful selection of critical excerpts dealing with Calvino's writings.

Benussi, Cristina. *Introduzione a Calvino.* Rome-Bari: Laterza, 1989. Solid and useful introduction to Calvino's writings, which are seen in a historical, cultural, and literary context. Valuable chronology and bibliography.

Bonura, Guiseppe. *Invito alla lettura di Italo Calvino.* Milan: Mursia, 1987. Valuable introduction to Calvino's life, works, and themes. A short anthology of criticisms, chronology, and bibliography are included.

Calligaris, Contardo. *Italo Calvino.* Rev. ed. Milan: Mursia, 1985. Last chapter is by Gian Piero Bernasconi. Dialectical comparison between formal elements and historical situation. Calvino's narratives reflect a precise relationship between subject and history.

Cannon, JoAnn. *Italo Calvino: Writer and Critic.* Ravenna: Longo Editore, 1981. Extremely useful analysis combined with theoretical implications of the text and the role of the reader.

Carter, Albert Howard, III. *Italo Calvino: Metamorphoses of Fantasy.* Ann Arbor: UMI Research Press, 1987. Fantasy as a creative core in Calvino's narrative. Focuses on the rhetorical success of his texts in establishing fantasies for the readers to follow. Examines the relationship between fantasy and science.

DeVivo, Alberto. *Il tempo: ordine e durata nei "Racconti" di Italo Calvino.* Abano Terme: Piovan Editore, 1990. A perceptive examination of the dualistic and dialectical function of time in Calvino's 1945–1958 short narratives.

Di Carlo, Franco. *Come leggere "I nostri antenati" di Italo Calvino.* Milan: Mursia, 1978. Though a bit dated, a useful introduction to the trilogy.

Ferretti, Gian Carlo. *Le capre di Bikini. Calvino giornalista e saggista 1945–1985.* Rome: Editori Riuniti, 1989. Analysis of Calvino's political and literary contributions to newspapers and periodicals in the context of his creative writings.

Milanini, Claudio. *L'utopia discontinua: Saggio su Italo Calvino.* Milan: Garzanti, 1990. An analysis of the key stages in Calvino's literary production, seen as transcending Italy's cultural milieu.

Napoletano, Francesca Bernardini. *I segni nuovi di Italo Calvino. Da "Le Cosmicomiche" a "Le città invisibili."* Rome: Bulzoni, 1977. Calvino broadens his perspective into infinity, eliminating the past and returning to an indistinct state (base zero) where everything is once again possible. Identifies a condition of absolute potentiality.

Olken, Ilene T. *With Pleated Eye and Garnet Wing: Symmetries of Italo Calvino*. Ann Arbor: University of Michigan Press, 1984. Mainly a discussion of the author's critical essays and the trilogy. The premise of this original study is that an "organic order," a "geometry," underlies Calvino's writings, which are united by his "science of control."

Re, Lucia. *Calvino and the Age of Neorealism: Fables of Estrangement*. Stanford: Stanford University Press, 1990. Calvino's politically committed realism and the implications of literary estrangement are intelligently discussed via the latest contemporary literary theories. Re focuses on the first novel, where she discovers a "crucial point of origin" for his entire "ethics" of writing.

Ricci, Franco. *Difficult Games: A Reading of "I racconti" by Italo Calvino*. Waterloo, Ont.: Wilfrid Laurier University Press, 1990. Exploration of the psychological and existential motivations in *I racconti*—a synthesis of the anxieties of the early Calvino as well as of postwar Italy.

Roelens, Nathalie. *L'odissea di uno scrittore virtuale: Strategie narrative in 'Palomar' di Italo Calvino*. Florence: Franco Cesati Editore, 1989. Close semiotic and microtextual reading of the novel. We witness Mr. Palomar's observations even before he himself becomes consciously aware of them.

Woodhouse, J. R. *Italo Calvino: A Reappraisal and an Appreciation of the Trilogy*. Hull: University of Hull, 1968. Counteracts some misinterpretations of the novels. Calvino's attitudes in the trilogy are consistent with those reflected in his other narrative works.

Articles and Chapters

Bencivenga, Nuccia. "Caliphs, Travelers, and Other Stories." *Forum Italicum* 20 (1986): 3–15. Close reading of *If on a winter's night a traveler*. The reading and the writing of a book are a falsification of it.

Biasin, Gian Paolo. "La superficie delle cose." *Forum Italicum* 19 (1985): 152–57. Careful reading of *Palomar* and the significance of Albrecht Dürer's painting on the cover.

Borutti, Silvana. "Metafisica dei sensi e filosofia involontaria nell'ultimo Calvino." *Autografo* 4 (Mar. 1987): 3–18. Close reading of *Under the Jaguar Sun;* impact of *Palomar*.

Breiner, Laurence A. "Italic [sic] Calvino: The Place of the Emperor in *Invisible Cities*." *Modern Fiction Studies* 34 (Winter 1988): 559–73. The novel is remarkable because "true narration is for the most part absent from both the frame and the framed."

Cannon, JoAnn. "Calvino's Latest Challenge to the Labyrinth: A Reader of *Palomar*." *Italica* 62 (1985): 189–200. Traces the various stages in Palomar's search for an intelligible reality; shows how "defamiliarization and enumeration" relate to this quest.

―――― . "Italo Calvino: *Mr. Palomar* and *Collezione di sabbia*." In her *Postmodern Italian Fiction: The Crisis of Reason in Calvino, Eco, Sciascia, Malerba*. Rutherford, N.J.: Fairleigh Dickinson University Press, 1989. 95–115, 128–30. Palomar's "nostalgia for totalizing structures coexists" with the possibility that they might be "heuristic fictions." The same crisis of the "legitimation of knowledge" characterizes Calvino's collection of essays.

Carlton, Jill Margo. "The Genesis of *Il barone rampante*." *Italica* 61 (1984): 195–206. Eighteenth-century literary sources.

Cases, Cesare. "Calvino e il 'pathos della distanza!' " In *I metodi attuali della critica*, ed. Maria Corti and Cesare Segre. Turin: Edizioni RAI, 1970. 53–59. Originally in *Città aperta* 7–8 (1958): 33–35. The Nietzschean "pathos of distance" is identified as the most vital nucleus of Calvino's art.

Cerina, Giovanna. "L'eroe, lo spazio narrativo e la costruzione del significato. Lettura di 'Ultimo viene il corvo.' " *Dalla novella rusticale al racconto neorealista*, ed. Sandro Maxia and Giovanni Pirodda. Rome: Bulzoni Editore, 1979. 115–153. Structural analysis of "The Crow Comes Last."

Cipolla, Gaetano. "Rhetorical Strategies in Calvino's Narrative." In his *Labyrinth: Studies on an Archetype*. New York and Toronto: Legas, 1987. 132–42. Identifies a manneristic substratum which conditioned Calvino's choices in writing his last three novels.

Corti, Maria. *Il viaggio testuale*. Turin: Einaudi, 1978. 169–220. Important semiotic readings of *The Castle of Crossed Destinies*, *Marcovaldo*, and the opera *La panchina*.

De Lauretis, Teresa. "Narrative Discourse in Calvino: Praxis or Poiesis?" *PMLA* 90 (1975): 414–25. A semiotic analysis: Calvino exposes the paradoxical nature of writing in the dialectics of signification; he breaks down the barrier separating high literature from popular culture.

―――― . "Calvino and the Amazons: Reading the (Post) Modern Text." In *Technologies of Gender: Essays on Theory, Film, and Fiction*. Bloomington: Indiana University Press, 1987. 70–83. Feminist reading of *If on a winter's night a traveler*.

De Vivo, Albert. "Calvino: politica e segni letterari." *Forum Italicum* 25 (1991): 40–56. Relationship between politics and literature. Interesting study of "The Name, the Nose."

Falaschi, Giovanni. "Ritratti critici di contemporanei: Italo Calvino." *Belfagor* 27 (1972): 530–50. Autobiographical elements in Calvino's narratives.

Gardner, James. "Italo Calvino 1923–1985." *The New Criterion* 4 (Dec. 1985): 6–13. Shows need to focus more on Calvino's early works. Critical of Calvino's scientific knowledge.

Ghidetti, Enrico. "Il fantastico ben temperato di Italo Calvino." *Il ponte* 43 (1987): 109–23. Calvino's "fantastic" is tempered because it is balanced by an innate realistic sense.

Hume, Kathryn. "Science and Imagination in Calvino's Cosmicomics." *Mosaic* 15 (Dec. 1982): 47–58. Calvino's lack of theological impetus. He forces the reader to "face the full scientific complexity" of the universe.

———. "Italo Calvino's Cosmic Comedy: Mythography for the Scientific Age." *Papers on Language and Literature* 20 (Winter 1984): 80–95. The mythic dimension of the cosmic tales, their philosophical contribution, and the relationship of human consciousness to the phenomenal world.

———. "Calvino's *La memoria del mondo:* The Forgotten Record of Lost Worlds." In *Calvino Revisited,* ed. Franco Ricci. University of Toronto Italian Studies 2. Toronto: Dovehouse, 1989. 85–102. This group of stories is seen as a turning point in his cosmic creations. Emotions and change in the universe are paramount in *Cosmicomics; t zero* focuses on death and offers "as answer the consolation of transformation and the creation of the new"; *La memoria* stories aim toward intellectual responses and do not limit themselves to how one relates to the universe: "we tell ourselves about the world and ourselves."

Hutcheon, Linda. "Actualizing Narrative Structures: Detective Plot, Fantasy, Games, and the Erotic." In her *Narcissistic Narrative: The Metafictional Paradox.* London: Routledge, 1984. 71–86. Underscores the self-reflexive nature of *Cosmicomics, t zero,* and *Invisible Cities.*

Illiano, Antonio. "Per una definizione della vena cosmogonica di Calvino: Appunti su *Le cosmicomiche e Ti con zero." Italica* 49 (1972): 291–301. Traces the sources of Calvino's cosmic tales.

Jeannet, Angela. "Italo Calvino's Invisible City." *Perspectives on Contemporary Literature* 3 (May 1977): 38–49. The "city," a major presence in Calvino's writings, is a privileged creation of human consciousness. In *Invisible Cities* the invisible is made visible, and the visible is pushed aside to allow more important discoveries.

Markey, Constance. "Calvino and the Existential Dilemma: The Paradox of Choice." *Italica* 60 (1983): 55–70. Dilemma of choice in the face of unpredictable and illusory reality, especially in *The Castle of Crossed Destinies.*

———. "The Tarot Cards as a Subversive Tool in Italo Calvino." *Aspects of Fantasy: Selected Essays from the Second International Conference on the Fantastic in Literature and Film,* ed. William Coyle. Westport, CT: Greenwood Press, 1986. 181–86. Calvino's dualistic and subversive use of the cards is "integral to the novel's dialectical approach to the quest or monomyth." However, the cards remain subjective in interpretation and defy final meaning.

Mengaldo, Pier Vincenzo. "L'arco e le pietre (Calvino, *Le città invisibili*)." In *La tradizione del Novecento: Da D'Annunzio a Montale.* Milan: Feltrinelli, 1975. 406–26. Focuses on Calvino's "poetics of estrangement." Tendency to work through combinations consisting of unities or simple semiological opposites—life–death, celestial–underworld etc.

Musalla, Ulla. "Duplication and Multiplication: Postmodernist Devices in the Novels of Italo Calvino." *Approaching Postmodernism.* Papers presented at a Workshop on

Postmodernism, 21–23 Sept. 1984, University of Utrecht, ed. Douwe Fokkema and Hans Bertens. Amsterdam and Philadelphia: Benjamins, 1986. 135–155. Focuses on *If on a winter's night.*

Ossola, Carlo. "L'invisibile e il suo 'dove': 'geografia interiore' di Italo Calvino." *Lettere Italiane* 39 (Apr.–June 1987): 220–51. Queneau's influence on Calvino.

Ozick, Cynthia. "Mouth, Ear, Nose." *The New York Times Book Review* 23 Oct. 1988: 7. Valuable and interesting review of *Under the Jaguar Sun.*

Pavese, Cesare. *"Il sentiero dei nidi di ragno." L'Unità* 26 Sept. 1947. Important review of the novel which helped promote Calvino's career and identified the fabulistic quality of his narratives.

Ragusa, Olga. "Italo Calvino: The Repeated Conquest of Contemporaneity." *World Literature Today* 57 (Spring 1982): 195–201. Calvino's writings are in tune with the contemporary world. Excellent overview of his writings.

Ravazzoli, Flavia. *"Le città invisibili* di Calvino: utopia linguistica e letteratura." *Strumenti Critici* 54 n.s. 2 (May 1987): 193–201. A book of fables with no action held together by deceit of aesthetic fiction, irony as literary lie, and the deceit of sensorial perception.

Rushdie, Salman. "Calvino." *London Review of Books* 17–30 Sept. 1981: 16–17. *If on a winter's night a traveler* is characterized as an outrageous fiction about fiction.

Sage, Lorna. "From the Mind's Balcony." *Times Literary Supplement* 5–11 Oct. 1990: 1060. Excellent review of *La strada di San Giovanni.*

Schneider, Marilyn. "Calvino at a Crossroads: *Il castello dei destini incrociati.*" *PMLA* 95 (1980): 73–90. The characters delimit two coinciding and overlapping narrative voices; the ever-changing sequences of the cards allegorize the making of fiction.

Shulman, Alix Kates. "Senses and Sensibility: Italo Calvino Solves the Mind-Body Problem." *Village Voice* 14 Feb. 1989: 53–54. Analysis of *Under the Jaguar Sun* and *Mr. Palomar.* She admires Calvino's "vibrantly sensual prose" with which he tries to apprehend the world and infer the past. At the core of both books there is a deep concern with the relation between perception, imagination, self, and the world.

Siegel, Kristi. "Italo Calvino's *Cosmicomics:* Qfwfq's [sic] Postmodern Autobiography." *Italica* 68 (1991): 43–59. *Cosmicomics* foregrounds unanswerable ontological questions characteristic of postmodernism.

Springer, Carolyn. "Textual Geography: The Role of the Reader in *Invisible Cities.*" *Modern Language Studies* 15 (Fall 1985): 289–99. Reader response approach to the novel, which is seen as an epistemological puzzle.

Updike, John. "Calvino, Grass, Böll." *Hugging the Shore: Essays and Criticism* (New York: Knopf, 1983). 457–77. Excellent reviews of *Invisible Cities, The Castle of Crossed Destinies,* and *If on a winter's night a traveler.*

Wood, Michael. "Fortune Hunting." *New York Review of Books* 12 May 1977: 36–39. Valuable review of *The Castle of Crossed Destinies.*

Zangrilli, Franco. "Pirandello e Calvino." In his *Linea pirandelliana nella narrativa contemporanea*. Ravenna: Longo Editore, 1990. 35–60. Points out a pronounced Pirandellian "umorismo" (humor) in Calvino.

Interviews

Almansi, Guido. "Intervista a Italo Calvino." *Nuova Corrente* 35 (1988): 387–408.
Calvino, Italo. "Chi cattura chi? Risposte di Italo Calvino." *L'approdo letterario* 14 (Jan./Mar. 1968): 105–110.
———. "Italo Calvino/ L'uomo di Neanderthal" and "Italo Calvino/ Montezuma." *Le interviste impossibili*. Milan: Bompiani, 1975. 5–12, 83–93. Imaginary interviews.
Corti, Maria. "Intervista: Italo Calvino." *Autografo* 2 (Oct. 1985): 47–53.
du Plessix Gray, Francine. "Visiting Italo Calvino." *New York Times Book Review* 21 June 1981: 1, 22–23.
Fournel, Paul. "Italo Calvino: cahiers d'exercice." *Magazine Littéraire* June 1985: 84–89.
Lucente, Gregory. "An Interview with Italo Calvino." *Contemporary Literature* 26 (1985): 244–53.
Nascimbeni, Giulio. "A colloquio con lo scrittore in occasione dell'uscita di *Cosmicomiche vecchie e nuove*." *Corriere della sera* 5 Dec. 1984: 3.
Stille, Alexander. "An Interview with Italo Calvino." *Saturday Review* Mar.-Apr. 1985: 37–39.
Weaver, William. "Calvino: an interview and its story." *Calvino Revisited*, ed. Franco Ricci. University of Toronto Italian Studies 2. Toronto: Dovehouse, 1989. 17–31.

Symposia Proceedings

Italo Calvino: la letteratura, la scienza, la città (Atti del Covegno nazionale di studi di Sanremo, 28–29 novembre 1986), ed. Giorgio Bertone. Genoa: Marietti 1988. Contributions by G. Bertone, N. Sapegno, E. Gioanola, V. Coletti, G. Conte, P. Ferrua, M. Quaini, F. Biamonti, G. Dossena, G. Celli, A. Oliverio, R. Pierantoni, G. Dematteis, G. Poletto, L. Berio, G. Einaudi, E. Sanguineti, E. Scalfari, D. Cossu, G. Napolitano, M. B. Bestagno, S. Dian, L. Lodi, S. Perella, L. Surdich. Includes extensive bibliography prepared by Giorgio Bertone.
Italo Calvino: Atti del Convegno internazionale (Firenze, Palazzo Medici-Riccardi 26–28 febbraio 1987), ed. Giovanni Falaschi. Milan: Garzanti, 1988. Contributions by L. Baldacci, G. Bárberi Squarotti, C. Bernardini, G. R. Cardona, L. Caretti, C. Cases, P. Daros, D. Del Guidice, A. M. Di Nola, A. Faeti, G. Falaschi, G. C. Ferretti, F. Fortini, M. Fusco, Jean-Michel Gardair, E. Ghidetti, L. Malerba, P. V. Mengaldo, G. Nava, G. Pampaloni, L. W. Petersen, R. Pierantoni, S. Romagnoli, A. A. Rosa, J. Risset, G. C. Roscioni, A. Rossi, G. Sciloni, V. Spinazzola, C. Varese.

Narratori dell'invisibile. Simposio in memoria di Italo Calvino. (Sassuolo, Palazzo Ducale, 21/22/23 febbraio 1986), ed. B. Cottafavi and M. Magri. Modena: Mucchi Editore, 1987. Contributions by R. Pierantoni, P. Fabbri, R. Bergamini, P. D. Napolitani, P. Borroni, A. Ogliari, A. Sparzani, G. Gramigna, G. Agamben, G. Celati, G. Scabia, G. Bompiani, D. Del Giudice, N. Orengo, E. Melandri.

Inchiesta sulle fate. Italo Calvino e la fiaba, ed. Delia Frigessi. Bergamo: Pierluigi Lubrina Editore, 1988. Symposium held at S. Giovanni Valdarno (Arezzo). Preface by C. Segre; contributions by A. M. Cirese, M. Barenghi, B. Falcetto, C. Pagetti, L. Clerici, H. Rölleke, G. Cusatelli, P. Clemente, F. Mugnaini, P. Boero, E. Casali, J. Despinette.

Special Issues

The Review of Contemporary Fiction 6 (Summer 1986): 6–167. Contributions by H. Mathews, J. A. Varsava, S. T. Friedman, J. E. Joseph, F. Ricci, F. La Polla, J. Byrne, F. Guardiani, M. Stephens, K. Hume, W. F. Motte Jr., C. P. James, L. Marello, G. Green, C. D. Malmgren, M. C. Olds, I. Rankin, C. Pierce, G. Scalise.

Nuova Corrente 34. 99 (1987): 1–212, ed. Mario Boselli. Contributions by I. Calvino, B. Falcetto, C. Milanini, K. Hume, M. Carlino, L. Gabellone, F. Muzzioli, M. Barenghi, Mario Boselli, E. Testa.

Nuova Corrente 34. 100 (1988): 227–419. Contributions by G. Celati, A. Prete, S. Verdino, E. Gionanola, V. Coletti, G. Patrizi, G. Guglielmi, G. Gramigna, G. Terrone, R. West; interviews with G. L. Lucente, G. Almansi; six letters by Calvino are included.

Nuova civiltà delle macchine 5 (1987). Contributions by G. Giorello, A. Battistini, G. Gabbi, G. Bonura, L. Valdrè, G. Bàrberi Squarotti, R. Campagnoli.

Calvino Revisited, ed. Franco Ricci. University of Toronto Italian Studies 2. Toronto: Dovehouse, 1989. Contributions by R. Barilli, W. Weaver, J. R. Woodhouse, JoAnn Cannon, R. Capozzi, K. Hume, P. Perron, W. F. Motte Jr., T. de Lauretis, W. Feinstein, G. P. Biasin, M. Schneider, F. Ricci, A. M. Jeannet.

INDEX

The index does not include references to material in the notes.